Bloom's Modern Critical Interpretations

Bloom's Modern Critical Interpretations

Jane Austen's
PERSUASION

Edited and with an introduction by

Harold Bloom
Sterling Professor of the Humanities
Yale University

CHELSEA HOUSE
P U B L I S H E R S
A Haights Cross Communications Company

Philadelphia

A Haights Cross Communications ✦ Company

Printed and bound in the United States of America.

10 9 8 7 6 5 4 3 2 1

Library of Congress Cataloging-in-Publication Data

Persuasion / edited and with introduction by Harold Bloom.
           p. cm. — (Bloom's modern critical interpretations) Includes
bibliographical references and index.
     ISBN 0-7910-7585-0
   1. Austen, Jane, 1775–1817. Persuasion. I. Bloom, Harold. II.
Series.

     PR4034.P43P47 2003
     823'.7—dc21

                                               2003009471

Contributing editor: Jesse Zuba

Cover design by Terry Mallon

Cover: © Hulton-Archive/Getty Images, Inc.

Layout by EJB Publishing Services

Chelsea House Publishers
1974 Sproul Road, Suite 400
Broomall, PA 19008-0914

www.chelseahouse.com

Contents

Editor's Note

My Introduction relates Jane Austen's portrait of Anne Elliot to Shakespeare's vision of Rosalind in *As You Like It*.

Anne Elliot receives what I regard as her classical critique from Stuart M. Tave, who regards her depth of feeling as controlled by a matching depth of integrity.

A. Walton Litz rightly emphasizes that *Persuasion* ends openly and ambiguously, compared to Austen's other major novels, while Gene W. Ruoff finds in the novel's conclusion something like a Wordsworthian myth of memory.

The prophetic sense of the decline of marriage as a societal covenant in the nineteenth century is ascribed by Julia Prewitt Brown to *Persuasion*, after which Susan Morgan sees perception as the true guide to character in this novel.

In a brilliant reading, the late Tony Tanner identifies Anne Elliot as a threshold figure, poised in between two houses, her father's and her prospective husband's.

To Claudia L. Johnson, *Persuasion* has subtle affinities with William Blake's dissent from "mind-forged manacles," while John Wiltshire finds in this novel what the great poet Elizabeth Bishop termed "the art of losing."

Adela Pinch strikingly increases our awareness of how Anne Elliot's experiences resemble the role of a reader in regard to books, after which Claude Rawson culminates this volume with the interplay of satire and augmented perceptiveness in *Persuasion*.

HAROLD BLOOM

Introduction

"Persuasion" is a word derived from the Latin for "advising" or "urging," for recommending that it is good to perform or not perform a particular action. The word goes back to a root meaning "sweet" or "pleasant," so that the good of performance or non-performance has a tang of taste rather than of moral judgment about it. Jane Austen chose it as the title for her last completed novel. As a title, it recalls *Sense and Sensibility* or *Pride and Prejudice* rather than *Emma* or *Mansfield Park*. We are given not the name of a person or house and estate, but of an abstraction, a single one in this case. The title's primary reference is to the persuasion of its heroine, Anne Elliot, at the age of nineteen, by her godmother, Lady Russell, not to marry Captain Frederick Wentworth, a young naval officer. This was, as it turns out, very bad advice, and, after eight years, it is mended by Anne and Captain Wentworth. As with all of Austen's ironic comedies, matters end happily for the heroine. And yet each time I finish a rereading of this perfect novel, I feel very sad.

This does not appear to be my personal vagary; when I ask my friends and students about their experience of the book, they frequently mention a sadness which they also associate with *Persuasion*, more even than with *Mansfield Park*. Anne Elliot, a quietly eloquent being, is a self-reliant character, in no way forlorn, and her sense of self never falters. It is not *her* sadness we feel as we conclude the book: it is the novel's somberness that impresses us. The sadness enriches what I would call the novel's canonical persuasiveness, its way of showing us its extraordinary aesthetic distinction.

From *The Western Canon*. © 1994 by Harold Bloom.

Persuasion is among novels what Anne Elliot is among novelistic characters—a strong but subdued outrider. The book and the character are not colorful or vivacious; Elizabeth Bennet of *Pride and Prejudice* and Emma Woodhouse of *Emma* have a verve to them that initially seems lacking in Anne Elliot, which may be what Austen meant when she said that Anne was "almost too good for me." Anne is really almost too subtle for us, though not for Wentworth, who has something of an occult wavelength to her. Juliet McMaster notes "the kind of oblique communication that constantly goes on between Anne Elliot and Captain Wentworth, where, though they seldom speak to each other, each constantly understands the full import of the other's speech better than their interlocutors do."

That kind of communication in *Persuasion* depends upon deep "affection," a word that Austen values over "love." "Affection" between woman and man, in Austen, is the more profound and lasting emotion. I think it is not too much to say that Anne Elliot, though subdued, is the creation for whom Austen herself must have felt the most affection, because she lavished her own gifts upon Anne. Henry James insisted that the novelist must be a sensibility upon which absolutely nothing is lost; by that test (clearly a limited one) only Austen, George Eliot, and James himself, among all those writing in English, would join Stendhal, Flaubert, and Tolstoy in a rather restricted pantheon. Anne Elliot may well be the one character in all of prose fiction upon whom nothing is lost, though she is in no danger of turning into a novelist. The most accurate estimate of Anne Elliot that I have seen is by Stuart Tave:

> Nobody hears Anne, nobody sees her, but it is she who is ever at the center. It is through her ears, eyes, and mind that we are made to care for what is happening. If nobody is much aware of her, she is very much aware of everyone else and she perceives what is happening to them when they are ignorant of themselves ... she reads Wentworth's mind, with the coming troubles he is causing for others and himself, before those consequences bring the information to him.

The aesthetic dangers attendant upon such a paragon are palpable: how does a novelist make such a character persuasive? Poldy, in Joyce's *Ulysses*, is overwhelmingly persuasive because he is so complete a person, which was the largest of Joyce's intentions. Austen's ironic mode does not sanction the representation of completeness: we do not accompany her characters to the bedroom, the kitchen, the privy. What Austen parodies in *Sense and Sensibility* she raises to an apotheosis in *Persuasion*: the sublimity of a particular, inwardly isolated sensibility. Anne Elliot is hardly the only figure in Austen who has an understanding heart. Her difference is in her almost preternatural acuteness of perception of others and of the self, which are surely the qualities that most distinguish Austen as a novelist. Anne Elliot is to Austen's work what Rosalind of *As You Like It* is to Shakespeare's: the character who almost reaches the mastery of perspective that can be available only to the novelist or playwright, lest all dramatic quality be lost from the novel or play. C. L. Barber memorably emphasized this limitation:

> The dramatist tends to show us one thing at a time, and to realize that one thing, in its moment, to the full; his characters go to extremes, comical as well as serious; and no character, not even a Rosalind, is in a position to see all around the play and so be completely poised, for if this were so the play would cease to be dramatic.

I like to turn Barber's point in the other direction: more even than Hamlet or Falstaff, or than Elizabeth Bennet, or than Fanny Price in *Mansfield Park*, Rosalind and Anne Elliot are almost completely poised, nearly able to see all around the play and the novel. Their poise cannot transcend perspectivizing completely, but Rosalind's wit and Anne's sensibility, both balanced and free of either excessive aggressivity or defensiveness, enable them to share more of their creators' poise than we ever come to do.

Austen never loses dramatic intensity; we share Anne's anxiety concerning Wentworth's renewed intentions until the novel's conclusion. But we rely upon Anne as we should rely upon Rosalind; critics would see the rancidity of Touchstone as clearly as they see the vanity of Jacques if they placed more confidence in Rosalind's reactions to everyone else in the play, as well as to herself. Anne Elliot's reactions have the same winning authority; we must try to give the weight to her words that is not extended by the other persons in the novel, except for Wentworth.

Stuart Tave's point, like Barber's, is accurate even when turned in the other direction; Austen's irony is very Shakespearean. Even the reader must fall into the initial error of undervaluing Anne Elliot. The wit of Elizabeth Bennet or of Rosalind is easier to appreciate than Anne Elliot's accurate sensibility. The secret of her character combines Austenian irony with a Wordsworthian sense of deferred hope. Austen has a good measure of Shakespeare's unmatched ability to give us persons, both major and minor, who are each utterly consistent in her or his separate mode of speech, and yet completely different from one another. Anne Elliot is the last of Austen's heroines of what I think we must call the Protestant will, but in her the will is modified, perhaps perfected, by its descendant, the Romantic sympathetic imagination, of which Wordsworth, as we have seen, was the prophet. That is perhaps what helps to make Anne so complex and sensitive a character.

Jane Austen's earlier heroines, of whom Elizabeth Bennet is the exemplar, manifested the Protestant will as direct descendants of Samuel Richardson's Clarissa Harlowe, with Dr. Samuel Johnson hovering nearby as moral authority. Marxist criticism inevitably views the Protestant will, even in its literary manifestations, as a mercantile matter, and it has become fashionable to talk about the socioeconomic realities that Jane Austen excludes, such as the West Indian slavery that is part of the ultimate basis for the financial security most of her characters enjoy. But all achieved literary works are founded upon exclusions, and no one has demonstrated that increased consciousness of the relation between culture and imperialism is of the slightest benefit whatsoever in learning to read *Mansfield Park*. *Persuasion* ends with a tribute to the British navy, in which Wentworth has an honored place. Doubtless Wentworth at sea, ordering the latest batch of disciplinary floggings, is not as pleasant as Wentworth on land, gently appreciating the joys of affection with Anne Elliot. But once again, Austen's is a great art founded upon exclusions, and the sordid realities of British sea power are no more relevant to *Persuasion* than West Indian bondage is to *Mansfield Park*. Austen was, however, immensely interested in the pragmatic and secular consequences of the Protestant will, and they seem to me a crucial element in helping us appreciate the heroines of her novels.

Austen's Shakespearean inwardness, culminating in Anne Elliot, revises the moral intensities of Clarissa Harlowe's secularized Protestant martyrdom, her slow dying after being raped by Lovelace. What removes Clarissa's will to live is her stronger will to maintain the integrity of her being. To yield to the repentant Lovelace by marrying him would compromise the essence of her being, the exaltation of her violated will. What is tragedy in Clarissa is converted by Austen into ironic comedy, but the will's drive to maintain itself scarcely alters in this conversion. In *Persuasion* the emphasis is on a willed exchange of esteems, where both the woman and the man estimate the value of the other to be high. Obviously outward considerations of wealth, property, and social standing are crucial elements here, but so are the inward considerations of common sense, amiability, culture, wit, and affection. In a way (it pains me to say this, as I am a fierce Emersonian) Ralph Waldo Emerson anticipated the current Marxist critique of Austen when he denounced her as a mere conformist who would not allow her heroines to achieve the soul's true freedom from societal conventions. But that was to mistake Jane Austen, who understood that the function of convention was to liberate the will, even if convention's tendency was to stifle individuality, without which the will was inconsequential.

Austen's major heroines—Elizabeth, Emma, Fanny, and Anne—possess such inward freedom that their individualities cannot be repressed. Austen's art as a novelist is not to worry much about the socioeconomic genesis of that inner freedom, though the anxiety level does rise in *Mansfield Park* and *Persuasion*. In Austen, irony becomes the instrument for invention, which Dr. Johnson defined as the essence of poetry. A conception of inward freedom that centers upon a refusal to accept esteem except from one upon whom one has conferred esteem, is a conception of the highest degree of irony. The supreme comic scene in all of Austen must be Elizabeth's rejection of Darcy's first marriage proposal, where the ironies of the dialectic of will and esteem become very nearly outrageous. That high comedy, which continued in *Emma*, is somewhat chastened in *Mansfield Park*, and then becomes something else, unmistakable but difficult to name, in *Persuasion*, where Austen has become so conscious a master that she seems to have changed the nature of willing, as though it, too, could be persuaded to become a rarer, more disinterested act of the self.

No one has suggested that Jane Austen becomes a High Romantic in *Persuasion*; her poet remained William Cowper, not Wordsworth, and her favorite prose writer was always Dr. Johnson. But her severe distrust of imagination and of "romantic love," so prevalent in the earlier novels, is not a factor in *Persuasion*. Anne and Wentworth maintain their affection for each other throughout eight years of hopeless separation, and each has the power of imagination to conceive of a triumphant reconciliation. This is the material for a romance, not for an ironical novel. The ironies of *Persuasion* are frequently pungent, but they are almost never directed at Anne Elliot and only rarely at Captain Wentworth.

There is a difficult relation between Austen's repression of her characteristic irony about her protagonists and a certain previously unheard plangency that hovers throughout *Persuasion*. Despite Anne's faith in herself she is very vulnerable to the anxiety, which she never allows herself to express, of an unlived life, in which the potential loss transcends yet includes sexual unfulfillment. I can recall only one critic, the Australian Ann Molan, who emphasizes what Austen strongly implies, that "Anne ... is a passionate woman. And against her will, her heart keeps asserting its demand for fulfillment." Since Anne had refused Wentworth her esteem eight years before, she feels a necessity to withhold her will, and thus becomes the first Austen heroine whose will and imagination are antithetical.

Although Austen's overt affinities remained with the Aristocratic Age, her authenticity as a writer impelled her, in *Persuasion*, a long way toward the burgeoning Democratic Age, or Romanticism, as we used to call it. There is no civil war within Anne Elliot's psyche, or within Austen's; but there is the emergent sadness of a schism in the self, with memory taking the side of imagination in an alliance against the will. The almost Wordsworthian power of memory in both Anne and Wentworth has been noted by Gene Ruoff. Since Austen was anything but an accidental novelist, we might ask why she chose to found *Persuasion* upon a mutual nostalgia. After all, the rejected Wentworth is even less inclined to will a renewed affection than Anne is, and yet the fusion of memory and imagination triumphs over his will also. Was this a relaxation of the will in Jane Austen herself? Since she returns to her earlier mode in *Sanditon*, her unfinished novel begun after *Persuasion* was completed, it may be that the story of Anne Elliot was an excursion or indulgence for the novelist. The parallels between Wordsworth and *Persuasion* are limited but real. High Romantic novels in England, whether of the Byronic kind like *Jane Eyre* and *Wuthering Heights* or of a Wordsworthian sort like *Adam Bede*, are a distinctly later development. The ethos of the Austen heroine does not change in *Persuasion*, but she is certainly a more problematic being, tinged with a new sadness concerning life's limits. It may be that the elegant pathos *Persuasion* sometimes courts has a connection to Jane Austen's own ill health, her intimations of her early death.

Stuart Tave, comparing Wordsworth and Austen, shrewdly noted that both were "poets of marriage" and both also possessed "a sense of duty understood and deeply felt by those who see the integrity and peace of their own lives as essentially bound to the lives of others and see the lives of all in a more than merely social order." Expanding Tave's insight, Susan Morgan pointed to the particular affinity between Austen's *Emma* and Wordsworth's great "Ode: Intimations of Immortality from Recollections of Earliest Childhood." The growth of the individual consciousness, involving both gain and loss for Wordsworth but only gain for Austen, is the shared subject. Emma's consciousness certainly does develop, and she undergoes a quasi-Wordsworthian transformation from the pleasures of near solipsism to the more difficult pleasures of sympathy for others. Anne Elliot, far more mature from the beginning, scarcely needs to grow in consciousness. Her long-lamented rejection of Wentworth insulates her against the destructiveness of hope, which we have seen to be the frightening emphasis of the earlier Wordsworth, particularly in the story of poor Margaret. Instead of hope, there is a complex of emotions, expressed by Austen with her customary skill:

> How eloquent could Anne Elliot have been,—how eloquent, at
> least, were her wishes on the side of early warm attachment, and

a cheerful confidence in futurity, against that over-anxious caution which seems to insult exertion and distrust Providence!— She had been forced into prudence in her youth, she learned romance as she grew older—the natural sequel of an unnatural beginning.

Here learning romance is wholly retrospective; Anne no longer regards it as being available to her. And indeed Wentworth returns, still resentful after eight years, and reflects that Anne's power with him is gone forever. The qualities of decision and confidence that make him a superb naval commander are precisely what he condemns her for lacking. With almost too meticulous a craft, Austen traces his gradual retreat from this position, as the power of memory increases its dominance over him and as he learns that his jilted sense of her as being unable to act is quite mistaken. It is a beautiful irony that he needs to undergo a process of self-persuasion while Anne waits, without even knowing that she is waiting or that there is anything that could rekindle her hope. The comedy of this is gently sad, as the reader waits also, reflecting upon how large a part contingency plays in the matter.

While the pre-Socratics and Freud agree that there are no accidents, Austen thinks differently. Character is fate for her also, but fate, once activated, tends to evade character in so overdetermined a social context as Austen's world. In rereading *Persuasion*, though I remember the happy conclusion, I nevertheless feel anxiety as Wentworth and Anne circle away from each other in spite of themselves. The reader is not totally persuaded of a satisfactory interview until Anne reads Wentworth's quite agonized letter to her:

"I can listen no longer in silence. I must speak to you by such means as are within my reach. You pierce my soul. I am half agony, half hope. Tell me not that I am too late, that such precious feelings are gone for ever. I offer myself to you again with a heart more your own, than when you almost broke it eight years and a half ago. Dare not say that man forgets sooner than woman, that his love has an earlier death. I have loved none but you. Unjust I may have been, weak and resentful I have been, but never inconstant. You alone have brought me to Bath. For you alone I think and plan.—Have you not seen this? Can you fail to have understood my wishes?—I had not waited even these ten days, could I have read your feelings, as I think you must have penetrated mine. I can hardly write. I am every instant hearing something which overpowers me. You sink your voice, but I can distinguish the tones of that voice, when they would be lost on others.—Too good, too excellent creature! You do us justice indeed. You do believe that there is true attachment and constancy among men. Believe it to be most fervent, most undeviating in

"I must go, uncertain of my fate; but I shall return hither, or follow your party, as soon as possible. A word, a look will be enough to decide whether I enter your father's house this evening or never."

I cannot imagine such a letter in *Pride and Prejudice*, or even in *Emma* or *Mansfield Park*. The perceptive reader might have realized how passionate Anne was, almost from the start of the novel, but until this there was no indication of equal passion in Wentworth. His letter, as befits a naval commander, is badly written and not exactly Austenian, but it is all the more effective thereby. We come to realize that we have believed in him until now only because Anne's love for him provokes our interest. Austen wisely has declined to make him interesting enough on his own. Yet part of the book's effect is to persuade the reader of the reader's own powers of discernment and self-persuasion; Anne Elliot is almost too good for the reader, as she is for Austen herself, but the attentive reader gains the confidence to perceive Anne as she should be perceived. The subtlest element in this subtlest of novels is the call upon the reader's own power of memory to match the persistence and intensity of the yearning that Anne Elliot is too stoical to express directly.

The yearning hovers throughout the book, coloring Anne's perceptions and our own. Our sense of Anne's existence becomes identified with our own consciousness of lost love, however fictive or idealized that may be. There is an improbability in the successful renewal of a relationship devastated eight years before which ought to work against the texture of this most "realistic" of Austen's novels, but she is very careful to see that it does not. Like the author, the reader becomes persuaded to wish for Anne what she still wishes for herself. Ann Molan has the fine observation that Austen "is most satisfied with Anne when Anne is most dissatisfied with herself." The reader is carried along with Austen, and gradually Anne is also persuaded and catches up with the reader, allowing her yearning a fuller expression.

Dr. Johnson, in *The Rambler* 29, on "The folly of anticipating misfortunes," warned against anxious expectations of any kind, whether fearful or hopeful:

because the objects both of fear and hope are yet uncertain, so we ought not to trust the representations of one more than the other, because they are both equally fallacious; as hope enlarges happiness, fear aggravates calamity. It is generally allowed, that no man ever found the happiness of possession proportionate to that expectation which incited his desire, and invigorated his pursuit; nor has any man found the evils of life so formidable in reality, as they were described to him by his own imagination.

This is one of a series of Johnsonian pronouncements against the dangerous prevalence of the imagination, some of which his disciple Austen had certainly read. If you excluded such representations, on the great critic's advice, then Wordsworth could not have written at all, and Austen could not have written *Persuasion*. Yet it was a very strange book for her to write, this master of the highest art of exclusion that we have known in the Western novel. Any novel by Jane Austen could be called an achieved ellipsis, with everything omitted that could disturb her ironic though happy conclusions. *Persuasion* remains the least popular of her four canonical novels because it is the strangest, but all her work is increasingly strange as we approach the end of the Democratic Age that her contemporary Wordsworth did so much to inaugurate in literature. Poised as she is at the final border of the Aristocratic Age, she shares with Wordsworth an art dependent upon a split between a waning Protestant will and a newly active sympathetic imagination, with memory assigned the labor of healing the divide. If the argument of my book has any validity, Austen will survive even the bad days ahead of us, because the strangeness of originality and of an individual vision are our lasting needs, which only literature can gratify in the Theocratic Age that slouches toward us.

STUART M. TAVE

Anne Elliot, Whose Word Had No Weight

A fitting close to this consideration of the weight carried by some of Jane Austen's words is a quiet look, appropriately brief, at a heroine who had great difficulties in making herself heard. The first sentence that introduces Anne Elliot's name tells us that with either her father or her sister "her word had no weight ... she was only Anne" (P 5). One way of describing the action of *Persuasion* is to say that it begins when Anne's word has no weight and it ends when her word pierces a man's soul (237). Anne has so many of the admirable accomplishments, a real elegance, and the best sort of imagination, and she is exemplary in exertion; but, until the end, there is no one to do her justice.

Nobody hears Anne, nobody sees her, but it is she who is ever at the center. It is through her ears, eyes, and mind that we know most of what we know and that we are made to care for what is happening. If nobody is much aware of her, she is very much aware of everyone else and she perceives that is happening to them when they are ignorant of themselves. She knows more of the characters of the members of her family, of her father and Elizabeth, and of the dangers that threaten them, than they do. She understands Benwick's wounded mind, how far it is to be taken seriously, and how to prescribe for it, better than he does, better than his closest friends. She can define what the Musgrove girls are feeling and the reasons, when they are drawn to Captain Wentworth, though they are not capable of it themselves.

From *Some Words of Jane Austen*. © 1973 by The University of Chicago.

And she reads Wentworth's mind, with the coming troubles he is causing for others and himself, before those consequences bring the information to him. Furthermore, she is an excellent listener and it is to her that others turn when they have something to say which no one else will hear; it is a special sign of the moral obtuseness of her father and elder sister that they are exceptions to this general rule when it is they who, by natural ties and their particular needs, could most profit from this valuable quality in her. Charles Musgrove brings to her his complaints about Mary, and Mary hers about Charles. Mary confides to her what is wrong with Mrs. Musgrove, and Mrs. Musgrove and her daughters what is wrong with Mary. "She could do little more than listen patiently" and give each of them the appropriate sorts of hints (46). Captain Benwick finds in her his best audience, the opportunity for feelings glad to burst their usual restraints, and she tries to be of real use to him, with a certain amount of irony directed at herself (100–101). The next morning it is Henrietta who chooses her as confidante and, smiling to herself, Anne enters into the subject, as ready to do good by entering into the feelings of a young lady as of a young man (103). How right it is, in the scene at the White Hart, that her own opportunity to utter her large emotional speech comes to her when Captain Harville wants to confide in Anne, looks at her with a smile and a little motion of the head which expresses, "Come to me, I have something to say" (231).

Anne listens patiently at Uppercross. It is a noisy place at Christmas holidays, with much clamor, laughing, singing, dancing, even a roaring fire, and Lady Russell does not like it at all. But "Every body has their taste in noises" and sounds are quite innoxious or most distressing by their sort rather than their quantity. Lady Russell does not complain of the rumble, bawling, and clink of Bath, these being the noises she associates with her winter pleasures, and her spirits rise under them (135). But Anne listens patiently to others though her own pleasures can come, if at all, only obliquely. In the music-making at Uppercross Anne herself plays a great deal better than either of the Miss Musgroves, but "having no voice," nor anything else that would make a noise, no knowledge of the harp (the instrument of false elegance), no fond parents as an audience, her performance is little thought of, as she is well aware. Except for the one short period eight years ago, the time Frederick Wentworth had been with her, since the age of fourteen and the loss of her mother, Anne had never known "the happiness of being listened to" (47). It is an admirable strength that despite her loneliness the fond partiality of the Musgroves for their own daughters' performance and their indifference to hers gives her more pleasure for their sake than mortification for her own. Anne plays that others may dance, and it is this that recommends her musical powers to Mr. and

Mrs. Musgrove: they notice how her little fingers fly about. They do not see her and they do not hear her.

It is to be expected of her father and sister and of the Musgroves that they should be imperceptive; they have never been different and they never will be. But Captain Wentworth is different, because there was that brief period eight years ago when he had listened, had encouraged by his just appreciation and real taste, when, in music, she had not been alone in the world. The common interest in music is important in their relation and it is at a concert in Bath, late in the book, that Anne learns, again, that he must love her. He is a perceptive man, but at his first appearance in the novel he has the closed, foolish mind that only a clever man can have. When they meet for the first time upon his return, a thousand feelings rush on Anne and she cannot organize herself completely; but "she heard his voice" (59). He, however, does not perceive her. He thinks her wretchedly altered, and he does so because he has thought himself ill-used by her. She had deserted him, he thinks, out of a feebleness of character, weakness, which his own decided, confident temper could not endure. He has come ashore now and intends to marry, ready to fall in love with all the speed which a clear head and quick taste will allow. He has a heart for any pleasing young woman who comes in his way, excepting only Anne Elliot, because he wants a strong mind with sweetness of manner: that is an excellent description of Anne and marks just low clear-headed he is or how bright his bright, proud eye is. He is convinced he is "nice," a man able to discriminate, make fine distinctions. If he is a fool in marrying, he says, he shall be a fool indeed, for he has thought on the subject more than most men (61–62). The next chapter shows how foolish he is, how nice.

From this time Anne and he are repeatedly in the same circle, but they have no conversation beyond what the commonest civility requires. He talks much, narrating his career to others; his profession qualified him, his disposition led him to talk (63); his voice does not falter and his eye does not wander, but Anne from her knowledge of his mind knows that when his narrative touches the year of their engagement they must have the same immediate associations, though not the same pain. At one time, in that year, of all the large party present they two would have found it most difficult to cease to speak to one another, being so similar, so loving; now they are more than strangers, since they can never become acquainted. When he talked "she heard the same voice, and discerned the same mind" (64). He is talking to the Musgrove girls about the navy, the same sort of talk that she had heard eight years ago when she had been as surprised and as ignorant of navy life as they are now. He fills the girls with amazement, pity, horror, as he tells them of his luck, his danger from leaky ships, storm, and enemy, his narrow escapes and his large successes as a commanding officer. His style is light, assured, fascinating to the girls, the too facile manner of the returned veteran. As he thrills his audience it is Anne who shudders to herself alone, unnoticed, because it is she who has most reason to be affected by his anecdotes of peril.

It is as he is at the height of this pleasurable performance, the lovely cruise in the *Laconia* when he made money so fast, luck upon luck, that Mrs. Musgrove interrupts with a word of how lucky it was for them when Captain Wentworth took command of the *Laconia*, because Dick Musgrove was a midshipman in her. Mrs. Musgrove's feelings make her speak low; this is not something she does often, because Mrs. Musgrove, like all her family, is rather loud, and it is more in her normal style that when she attempts to moderate her voice it carries only too well in the scene at the White Hart when she is talking to Mrs. Croft it is just in that inconvenient tone of voice which is perfectly audible while it pretends to be a whisper, a powerful whisper. But she does feel for her lost son; extraordinary bursts of mind do occur and there is some part of real feeling for him at the moment. Captain Wentworth, in the full flow of his own talk, "hearing only in part" (67) and not having Dick Musgrove at all in mind, is suspended and must wait for the explanation. When it comes his momentary expression, the glance of his bright eye and curl of his handsome mouth, is sufficient indication of what his real opinion of Dick Musgrove had been, but it is too transient an indulgence in self-amusement to be detected by anyone who understands him less than Anne. It is a creditable action in Wentworth that he ceases this self-amusement of the kind he has been indulging throughout the evening and, perfectly collected and serious, sits on the sofa next to Mrs. Musgrove and enters into conversation with her, "in a low voice"; he does it with so much sympathy and natural grace as to show the kindest consideration for all that was real and unabsurd in her feelings. It is something that helps save him in our opinion; we have seen him triumphant, displaying some of the flashing and handsome qualities that make him attractive, make evident how any woman could be drawn to him, but it has all been rather too attractive, too easy. It has all been an exterior show. His response to Mrs. Musgrove shows that the man has other qualities of greater importance, both natural and moral. It also shows a higher quality of mind, an ability to make the important distinctions between what is absurd in Mrs. Musgrove and what is real. We understand better why a woman like Anne Elliot can love him, and it is necessary that we think well of him, think him worthy of Anne, if her feelings are to be important to us and if we are to desire their union.

It is at this point that there is a brief passage which may be rather disconcerting to the reader, the bit on the large, fat sighings of Mrs.

Musgrove. There is nothing soft in Jane Austen but there is nothing cruel and there is no need to explain away the passage. What she says of Mrs. Musgrove is perfectly accurate. What she says of personal size and mental sorrow—that they have certainly no necessary proportions—is clearly right and no one can quarrel with it. And what she says of the unbecoming conjunctions of bulky figure and deep affliction, that taste cannot tolerate and ridicule will seize, is an observation of general conduct and specifically not an endorsement that it is fair or reasonable. But the main point here is not the generalization but the application to the immediate dramatic moment. We see the scene with Anne. As Wentworth shows the kindest consideration for Mrs. Musgrove and her real feelings and sits next to her, the significant thing is that he and Anne are now actually sitting on the same sofa. They are divided only by Mrs. Musgrove, but that is no insignificant barrier. While Wentworth is so kind to Mrs. Musgrove he typically cannot see: the agitations of Anne's slender form and pensive face are very completely screened from him. Wentworth must be allowed credit for the self-command with which he attends to the large, fat sighings of Mrs. Musgrove and he does not fall under the general observation of seizing on the ridiculousness of the unbecoming conjunction; we must think well of him because he is a superior man. But at the same time, with all his fine quality he does not see Anne, whose feelings are more worthy of his attention and far more intimately a part of his career. The scene defines at once his excellence and his deficiency (67–68).

The point is reinforced by what follows immediately, when Admiral Croft interrupts because he is unobservant. He is not so fine a man as Wentworth, but he has the simple good sense a more refined man may lack when the fine man makes unimportant or wrong distinctions. Captain Wentworth will not willingly take lady passengers on board a ship of his, not because he lacks gallantry, as the Admiral thinks at first, but rather from feeling that it is impossible to make the accommodations on board such as a woman ought to have; his gallantry is high. This brings his sensible sister upon him, to attack his idle gallantry, his superfine, extraordinary gallantry. She hates to hear him talking like a fine gentleman and as if all women were fine ladies instead of rational creatures (68–70). This is the same Wentworth that we have seen so kind to Mrs. Musgrove, not seeing Anne, very fine and missing the essentials. When the evening ends with dancing, Anne offers her services, as usual, to play the music as others dance; her eyes sometimes fill with tears but she is glad to be employed and unobserved. She is indeed unobserved in a merry, joyous party and no one is in higher spirits than Captain Wentworth, the center of general attention and deference and especially the attention of all the young women, a little spoilt by such universal, such eager admiration, as Anne notes without wonder. Once he looks at her, to observe her altered features, perhaps; once he speaks of her to his dancing partner, to find out that Anne never dances now; once he speaks to her, only of necessity and with a studied politeness, cold and ceremonious, worse than anything; each occasion emphasizes how little he can see or hear her (71–75).

What he is doing is dangerous, both for himself and others. He is flattered and bewitched by the attention he is receiving, as the next chapter begins (73), and, without knowing it, he is making trouble. He is disturbing the potential match between Henrietta Musgrove and Charles Hayter and he is doing it not only in ignorance of their prior relation but in ignorance of his own mind. It is doubtful which of the two sisters he prefers; one is more gentle, the other more lively, and Anne, observing all this, does not know which is more likely to attract him now; he himself cannot know. Nor is it important which he prefers, because there is little to choose between them; as Admiral Croft says, later, we hardly know one from the other. What is more important, as Anne thinks, is that Wentworth should know his own mind and not endanger the happiness of either sister or impeach his own honor. He, however, is unaware and his mistaken self-confidence is stamped with a light arrogance by the incident that closes the chapter, when he finds himself unexpectedly alone with Anne. After a few words to her he is silent. Charles Hayter enters and Wentworth, not knowing Charles's feelings, is disposed for conversation with him; but Charles soon puts an end to that. Wentworth's silence to Anne and his readiness to converse with Hayter is a compounding of his confusion without his knowing it. The next moment defines him more precisely, when, as Anne kneels to attend the injured older Musgrove boy, the younger pest climbs on her back, fastens his hands around her neck, and will not obey. Charles Hayter tries to order him down—"Do not you hear your aunt speak?"—but the child will not stir. It is Wentworth, kind and resolute, who takes the child away. He does it silently and he acts well in comparison with Charles Hayter, who, knowing that he should have acted himself, is left with only a vexed tone of voice. Wentworth not only does it silently, however, but the conviction is soon forced on Anne "by the noise he was studiously making with the child, that he meant to avoid hearing her thanks" and it testifies that her conversation is the last of his wants. The mixture of the rightness of his small action and the self-created deafness to a larger issue is more than a trifle, though Anne, ashamed of being so much affected by it, tries to think that it is (78–80).

It is Anne who hears, it is Anne who is unheard. Her unintentional bit of eavesdropping from behind the hedgerow in the next chapter, a convenient device for novelists, is in this novel an explicit representation of the moral awareness of the characters. As Anne has continued to observe Wentworth she sees that Louisa is the favorite and her observations are precise in definition and in coming to the exact word. Louisa is the favorite, but Wentworth is not in love; it is the sisters who are in love with him, and yet it is not love but a little fever of admiration. Wentworth is not aware of the pain he is causing Hayter, but he is wrong in accepting the attentions "(for accepting must be the word)" of the two women (82). As she is walking with them on a November day it is a melancholy time for Anne, though not so sad as she thinks. She wants to be out of the way of anybody and her pleasure is in viewing the tawny leaves and withered hedges and in occupying her mind with poetic quotations on the season. That is not what her mind should be on and in fact it is not possible that when near Wentworth's conversation with the Musgrove girls she should not try to hear it. There is little of importance to hear, but it is now certainly Louisa who is engaging more of his attention; a feeling seems to develop between him and Louisa, as she speaks with loud enthusiasm of how bravely and inseparably she could love and he catches her tone. That development stops Anne's autumnal quotations for a bit. She rouses herself to point out the direction the walk has taken, to Winthrop. "But nobody heard, or, at least, nobody answered her" (85). It is not quite clear at this moment why the direction of the walk is important and its immediate effect will be to Anne's disadvantage, but the farmer is at work plowing a fresh path, counteracting the autumnal quotations because he means to have spring again. It develops that the walk has been to Winthrop to enable Henrietta to return her affection to Charles Hayter. Anne learns this as she sits under the hedgerow and, unseen, hears Wentworth and Louisa behind her. She distinguishes Louisa's voice first and from her speech it appears that Louisa has made Henrietta go, not allowed Henrietta to be persuaded into giving up her intention of returning to Charles Hayter by the snobbish pride of Mary Musgrove. Wentworth admires Louisa's mind, her fortitude, strength, resolution, decision, firmness. He delivers with playful solemnity his sermon on the beautiful nut which by its strength has outlived all the storms of autumn and possessed happiness, and he recommends its firm example to Louisa if she wishes to be beautiful and happy in her November of life. His playfulness is a saving grace, but he is quite serious in his moral judgments, and quite wrong in their application. What he does not know is that Louisa's firm powers of mind have been used to eliminate her sister from the competition and leave Captain Wentworth all for herself. More seriously, he is not only mispraising and misleading Louisa but the obvious contrast between her and Anne which he has in mind is a blind reversal of truths. Anne at the moment is protected by a bush of holly; he has yet to learn of her November (87–88).

It was evidently Jane Austen's first intention that the ending of the novel should follow this same pattern, of Anne the overhearer and the unheard. In the original Chapter X of Volume II Anne is once again, unwillingly but typically, placed in a situation where she listens to others, this time through a very firmly closed door. It has been closed by Wentworth, who wants to keep her from hearing and who speaks in a love tone, but who cannot check the unmanaged and natural voice of Admiral Croft. It is impossible for Anne not to distinguish parts of their conversation and she hears her own name. The important difference between the succeeding scene of Anne and Wentworth and their earlier scenes is that by this time Wentworth's unwillingness to speak or hear is in his knowledge of his own awkwardness and inferiority. But it is still he who does almost all the talking, as he must in this situation, who must say that "a very few words" from her will be sufficient. "Anne spoke a word or two, but they were unintelligible," and he speaks again, before she can command herself, to dictate to her the form of her answer: if she will only tell him that the Admiral may address a line to Sir Walter, giving up the lease to Kellynch, it mill be enough; "Pronounce only the words, *he may*." At that point Anne speaks out and the truth is revealed. His eyes, with all their power and keenness blind for most of the novel, for the first time see the truth; his expression has something more than penetration in it, something softer which they have been wanting. What ensues is "a silent but very powerful dialogue" and then on his part a bursting forth in the fullness of exquisite feeling (258). It is a grand scene, but not good enough for Jane Austen.

The revision is in many ways more satisfying, but the one point that is relevant here is the difference in the weight of Anne's word. The arrival of the additional characters from Uppercross puts Anne and Wentworth in a large company once again, as they had been at Uppercross in the recent past, and the marked difference is that now Wentworth is alive to every opportunity of understanding Anne. As Anne speaks to Mary Musgrove about Mr. Elliot, she feels that Wentworth is looking at her, as he is, to understand how she feels toward Mr. Elliot (222). As Charles Musgrove talks of Mr. Elliot, Anne sees that, for the same reason, Wentworth is all attention, "looking and listening with his whole soul" (224) and turning his inquiring eyes from Charles to herself. When she speaks on the subject she is conscious that "her words were listened to" (225). Tentative, broken conversation between them—open to some misconstruction on his part, Anne fears, hearing the sounds he utters—is interrupted first by Henrietta, then by more alarming sounds as her father and sister arrive to reduce the room to a hush, determined silence, or insipid talk. When Mary whispers very audibly her mistaken conviction of Wentworth's delight at her father's and sister's attentions, Anne turns away that she may neither see nor hear more to vex her and she goes home to be sure of being as silent as she chooses. But her vexation is not entirely justified, or is so only because Wentworth is now listening to her and she is anxious that he hear the right sounds.

In the climactic scene of the revision, the next day Anne at the White Hart is in her characteristic posture, alone in a group. Wentworth, engrossed in writing a letter for Harville, nearly turns his back on them all. Mrs. Musgrove is talking to Mrs. Croft in her inconvenient tone of voice, the perfectly audible whisper, and Anne cannot avoid hearing. But the conversation is unexpectedly interesting, because it turns on the unadvisability of long engagements and Anne feels its application to herself; it becomes more interesting when she sees that Wentworth has paused to listen, and to give one quick, conscious look at her. Harville, wrapped in his own thoughts, has heard none of it and now invites Anne to come listen to him, nearer to Wentworth. They talk of Fanny Harville, how she who has been forgotten would not have forgotten so soon, he speaking in a deep tone, Anne "in a low feeling voice" (232), and by Anne's generalization they turn the instance to the nature of a woman's feelings. The tenderness and long life of those feelings are a subject Anne knows well and as she goes on she talks "with a faltering voice" (233). At that point a slight noise calls their attention to Captain Wentworth, whose pen has fallen, startling Anne, who had not thought him so close and who suspects that his pen has fallen because he has been "striving to catch sounds, which yet she did not think he could have caught" (234). She is underestimating him. Harville and Anne continue to talk, in varied tones as the emotion builds, until Anne claims for her sex the unenviable privilege of loving longest when hope is gone and she cannot utter another sentence because her heart is too full, her breath too oppressed. Harville cannot quarrel with her; his tongue is tied. Wentworth is impatient to be gone, which Anne does not know how to understand, and he leaves without a word or a look. Her understanding comes when she hears footsteps and he returns to place his letter before her with glowing eyes. It is the letter that reveals the effect her words have had on him, and the effect has been great. The man who at the beginning had said no more to her than civility required, who deliberately wanted to avoid hearing her, can now no longer listen in silence and must speak to her by such means as are within his reach. She has pierced his soul. The man who has talked so well and easily now finds that he can hardly write because he is every instant hearing something that overpowers him. To that voice he did not want to hear he is now perfectly attuned: "You sink your voice, but I can distinguish the tones of that voice, when they would be lost on others" (237). He is now alive to the smallest sign from her, and it will be decisive in his life: "A word, a look will be enough to decide" (238). An essential difference in the new ending is the reversal of the positions of Anne and Wentworth. The final understanding does not begin with her listening to him through a closed door; we know already her ability to hear him through barriers, to read his mind, the loving anxious perception that makes it possible. His footsteps behind her, as he approaches to know her answer, are what she has always heard, "a something of familiar sound" (239). But what we see for the first time in the revision is his ability to hear her.

This importance throughout the novel of the finely attuned ear is one of the things that makes the Mrs. Smith of Chapter IX a tiresome character. It is in that chapter immediately preceding the revised ending that Anne learns the truth about Mr. Elliot and it is right that she should. At the beginning of that chapter she feels a great deal of good will toward him, because of his understanding of the dangers of Mrs. Clay, feels also she owes him gratitude and regard, in return for his affection to herself, and perhaps compassion, if he is to suffer because she cannot return his feeling. After hearing Mrs. Smith's story she is relieved in one point; no tenderness is due him and no pity. Mr. Elliot has been a threat to Anne's family and to herself. He holds out to her the possibility of becoming Lady Elliot and mistress of Kellynch, of becoming what her mother had been and to Anne that is a moving possibility. She must learn the truth about him and Mrs. Smith is able to tell her what no one else could have told her; it is a reward for Anne's attentions to her old friend and it is to that degree a result of her own effort. It is also true that Mrs. Smith begins to tell her story because she needs Anne's help and to that degree Anne is in a familiar listening posture. But the Anne we have come to see in the novel is quite capable of learning for herself what must be known without this long, circumstantial narrative of details and documents of the dead; the story itself is uninteresting and burdensome for its function in the novel, but its chief fault is that it works by way of direct revelation, pouring out upon Anne a stream of information in a novel where the characteristic and significant mode of learning is indirection. The listening ear hears the significant detail. It is uncomfortable for the reader to find someone saying to Anne, to give her essential information, "Hear the truth, therefore, now ... Oh! he is black at heart, hollow and black!" (199).

ANNE needs neither such imperatives nor such unmodulated language to reach her. She hears well because she knows how to "submit." The word does not mean weak and it does not mean passive. The right kind of submission requires strength. It requires self-command and self-knowledge. When she hears that Wentworth, having seen her again for the first time in eight years, thought her altered beyond his knowledge, "Anne fully submitted, in silent, deep mortification" (60–61). Every word is important. The *mortification* is the painful recognition of one's own deficiencies which only the best can learn from. Anne's is *deep*, because it goes to her deepest desires, tells her that the loved woman she was once has been destroyed. That it is *silent* is in her best mode of isolated knowledge and contained suffering. She admits fully, without any reservations that might protect herself by timidity or reaction. She *submits* to the necessity and undergoes the truth. She does not deny it— doubtless it was so; and she does not attempt to revenge herself by a return in kind upon him. Her reward is that his reported words have a value for her in that they allay her agitation, compose her and consequently, she thinks, must make her happier. If her future is to be more agitated and her happiness of a different and better sort than she anticipates at the moment, the manner of her response is the right one and it is the only way she will find her happiness. She may not find it at all, but she will never find it in any other way. She will have to face suffering, but to try to avoid it will be worse. In thinking over the past, at the end, after her happiness has been assured, and trying impartially to judge the right and wrong of her own action, she must believe that she was right in being guided by Lady Russell, much as she suffered from it. Lady Russell was in the place of a parent to her. Not that the advice was right, "But I mean, that I was right in submitting to her." If she had done otherwise she should have suffered more in continuing the engagement than she did even in giving it up, because she should have suffered in her conscience (246).

The most interesting function of Mrs. Smith in the novel is not in providing information but in bringing out the particular quality of Anne as one who can bear suffering. For Mrs. Smith has more serious physical and economic ills to face than Anne has, and is even more alone in the world. Yet her spirits are high and her enjoyments more than her depression. How this can be is a matter of much interest to Anne, who watches, observes, reflects, and finds that there is in Mrs. Smith an elasticity of mind, a disposition to be comforted, a power of turning readily from evil to good, of finding employment, which comes from Nature alone, and is the choicest gift of Heaven. The gifts of Nature and Heaven are mercies and in that sense Mrs. Smith has something more than Anne (154). What Anne has is a "submissive spirit" that is patient and a strong understanding that supplies resolution, but these are the qualities that give her a value superior to Mrs. Smith and make her worth watching. Mrs. Smith responds to adversity with a natural elasticity but Anne must earn her way by fortitude and by resignation and that is a process that takes struggle and time. Mrs. Smith has one fine gift and a single value but Anne must work with a combination of opposing and complementary qualities. It is something Captain Wentworth does not understand.

Anne's gentle submission is coordinate with her strength and resolution and it is essential in that fineness of mind that enables her to make distinctions. It is the essential first condition for the listening ear. When she arrives at the White Hart for the beginning of what becomes the proposal scene, her mind filled with her own keen interest, she finds the others engaged in talk of their own concerns—Mrs. Musgrove with Mrs. Croft, Captain Harville with Captain Wentworth—and she finds that Mary and Henrietta, too impatient to wait, have gone out but have left strictest injunctions that Anne must be kept until they return. It is the situation she knows well. "She had only to submit, sit down, be outwardly composed, and feel herself plunged at once in all the agitations ..." (229). The agitations of Anne, here as elsewhere, are not the nervous affliction of a weak creature, without cause and without issue. The causes are the real difficulties of her situation and the mixed feelings they produce, the issue is a continual effort to submit to her necessity, hold the conflicting emotions without being false to them and to distinguish the exact elements. Captain Wentworth is a clear-headed man, a decisive man, one who knows his own mind and has no doubts of his ability to make moral distinctions for himself and for others. He lectures well, as Louisa Musgrove knows. He is a fine dashing fellow, as Dick Musgrove wrote home—in one of the few letters he wrote, under the influence of his excellent captain; "only," as Dick said in the only insight ever recorded in his spelling, "two perticuler about the school-master" (52). Captain Wentworth knows rather too much too easily. He is a lucky man. But he has always been used to the gratification of believing himself to have earned every blessing he enjoys, valuing himself on honorable toils and just rewards. His toils assuredly have been honorable and he and his profession, Anne sees, deserve their rewards, while her useless father is unworthy to hold what he has inherited. But Wentworth also realizes, by the end, and it is a sort of pain which is new to him, that in gaining Anne after so misvaluing her, and after missing the opportunity to act, he has been given more than he has earned. "'Like other great men under reverses,' he added with a smile, 'I must endeavour to subdue my mind to my fortune. I must learn to brook being happier than I deserve'" (247). The smile, the wit, turned properly upon himself in recognition of his own failures, make us know again how this man can be loved. The notion of Captain Wentworth endeavoring to subdue his mind to his fortune is both amusing and serious and that tone gives us the degree to which he has been made to undergo the experience of Anne's submission. Like other great men under reverses, he says; like one small woman, we know.

Anne is not lucky like him, not gifted like Mrs. Smith; she is the one who must earn her blessings. She is not the schoolmaster of others that he is;

she, as we are told on the same page (52), "must teach herself" to sustain the trial, the nerves, to enure herself. It must be done with complete acceptance, without the easier devices of turning the blame and the burden upon another. This is more than Wentworth can do. When Elizabeth Elliot lacked the moral strength to solve her own problem "She felt herself ill-used," as did her father (11). Mary Musgrove is a weak and querulous creature forever fancying that she is being "ill-used" when it is absurdly plain that it is she who imposes on others and especially on Anne (37, 107, 221). Mrs. Bennet (PP 129) and Margaret Watson (MW 351) are similar nervous females who enjoy feeling ill-used. But it is somewhat startling to find that the strong-minded Wentworth applies the same word to his needs. Anne had given up their engagement because she believed she was being prudent and self-denying for his advantage, but he added to her pain, being totally unconvinced and unbending, and "feeling himself ill-used" (28). The words he spoke, when he returned, to which she fully submitted, had been spoken quickly and as he felt; he had not forgiven her; "she had used him ill" (61; cf. 172). Anne had stood with him on one side of her and Lady Russell on the other when her early decision had to be made. It was a vexed problem and though she knows at the end that she was right in what she had done, Lady Russell's advice was perhaps in error or was good or bad only as the event decided, and was certainly not the advice Anne herself would give in similar circumstances. The important point, the one the novel concentrates on, is not the rights or wrongs of the distant and difficult originating event, but the manner in which the participants were able to sustain its lengthy consequences. Captain Wentworth could not forgive either Anne or Lady Russell and thought himself ill-used by a weak woman. Lady Russell, who never understood anyone so different from herself as Wentworth, saw him as dangerous. When she sees him eight years later seemingly attached to Louisa Musgrove she listens composedly and says she wishes them happy; but she sees his present unworthy taste as her justification and internally her heart revels in angry pleasure, in pleased contempt (125). Both Captain Wentworth and Lady Russell are excellent people and Anne loves them both, but neither is capable of Anne's submissive integrity that never requires a feeling of being ill-used or the vindication of contempt.

Anne's position in the novel, again and again, is to stand between opposed forces, neither understanding her and both putting pressure on her, without succumbing, without losing her ability to judge. She stands at various times between Wentworth and Lady Russell, between this Musgrove and that, between Kellynch and Uppercross, between her father and the several threats to him and his position. She stands between the navy and Kellynch, as the one takes over the other, and it is the active virtues of the navy she comes to regard more highly; the action begins when Anne loses one home and ends when she finds another. But what is more important in the course of the novel is that Anne is not herself properly valued by either her family or her naval captain, both sides thinking she falls, faded and weak, below their own high standards. She, of course, embodies in practice the best values of each force better than its self-assured representative, takes the best from each without ever misjudging the other or resenting it, or collapsing, or giving up a part of her own best self. As she moves about in the novel, going from Kellynch to Uppercross, to Lyme, to Kellynch, to Bath, she is aware that she removes each time from one set of people to another, that, however short the distance, she moves into a total change of conversation, opinion, and ideas, that she moves into another social commonwealth (42–43, 124). Anne's accomplishment in making the movement into a new society is in realizing "she must now submit to feel that another lesson, in the art of knowing our own nothingness beyond our own circle, was become necessary for her." The art of knowing our own nothingness is the art that can enter into another circle, make its concerns and its discourse our own, hope to become a not unworthy member of the commonwealth into which we are transplanted. Emma Woodhouse with so much imagination had no art to see beyond one circle, but Anne has, more than anyone in Jane Austen, the right kind of imagination. She knows when it is incumbent on her "to clothe her imagination, her memory, and all her ideas" in as much of the new commonwealth as she can. She has the strength and capacity of mind to hold varied and conflicting forces while never losing her own integrity.

This control of confusion is going on continually within her own feelings. When she is to see Wentworth again for the first time after so long a separation, at Uppercross Cottage with Mary, he provides her with a two-minute warning of his coming; Mary takes this as a gratifying attention to herself, is delighted to receive him, and has no reason for a more complicated reaction; but "a thousand feelings rushed on Anne." Her eye half met his, she heard his voice as he talked to Mary and the Miss Musgroves: "the room seemed full—full of persons and voices" (59). When it is over, as it is in a few minutes, Anne begins to reason with herself and tries to be feeling less. It is absurd to be resuming the agitation that eight years, nearly a third of her life, have banished into distance and indistinctness. But she soon finds that to retentive feelings the eight years are little more than nothing. The agitations are the thronging of emotions in a sensitive mind that forgets nothing and is aware of the weight of every moment, its history and its gestures, but the response is an activity that is always working for meaning and for control by making the distinctions. At the moment when Wentworth removes the troublesome little boy from her neck her sensations make her perfectly speechless, leave her with most disordered feelings; all the little particulars of the situation, each of which enables her to understand his feelings, produce a confusion of varying but very painful agitation: she must arrange her feelings, she is ashamed of being so nervous and overcome, and it requires a long application of solitude and reflection to recover (80–81). When, at the return from the walk to Winthrop, Wentworth places her in the Crofts' carriage, much is made apparent to her in this little circumstance. She understands him, both the unjust condemnation for the past and the warm impulse which is the remainder of a former sentiment; and that remainder she cannot contemplate without emotions so compounded of pleasure and pain that she knows not which prevailed (91). When they meet again in the shop at Bath, for the first time after learning that Louisa is to marry Benwick, it is Anne who has descried him first, "most decidedly and distinctly," walking down the street. The effect is to make her start, though this is perceptible only to herself. "For a few minutes she saw nothing before her. It was all confusion." She scolds back her senses. When they then meet "It was agitation, pain, pleasure, a something between delight and misery" (175). The ambiguities of "a something between" can be, in Jane Austen, treacherous ground, Mary Crawford's or Emma Woodhouse's evasion of responsible definition; Anne never seeks those moments of ambiguity and never avoids them, but bears them all as she must and until they can be brought to clarity. In the subsequent conversation with Wentworth, in the octagon room, she learns from what he says of Louisa and Benwick and of first attachments that his heart is returning to her; Anne hears it all: in spite of the agitation of his voice, in spite of "all the various noises of the room, the almost ceaseless slam of the door, and ceaseless buzz of persons walking through," Anne had "distinguished every word" and was struck, gratified, confused, and beginning to "feel an hundred things in a moment" (183). At the White Hart after she hears and feels the unexpected meaning in the conversation between Mrs. Musgrove and Mrs. Croft and sees that Wentworth is listening too, the talk continues but Anne now hears nothing distinctly; "it was only a buzz of words in her ear, her mind was in confusion" (231). At that point, however, the conversation is merely re-urging the admitted truths and Anne has heard them. For it is her ability to sustain the buzz and the confusion and to hear distinctly what must be heard, to make the right distinctions under the agitation of pain, of pleasure, of mixed feelings, that makes her so lovely. She has a power and it is what Wentworth, who thought her power with him gone forever (61), must learn from her.

The process begins for him when Louisa falls. It is his fault because he has encouraged her to think that being resolute, having her own way, is a virtue. The effect of the incident upon the clear and decided Captain is to take all his strength from him and when there is assurance that her injuries are not fatal he sits over a table "as if overpowered by the various feelings of his soul" (112). That overpowering is important because it is necessary for him to experience the variousness of feelings, to lose his clarity, to be plunged into confusion, before he can learn. It is an experience that comes to more than one character in this novel; it is sometimes objected that it is inconsistent in Mrs. Clay to run off with Mr. Elliot, after having been so calculating throughout, and perhaps she should not; but it is good to see that "her affections had overpowered her interest" (250) and it is a fitting punishment that the beginning of a human response is the cause of her fall. For Captain Wentworth the overpowering is the beginning of knowledge. By the time he meets Anne again in Bath he has learned much about himself. She has seen him coming and has regained her senses from confusion and passed the overpowering first effects before he sees her. He is more obviously struck and confused by the sight of her than she has ever seen him; for the first time in the novel she is betraying less sensibility than he is. He is now prepared to begin making distinctions. In their next conversation, in the octagon room (181–84), he returns to the events at Lyme, having hardly seen her since the day of the fall; he is afraid she must have suffered from the shock, the more from its not "overpowering" her at the time. She assures him she was well. We know that it was an overpowering moment for him, but not for her, who retained her presence of mind, who had not borne a responsibility for the event. He thinks she can have no liking for Lyme because of the distress she was involved in, the toll on mind and spirits, but she knows more of pain and pleasure than he does and can set him right: the last few hours were painful but when pain is over, the remembrance is often a pleasure; and one does not love a place less for having suffered in it, certainly not when there has been previous pleasure there. Lessons like this, in the careful discriminations of mixed feelings, are what she is best qualified to give and he, now, to receive. It is, then, in the scene at the White Hart that he finally hears her as he strives to catch the sounds. He is, he tells her in the letter, "half agony, half hope." He is every instant "hearing something which overpowers" him. She sinks her voice, but he can "at last distinguish the tones" of that voice (237). It has been a long course for him, as he explains it later, learning to do justice to her at Uppercross, and beginning to understand himself at Lyme. It was only through Louisa's fall and the time that followed, which enabled him to reflect, that he had learnt to distinguish between steadiness of principle and obstinacy of self-will, between the darings of heedlessness and the resolution of a collected mind (241–42). Nor had his education been completed when he made his proposal. He had been jealous of Mr. Elliot, who seemed so eligible a match, had been feeling a fool and looking on with agony, thinking that Lady Russell, who had once been so persuasive might be so again. "'You should have distinguished,' replied Anne": the case was different, her age was different; if she yielded once to persuasion it was on the side of safety and not risk; when she yielded it was to duty; in marrying Mr. Elliot, a man indifferent to her, all risk would have been incurred and all duty violated. But Wentworth had been unable to reason thus; all knowledge of Anne's character he had recently acquired had been overwhelmed, buried, lost in his earlier feelings under which he had been smarting for eight years (244–45). That exchange on duty prepares him to understand Anne's justification of her earlier conduct, her submission to Lady Russell; there she sorts out for him the right and the wrong, and then makes him feel the strong sense of duty she brings him as no bad part of her marriage portion (246).

The sense of duty is perhaps the strength one might expect to be the contribution of the naval hero, but, as so frequently, it is Anne who has more of the quality that other characters think they themselves have and which they put forward for display; it is Anne who really has the virtue and has it in its best form. Her father and sister are proud people, with high ideas of their own situation in life; but when Anne sees them for the first time in contact with nobility, with their cousins Lady Dalrymple and Miss Carteret, she forms a wish she had never foreseen—a wish that they had more pride (148). Mr. Elliot, with more sense than Sir Walter and Elizabeth but an ever sharper sense of the advantages of rank, tries to point out to her the value of these cousins. Anne replies, "I suppose (smiling) I have more pride than any of you" (151) . It is Captain Benwick who is the man of feeling, so regarded by all his friends and acquaintance and by himself, looking so entirely as if he would be understood. But he is the quick forgetter, easily comforted by a less worthy woman than the one he has lost, and it is the submissive and unheard Anne who has the real retentive feeling. It is Louisa Musgrove who thinks of herself as the resolute woman, but she is in fact heedless and self-willed, as Wentworth comes to realize, and it is Anne who has the real resolution. It is a delicate justice at the end that when Captain Wentworth follows Anne and Charles Musgrove—he has written his letter but does not know how Anne has received it—he is "irresolute" whether to join them or to pass on. He can only look. Anne commands herself to receive that look—and he walked by her side (239–40). Because it is, finally, Wentworth, who has thought of her as weak and timid and himself as strong, who sees that he has been weak (237) and she strong. That kind of simple truth, Jane Austen always knew, is the most difficult to make real.

Persuasion is Anne Elliot's novel but the story is not at all obviously hers, as, say, *Pride and Prejudice* is Elizabeth Bennet's or *Emma* is Emma Woodhouse's. Jane Austen has of course made a deliberate choice, because the readiest way of telling the story would be to make it Frederick Wentworth's. It is he who has what is conventionally the central role of a comedy or romance: the young man who, because he acts foolishly or weakly or is blind to the truth, finds himself attracted to and involved with the wrong young lady; when he arrives at the realization of how wrong he has been, and he understands himself and understands the real value of the right young lady, he transfers his affections and secures his happy ending. To tell that story from the point of view of the woman who waits for him, when all the active doing—the mistaken decisions and the crisis of self-understanding and change of decision—belongs to him, is to tell it the hard way. It is not very helpful to talk of Jane Austen's work as, wisely or weakly, cautious in venture because restricted to a female viewpoint. It is not enlightening to note that she gives us no scene in which men converse without the presence of a woman, as though one had thereby pointed out a limitation. If that fact points to anything it is to one of the defining strengths. It could be used more effectively to support the observation of her extraordinary originality. "It was strange to think that all the great women of fiction were, until Jane Austen's day, not only seen by the other sex, but seen only in relation to the other sex." (Virginia Wolf, *A Room of One's Own*.) All histories are against you, Captain Harville says to Anne in their disagreement about man's nature and woman's nature, "all stories, prose and verse." He could bring fifty quotations in a moment to his side of the argument, from books, songs, proverbs. But they were all written by men. "Men have had every advantage of us in telling their own story," as Anne says (234). *Persuasion* is the story told by the woman.

Jane Austen had already told the stories of Elinor Dashwood and of Fanny Price, which presented similar problems, since they too, in the conventional mode, could have been the stories of Edward Ferrars and of Edmund Bertram. But *Persuasion* seems to solve the problem more successfully, partly because it sets for itself even greater difficulties. If the heroine of such a novel is to dominate it in spite of her restricted opportunities of action, then it is her mind and her feelings that must be at the center and the man's mind must become less interesting except as she is interested in him. The least successful part of *Sense and Sensibility* is the character of Edward. We must be convinced of Edward's value, not for his sake but because we must believe in Elinor's feelings, believe that her love is important because the man is important, that her suffering in the loss of him is deep because the man has depth. But the requirements of the plot are such that his secret engagement forces him to be reserved, dispirited, and dull and that flattens not only his spirits but his freedom to allow himself to be attractive to Elinor. The result is an unsolved problem and though he is a worthy young man we never see well how Elinor comes to feel so much for him. Edmund Bertram is allowed much more scope, but the problem with him is that he must be very like Fanny but a lesser version of her, similar in mind but not quite up to her level. The result there is that he does not have a different life and interest, and he sometimes seems obtuse in making poor judgments at the moment she is making the right ones on the same principles and the same evidence. But Captain Wentworth is able to hold the eye with the brightness of his own life, has another style and history from Anne's, gives every proof of a man who can be loved. That, by complicating the author's problem, helps to solve it; the novel becomes Anne's more convincingly when the man to whom the story might belong is impressive enough to give greater weight to her emotions for him. But that complicates the problem because then Anne herself must become even more impressive to maintain the center; her word must have great weight indeed.

Anne is "delicate," she has the real delicacy that is pained to see unfeeling conduct and she sympathizes with the sufferer (77); even the delicacy of her features is emphasized by the contrast with her family, with her father who cannot appreciate her delicacy because his own good looks are so totally different (6), with her older sister whose more fashionable beauty is more admired by men: "Anne is too delicate for them" (178). Anne is an "elegant little woman" (153), the most truly elegant of Jane Austen's women because hers is a fully represented quality of mind and character. Once again the contrast with her family illuminates its unusual beauty. Elizabeth and Sir Walter have the elegance of manner that is empty, fashionable, stupid, anxious, heartless (e.g., 9, 140, 141, 180, 184, 226). Anne from her first introduction to us has "an elegance of mind and sweetness of character" which must have placed her high with any people of real understanding, though with her father and sister her word had no weight (5). She has an "elegant and cultivated mind" (41), the "Elegance, sweetness, beauty" that Captain Benwick can see (131). But this little woman, delicate, elegant, sweet, has the kind of force the genuinely heroic Captain Wentworth has not. She is gentle, with her "gentle and embarrassed glance, and a 'good morning to you,'" (177) and her "gentle 'How do you do?'" (181); if that gentleness was once something that attracted him (74), he had in weakness and resentment come to see it as a deficiency in liveliness and in firmness of character. What he has not seen is the correlative of the gentleness. Anne has fortitude. The character he had judged to be of little "fortitude and strength of mind" (88) is at last fixed on his mind as perfection itself, "maintaining the loveliest medium of fortitude and gentleness" (241).

Fortitude is a cardinal virtue and the virtue a successful warrior has well been able to believe most especially his own. It is gentle Anne's, now, in a higher sense of heroism, in the patience that is the truest fortitude, as Milton might have said, patience the trial of fortitude that makes one his own deliverer and victor over fortune and over the temptation of sadness. "Fortitude is very becoming in both sexes," James Beattie said, and, unlike a more brutal courage, consistent with "a certain degree of timidity" and "gentleness of disposition" (*Elements of Moral Science*, Edinburgh 1790–93, is 302–4).

Other authors, especially the guides of the female mind, had recommended to young ladies the passive courage, "patience, and fortitude under sufferings" (Hester Chapone, *Letters on the Improvement of the Mind, Addressed to a Young Lady*, 1773, I: 125), and there was a religious history behind these moralists. There are, however, obvious difficulties here for authors who are interested in the varieties of human nature and its actions. Dr. Johnson, in the *Rambler* (no. 34), said he had been censured for having dedicated so few of his speculations to the ladies and he acknowledged a fault: "Yet it is to be considered, that masculine duties afford more room for counsels and observations, as they are less uniform, and connected with things more subject to vicissitude and accident; we therefore find that in philosophical discourses which teach by precept, or historical narratives that instruct by example, the peculiar virtues or faults of women fill but a small part." There would seem to be an opportunity here for the novelist, but there is still the problem of the lesser room afforded by feminine duties in a duller and unvaried life. "We live at home, quiet, confined," Anne says to Captain Harville. "You are forced on exertion" (232).

But within that confinement of the novel it is Anne who has the exertion. Man represents himself as characterized by superior fortitude, said Thomas Gisborne, but "Fortitude is not to be sought merely on the rampart, on the deck, on the field of battle. Its place is no less in the chamber of sickness and pain, in the retirements of anxiety, of grief, and of disappointment." (*An Enquiry into the Duties of the Female Sex*, 1797, p. 25.) What instances of ardent, disinterested, self-denying attachment there must be in a sick chamber, says Anne, instances of "heroism, fortitude, patience, resignation—of all the conflicts and all the sacrifices that ennoble us most. A sick chamber may often furnish the worth of volumes." Mrs. Smith, with more experience and more doubt, knows that human nature may be great in times of trial but generally it is its weakness and not its strength that appears in a sick chamber, its "selfishness and impatience rather than generosity and fortitude" (156). Anne is an instance of the heroism and fortitude, patience and all that ennoble us most, not because she is what women generally are, or what women are conventionally supposed to be, but because she has greatness in action. She furnishes the worth of her two volumes. Women may have fortitude not much inferior to that of "the other sex, on whom many more scenes of danger and of strenuous exertion are devolved," says Gisborne (p. 30). But no man exerts himself more than Anne.

If she has none of the glorious opportunities of Wentworth on the deck in stormy and embattled seas before he makes his entrance, within the novel it is she who acts, acts usefully, more than he, or anyone. (It is certainly one of the improvements of the revised ending that it is Anne's action, in her conversation with Captain Harville, that brings her and Wentworth together, as it was her action that wears earlier had separated them.) Captain Harville is an admirable man, as Anne sees him, living in rooms so small but turning the actual space to the best possible account; his home reflects his character and his profession, his life of active labor, his "mind of usefulness" (98–99). Within her own small room Anne has always had that mind of usefulness. She has no physical vigor to spare and is frequently more deserving of aid than those she aids, but it is extraordinary how whenever someone is ill it is Anne who nurses, whenever anyone falls it is Anne who is there to put things right. Mary's indispositions may be imaginary but it is only Anne who can make her well. Mary's son may have a real injury but it is only Anne who can nurse him properly. Whether it is Benwick's broken heart or Louisa's broken head (neither is made of durable stuff) Anne is the one who has the head and heart to say the necessary words and take the necessary actions when they must be said and done. Mrs. Smith seems to have no attraction, says Sir Walter, except that she is old and sickly, but Anne is not put off from what should be done. As always, the value of Anne is all the more precious in a family where, with great show, no one else does anything; where her father preserves his handsome appearance by his contempt for any man in a profession that "has its utility" (19) and where he is not even able to maintain himself in the position in life to which he has been born. Her older sister Elizabeth has had a life of elegance, prosperity, and nothingness, of vacancy, because "there were no habits of utility abroad," no talents or accomplishments for home (9). Her young sister Mary enjoys "the sense of being so very useful" to the injured Louisa that it helps make for her a really agreeable fortnight at Lyme (130), but we know how useless she has been even in caring for her own hurt child. It was Anne who "knew herself to be of the first utility to the child" (58). If there are few comforts for Anne in those first days at Uppercross, there are some and they are important; if her own happiness is not much, that does not reduce her to self-pity or uselessness. "Her usefulness to little Charles would always give some sweetness to the memory" of her visit (93); returning to Uppercross, when the family is in distress after the incident at Lyme, "she had the satisfaction of knowing herself extremely useful there" (121). It is Anne, and the useful Captain Harville and his wife (111, 121), who can exert themselves when they are needed. When Louisa falls it is not Captain Wentworth but Anne who takes charge, with strength and zeal and thought, while he and the others look to her for direction (111). Wentworth begins to see something of the strength he had thought was not there; she hears that he has expressed the hope of her not being the worse "for her exertions, and had spoken of those exertions as great." This is handsome and gives Anne more pleasure than almost anything else could have done (126).

Captain Wentworth's appreciation is the most pleasing repayment of her exertions and it looks forward to the happiness so much deserved by her; but it is dependent necessarily not on herself but on his growing understanding. His recognition must come only after the other repayments which are not dependent. She has always known the obligations and the pleasures of exertion and her action on a spectacular occasion has come from a mind that has always acted from the right impulse, usually unobtrusively and effectively, where others were not able. Wentworth himself has done much, in traveling to and staying long with his friend Benwick, for example, when Benwick suffered a serious loss; Anne, quietly, while Wentworth and Harville lead the talk on one side of the room, by her mildness and gentleness, encourages Benwick to talk and has her good effect on him; he turns out to be rather interesting and she is "well repaid the first trouble of exertion" (100). This private discovery of values in other people which would not otherwise have been made is another pleasing issue. The sweet memories created by her usefulness to others is still more intimate in its effect. But the most important repayment is not in the supervening reward, however sweet, but is intrinsic in the act itself. Her usefulness to others, her exertions, have risen from a self-command and a sense of duty that make the actions possible, and the reward is that the exertion in turn helps to create that conquest of self. For the last point must be that if Anne, as heroine, has what seem to be specifically feminine virtues of submission and patience, of feeling, and yet she has what may seem to be the masculine virtues of activity and usefulness, of exertion, the better definition of her heroism can only be that she makes these distinctions irrelevant to her comprehensive human greatness.

The greater tenderness and longer life of women's feelings, she says to Captain Harville, is perhaps the fate of women rather than their merit. They cannot help themselves. Because they live at home, quiet and confined, their feelings prey on them. Because men are forced on exertion, have a profession, pursuit, business of some sort or other to take them into the world immediately, the continued occupation and change soon weaken impressions. But the argument is not fully applicable to the present occasion. As Harville points out, it does not apply to Benwick, who was not forced on exertion but was merely a man of weak feeling. More importantly, as the reader can see, it does not apply to herself because she does not do justice to her own special strength; which comes not from being preyed upon by her feelings, or from simply the inferior position of women. It comes from a depth of feeling which does not reduce her to its passive prey but to which she has responded by a depth of control. She has responded by exertion, by continual occupation; moreover, the effect has not been the supposedly masculine repayment of a weakening of impression. Her feelings and her exertions have maintained an active and balanced integrity and neither can be explained away as woman's nature or as man's nature. Only Anne.

A. WALTON LITZ

Persuasion: *forms of estrangement*

Virginia Woolf, in her essay on Jane Austen in *The Common Reader* (1925), found that *Persuasion* was characterized by 'a peculiar beauty and a peculiar dullness.'

> The dullness is that which so often marks the transition between two different periods. The writer is a little bored. She has grown too familiar with the ways of her world; she no longer notes them freshly. There is an asperity in her comedy which suggests that she has almost ceased to be amused by the vanities of a Sir Walter or the snobbery of a Miss Elliot. The satire is harsh, and the comedy crude. She is no longer so freshly aware of the amusements of everyday life. Her mind is not altogether on her object. But, while we feel that Jane Austen has done this before, and done it better, we also feel that she is trying to do something which she has never yet attempted.

Most readers will agree with Virginia Woolf's response, whether or not they care to use the term 'dullness': Jane Austen has her eye on new effects in *Persuasion*, and situations or characters which yielded such rich comic pleasures in previous novels are given summary treatment. Most readers

From *Jane Austen: Bicentenary Essays*. © 1975 by Cambridge University Press.

would also agree that there is a 'peculiar' beauty in *Persuasion*, that it has to do with a new allegiance to feeling rather than prudence, to poetry rather than prose, and that it springs from a deep sense of personal loss. As Virginia Woolf phrases it, Jane Austen 'is beginning to discover that the world is larger, more mysterious, and more romantic than she had supposed.'

> We feel it to be true of herself when she says of Anne: 'She had been forced into prudence in her youth, she learned romance as she grew older—the natural sequel of an unnatural beginning.' She dwells frequently upon the beauty and the melancholy of nature, upon the autumn where she had been wont to dwell upon the spring. She talks of the 'influence so sweet and so sad of autumnal months in the country.' She marks 'the tawny leaves and withered hedges.' 'One does not love a place the less because one has suffered in it,' she observes. But it is not only in a new sensibility to nature that we detect the change. Her attitude to life itself is altered ... the observation is less of facts and more of feelings than is usual. There is an expressed emotion in the scene at the concert and in the famous talk about woman's constancy which proves not merely the biographical fact that Jane Austen had loved, but the aesthetic fact that she was no longer afraid to say so.

Persuasion has received highly intelligent criticism in recent years, after a long period of comparative neglect, and the lines of investigation have followed Virginia Woolf's suggestive comments. Critics have been concerned with the 'personal' quality of the novel and the problems it poses for biographical interpretation; with the obvious unevenness in narrative structure; with the 'poetic' use of landscape, and the hovering influence of Romantic poetry; with the pervasive presence of Anne Elliot's consciousness; with new effects in style and syntax; with the 'modernity' of Anne Elliot, an isolated personality in a rapidly changing society. Many of these problems were discussed in my own earlier study,[1] but I would like to consider them again, I hope with greater tact and particularity. Of all Jane Austen's major works, *Persuasion* suffers the most from easy generalizations, and requires the most minute discriminations. For example, my own remark that 'more than has been generally realized or acknowledged, [Jane Austen] was influenced by the Romantic poetry of the early nineteenth century'[2] has been frequently quoted with approval, but I now feel that it needs severe definition: What are the qualities of Romantic poetry reflected in Jane Austen's new attitudes toward nature and 'feeling'? How do these new effects in *Persuasion* differ from those in the earlier novels? The following pages offer no startlingly new perspectives, but rather a refinement of several familiar points of view.

In spite of Jane Austen's warning to a friend 'that it was her desire to create, not to reproduce,'[3] readers from her own day to the present have delighted in identifying Anne Elliot with Jane Austen. Anne is twenty-seven years old, a dangerous age for Jane Austen's young women; Charlotte Lucas is 'about twenty-seven' when she accepts the foolish Mr Collins, and Marianne in *Sense and Sensibility* laments that a 'woman of seven and twenty ... can never hope to feel or inspire affection again.'[4] Jane Austen's own broken 'romance,' the details of which are hopelessly obscure, seems to have taken place around 1802, when she was twenty-seven, and Virginia Woolf was probably justified in her belief that *Persuasion* confirms 'the biographical fact that Jane Austen had loved.' Other passages from Jane Austen's life are obviously driven deep into the life of the novel: the careers of her sailor brothers, and the pleasant days at Lyme Regis in the summer of 1804, when she explored the area with Cassandra and her brother Henry. These facts give a certain sanction to biographical speculation, if one cares for that sort of thing, but they do not explain the intensity with which readers have pursued the 'personal' element in *Persuasion*. That intensity comes from the fiction, not from a curiosity about the writer's life, and has to do with the lost 'bloom' of Anne Elliot.

If asked to summarize Jane Austen's last three novels in three phrases, one might say that *Mansfield Park* is about the loss and return of principles, *Emma* about the loss and return of reason, *Persuasion* about the loss and return of 'bloom.' To make these formulations, however crude they may be, is to appreciate the deeply physical impact of *Persuasion*. The motif words of the earlier novels are the value terms of the eighteenth century—sense, taste, genius, judgment, understanding, and so forth—and their constant repetition is a sign of Jane Austen's rational vision. But there is something idiosyncratic and almost obsessive about the recurrence of 'bloom' in the first volume of *Persuasion*. 'Anne Elliot had been a very pretty girl, but her bloom had vanished early,' while Elizabeth and Sir Walter remained 'as blooming as ever,' at least in their own eyes (p. 6). The word occurs six times in the first volume, culminating in the scene on the steps at Lyme where Anne, 'the bloom and freshness of youth restored by the fine wind,' attracts the admiration of Wentworth and Mr Elliot (p. 104). It then disappears from the novel, only to return in the 'blushes' which mark Anne's repossession of her lost love: 'Glowing and lovely in sensibility and happiness, and more generally admired than she thought about or cared for, she had cheerful or forebearing feelings for every creature around her' (p. 245).

But 'bloom' is only one of many physical metaphors which make the first half of *Persuasion* Jane Austen's most deeply felt fiction. A sense of the earth's unchanging rhythms, confined in earlier works to an occasional scene and usually presented in the 'picturesque' manner, provides a ground-rhythm for the first half of *Persuasion*.

> Thirteen years had seen [Elizabeth] the mistress of Kellynch Hall, presiding and directing with a self-possession and decision which could never have given the idea of her being younger than she was. For thirteen years had she been doing the honours, and laying down the domestic law at home, and leading the way to the chaise and four, and walking immediately after Lady Russell out of all the drawing-rooms and dining-rooms in the country. Thirteen winters' revolving frosts had seen her opening every ball of credit which a scanty neighbourhood afforded; and thirteen springs shewn their blossom, as she travelled up to London with her father, for a few weeks annual enjoyment of the great world. (pp. 6–7)

This marvellous passage, which acts out the progress of time and exposes the static lives of Kellynch Hall, would have been cast in a very different form in the earlier fictions. Narrative summary and authorial commentary have given way to a poetic sense of time's changes that commands the first volume of *Persuasion*. The chapters set in Somerset are pervaded with references to the autumnal landscape, which dominates Anne's emotions as she waits with little hope for 'a second spring of youth and beauty' (p. 124); while the scenes at Lyme are softened by the romantic landscape and the freshening 'flow of the tide' (pp. 95–6, 102). This poetic use of nature as a structure of feeling, which not only offers metaphors for our emotions but controls them with its unchanging rhythms and changing moods, comes to a climax in the scene where Anne's mind, depressed by the recent events at Lyme and her imminent departure for Bath, becomes part of the dark November landscape.

> An hour's complete leisure for such reflections as these, on a dark November day, a small thick rain almost blotting out the very few objects ever to be discerned from the windows, was enough to make the sound of Lady Russell's carriage exceedingly welcome; and yet, though desirous to be gone, she could not quit the mansion-house, or look an adieu to the cottage, with its black, dripping, and comfortless veranda, or even notice through the misty glasses the last humble tenements of the village, without a

saddened heart.—Scenes had passed in Uppercross, which made
it precious. It stood the record of many sensations of pain, once
severe, but now softened ... She left it all behind her; all but the
recollection that such things had been. (p. 123)

Such a passage fully justifies Angus Wilson's reply to those who say 'that
there is no poetry in Jane Austen.' The poetry is there in 'the essential
atmosphere of her novels—an instinctive response to those basic realities of
nature, the weather and the seasons.' All of Jane Austen's heroines, whether
declining like Fanny and Anne, or flourishing like Emma and Elizabeth, are
acutely conscious of their physical lives. The fact of 'being alive,' as Wilson
says, 'is never absent from the texture of the thoughts of her heroines.'[5]

Most readers of Jane Austen would agree with Wilson's claims, and
would also agree that *Persuasion* represents her most successful effort to build
this sense of physical life into the language and structure of a novel. If asked
for proof, they would point to the frequent allusions to the Romantic poets,
especially Byron and Scott, and to the famous passage (pp. 84–8) where
Anne's autumnal walk is permeated with poetic 'musings and quotations.' But
here they would be, I think, demonstrably wrong. Most of Jane Austen's
direct references to the Romantic poets in *Persuasion* are associated with
Captain Benwick, and have the same satiric intent—although they are
gentler in manner—as the references to contemporary poetry in *Sanditon*.
When Anne and Captain Benwick talk of 'poetry, the richness of the present
age,' his enthusiasm for Scott and Byron is so emotional that Anne ventures
to 'recommend a larger allowance of prose in his daily study' (p. 101), and
her caution is confirmed when Benwick's raptures on Byron's *The Corsair* are
interrupted by Louisa's rash jump to the Lower Cobb. Jane Austen has no
place in her world for the Byronic hero, and Wentworth is not—as one
recent critic has claimed—a successful recreation of Byron's Corsair.

Surely Angus Wilson is right in implying that Jane Austen's
assimilation of the new poetry is most profound when least obtrusive. 'If we
seek for any conscious concern for nature, we get either the Gilpin textbook
stuff of *Northanger Abbey* or the "thoughts from the poets" of Fanny or Anne
Elliot.'[6] A good example of Jane Austen's conscious concern for nature would
be the scene in *Mansfield Park* where Edmund joins Fanny at the window to
view the stars:

his eyes soon turned like her's towards the scene without, where
all that was solemn and soothing, and lovely, appeared in the
brilliancy of an unclouded night, and the contrast of the deep
shade of the woods. Fanny spoke her feelings. 'Here's harmony!'

said she, 'Here's repose! Here's what may leave all painting and all
music behind, and what poetry only can attempt to describe.
Here's what may tranquillize every care, and lift the heart to
rapture! When I look out on such a night as this, I feel as if there
could be neither wickedness nor sorrow in the world; and there
certainly would be less of both if the sublimity of Nature were
more attended to, and people were carried more out of
themselves by contemplating such a scene.' (p. 113)

This is a set-piece out of eighteenth-century aesthetics, in which Fanny
responds to the natural landscape with appropriate emotions of 'sublimity'
and transport. Even the descriptive details are heavily literary, drawn from
Shakespeare and Ann Radcliffe.[7] A different and more intimate sense of
landscape is displayed by the famous autumnal walk in *Persuasion*:

Her pleasure in the walk must arise from the exercise and the day,
from the view of the last smiles of the year upon the tawny leaves
and withered hedges, and from repeating to herself some few of
the thousand poetical descriptions extant of autumn, that season
of peculiar and inexhaustible influence on the mind of taste and
tenderness ... After one of the many praises of the day, which
were continually bursting forth, Captain Wentworth added:
     'What glorious weather for the Admiral and my sister! They
meant to take a long drive this morning; perhaps we may hail
them from some of these hills. They talked of coming into this
side of the country. I wonder whereabouts they will upset today.
Oh! it does happen very often, I assure you—but my sister makes
nothing of it—she would as lieve be tossed out as not.'
     'Ah! You make the most of it, I know,' cried Louisa, 'but if it
were really so, I should do just the same in her place. If I loved a
man, as she loves the Admiral, I would be always with him,
nothing should ever separate us, and I would rather be
overturned by him, than driven safely by anybody else.'
     ... Anne could not immediately fall into a quotation again. The
sweet scenes of autumn were for a while put by—unless some
tender sonnet, fraught with the apt analogy of the declining year,
with declining happiness, and the images of youth and hope, and
spring, all gone together, blessed her memory. She roused herself
to say, as they struck by order into another path, 'Is not this one
of the sways to Winthrop?' But nobody heard, or, at least, nobody
answered her.

> Winthrop ... was their destination; and after another half mile
> of gradual ascent through large enclosures, where the ploughs at
> work, and the fresh-made path spoke the farmer, counteracting
> the sweets of poetical despondence, and meaning to have spring
> again, they gained the summit of the most considerable hill,
> which parted Uppercross and Winthrop, and soon commanded a
> full view of the latter, at the foot of the hill on the other side. (pp.
> 84–5)

Fanny Price has three transparencies on the panes of her window, depicting Tintern Abbey, a cave in Italy, and a moonlit lake in Cumberland; the subjects may suggest Wordsworth, but her tastes are strictly for the picturesque and the academic sublime. The presentation of Anne Elliot's autumnal walk is much closer to a Wordsworthian view of nature, emphasizing as it does the responsive ego, yet it would be a mistake to identify Anne's thoughts on autumn with the powerful reactions of the great Romantic poets. Her 'poetical descriptions' are, most likely, culled from the popular magazine poets, and her literary taste is not necessarily superior to that of Fanny Price. What is different in *Persuasion* is the way in which two views of nature, both conventional, have been internalized to provide a complex and original impression. Whereas in *Sense and Sensibility* Marianne's sentimental effusions on nature are dramatically counterpointed to Edward's practical view, her sense of the picturesque set against his sense of the ordinary, the autumnal scene from *Persuasion* locates both responses within Anne's mind. After she has fallen sentimentally and self-indulgently into quotation, the sight of the farmer ploughing, 'meaning to have spring again,' rescues Anne from 'poetical despondence,' and restores her emotional composure. This passage is infused with a sense of immediate feeling absent from the description of Fanny's rapture, but it remains a consciously 'literary' construction, closer to Cowper than to Wordsworth. In the final scene at Uppercross already quoted, however, the effects are truly Wordsworthian. The cottage viewed on a 'dark November day' is a stock-piece of the picturesque, with its irregular shape and misty appearance, yet it is transformed by memory, by 'reflection' and 'recollection,' into a complex symbol of what 'had been.' In the opening chapters of *Persuasion* Jane Austen is most 'poetic,' most Wordsworthian, when she is willing to abandon the literary allusion and give herself to a direct passionate rendering of nature's changing face.

Our discussion of the romantic dimensions of *Persuasion* has been confined to the first half of the novel, the opening twelve chapters, and for good reason: the latter half of the novel is radically different in style and narrative method. Any census of the metaphors of natural change will find that they are concentrated in the first half, suggesting that *Persuasion* has a deliberate two-part structure that has been often overlooked. *Northanger Abbey*, its companion in the posthumous four-volume edition, was always intended as a two-part romance: the original version sold to the publisher Crosby in 1803 was described as 'a MS. Novel in 2 vol. entitled Susan.' All of Jane Austen's other novels were published in three parts, and designed to fit that pattern. Thus the three-part division of *Pride and Prejudice* follows the three-act structure of a stage comedy, and the three parts of *Emma* correspond to three successive stages in a process of self-discovery. But Jane Austen deliberately chose to construct *Persuasion* in two parts (the numbering of the cancelled last chapters proves this), and much of the apparent unevenness or 'dullness' of the novel is explained by this artistic decision.

The first half of *Persuasion* portrays Anne Elliot against a natural landscape, and it is there that Jane Austen's newfound Romanticism is concentrated. Once the action has moved to Bath a claustrophobic atmosphere descends, and the external world becomes insubstantial: Anne, without a human confidante but sustained by nature in the first volume, is left terribly alone in the second volume—only the reconciliation with Wentworth can save her from anonymity. The language of the second volume, although less satisfying to our modern taste, is deliberately fashioned to express this sense of personalities moving in a vacuum. The rich metaphors of Volume One are replaced by the eighteenth-century value terms of earlier novels, but—as Virginia Woolf noted—with a sense of perfunctory ritual. It is as if Jane Austen, hurrying to the final reunion, were at long last impatient with those weighty terms of judgment and admonition that had served her so well in earlier years. In a space of seven pages (pp. 140–7) the word 'sensible' occurs six times along with 'pride,' 'understanding,' 'decorum,' 'candid,' 'amiable,' 'sensibility,' and 'imaginations.' This is an aggressive return to the abstract language of the earlier fictions, but it is difficult to tell whether Jane Austen does so out of boredom—as Virginia Woolf seems to imply—or out of a desire to convey the eighteenth-century stasis of Bath. In any case, the contrast between the first and second volumes of *Persuasion* is profound in the realm of language and metaphor, reflecting the radical dislocation of Anne Elliot. And there are differences in narrative method as well. The first half of the novel presents Anne as the commanding center. As Norman Page has shown, the 'slanting of the narrative through the mental life of the principal character,' already developed in *Emma*, is the dominant mode in *Persuasion*; narrative, authorial comment, dialogue, and interior monologue merge into one another.[8] 'Free indirect speech,' in which lengthy dialogue is compressed and located within the central consciousness, is combined with more conventional narrative methods to give a sense of the entire novel taking place within the mind of the heroine. But this complex method of internalized presentation is most evident in the first volume, and in Volume Two—as Anne Elliot enters the alien environment of Bath—Jane Austen reverts to earlier and more objective methods. It is a sign of Anne's isolation that the revelation of William Elliot's true nature, and even of Wentworth's love, must come to her through letters, one of the most 'external' of fictional devices.

Another aspect of style in *Persuasion*, present in both volumes but more characteristic of the first, is a rapid and nervous syntax designed to imitate the bombardment of impressions upon the mind. A fine example occurs when Anne, a victim of the rambunctious child Walter, is rescued by Captain Wentworth.

> In another moment, however, she found herself in the state of being released from him; some one was taking him from her, though he had bent down her head so much, that his little sturdy hands were unfastened from around her neck, and he was resolutely borne away, before she knew that Captain Wentworth had done it. (p. 80)

Here the passive construction, the indefinite pronouns, and the staccato syntax all imitate the effect of the incident upon Anne's mind. Page is certainly right when he says that such passages, common in *Persuasion*, do not make statements about an emotional situation but suggest the quality of the experience through the movement of the prose.[9]

When we examine these details of sentence structure and punctuation, however, a certain caution is necessary. The sentences of *Persuasion* do, for the most part, move away from the Johnsonian norm, and in the revisions of the cancelled chapters one can see Jane Austen struggling toward a more expressive form. But one should remember that all of Jane Austen's manuscripts display a greater flexibility of sentence structure than her printed works, and although the cancelled chapters of *Persuasion* and the manuscript of *Sanditon* exhibit an extraordinary freedom, many of the same qualities are present in the manuscript of *The Watsons* (c. 1803–4). The printer of Jane Austen's day had great license with punctuation, paragraphing, and even sentence structure, and part of the 'flowing' quality of *Persuasion* may derive from a printer (T. Davison) whose standards and tastes differed from those of the printers who handled the earlier manuscripts. This does not affect the general import of Page's argument, but the dangers of relying too heavily on details of punctuation and sentence structure are evident in Page's comparison of a passage in the cancelled Chapter Ten with the revised version:[10]

> He found that he was considered by his friend Harville an engaged man. The Harvilles entertained not a doubt of a mutual attachment between him and Louisa; and though this to a degree was contradicted instantly, it yet made him feel that perhaps by *her* family, by everybody, by *herself* even, the same idea might be held, and that he was not *free* in honour, though if such were to be the conclusion, too free alas! in heart. He had never thought justly on this subject before, and he had not sufficiently considered that his excessive intimacy at Uppercross must have its danger of ill consequence in many ways; and that while trying whether he could attach himself to either of the girls, he might be exciting unpleasant reports if not raising unrequited regard.
>
> He found too late that he had entangled himself [cancelled version, p. 260 of Chapman's edition].

> 'I found,' said he, 'that I was considered by Harville an engaged man! That neither Harville nor his wife entertained a doubt of our mutual attachment. I was startled and shocked. To a degree, I could contradict this instantly; but, when I began to reflect that others might have felt the same—her own family, nay, perhaps herself, I was no longer at my own disposal. I was hers in honour if she wished it. I had been unguarded. I had not thought seriously on this subject before. I had not considered that my excessive intimacy must have its danger of ill consequence in many ways; and that I had no right to be trying whether I could attach myself to either of the girls, at the risk of raising even an unpleasant report, were there no other ill effects. I had been grossly wrong, and must abide the consequences.'
>
> He found too late, in short, that he had entangled himself ... [final version, pp. 242–3].

Page's comments upon the improved 'personal and dramatic form' of the revised version are just, but his observation that three long sentences have been broken up into nine shorter sentences falls away when we realize that the cancelled version, as Page quotes it, is actually reprinted from the 1870 *Memoir*, where Jane Austen's lively manuscript had been 'regularized' by the Victorian editor and printer. The actual passage from the manuscript, reproduced below, shows the nervous energy of Jane Austen's first draft, and reminds us that the relationship between Jane Austen's first drafts and the printed texts must often have been that of sketch to varnished canvas.

> He found that he was considered by his friend Harville, as an engaged Man. The Harvilles entertained not a doubt of a mutual attachment between him & Louisa—and though this to *a degree*, was contradicted instantly—it yet made him feel that perhaps by *her* family, by everybody, by *herself* even, the same idea might be held—and that he was not *free* in honour—though, if such were to be the conclusion, too free alas! in Heart.—He had never thought justly on this subject before—he had not sufficiently considered that his excessive Intimacy at Uppercross must have it's danger of ill consequence in many ways, and that while trying whether he c^d attach himself to either of the Girls, he might be exciting unpleasant reports, if not, raising unrequited regard!— He found, too late, that he had entangled himself—[11]

Persuasion reveals an author who is unusually sensitive to the forces of her time. Of all the novels, it is the only one where the action is precisely dated, and that date is 'the present' (1814–15). The other novels are slightly retrospective in their treatments of manners and events, but *Persuasion* is filled with references to contemporary history ('This peace will be turning all our rich Navy Officers ashore') and the most recent publications of the Romantic poets. These topical references are matched by certain passages in the novel which seem to reflect the events of 1815–16, when *Persuasion* was a work-in-progress. The description of the 'green chasms between romantic rocks' near Lyme may echo *Kubla Khan*, first published in 1816, although the chronology is doubtful and the whole passage strikes me as more picturesque than Coleridgean;[12] more likely is the influence of Scott's famous review in the *Quarterly* upon Jane Austen's retreat from 'prudence.' In Scott's review, which Jane Austen had read by 1 April 1816 (*Persuasion* was not completed until the summer), Jane Austen was characterized as anti-sentimental and anti-romantic, her novels bearing the same relation to those of the 'sentimental and romantic cast, that cornfields and cottages and meadows bear to ... the rugged sublimities of a mountain landscape.' Scott then went on to deplore the neglect of Cupid and romantic feelings, implying that Jane Austen coupled 'Cupid indivisibly with calculating prudence.'[13] This must have stung the creator of Anne Elliot, and we may take her passionate statement on 'romance' as a covert reply.

> How eloquent could Anne Elliot have been,—how eloquent, at
> least, were her wishes on the side of early warm attachment, and
> a cheerful confidence in futurity, against that over-anxious
> caution which seems to insult exertion and distrust Providence!—
> She had been forced into prudence in her youth, she learned
> romance as she grew older—the natural sequel of an unnatural
> beginning. (p. 30)

Unlike Jane Austen's other major works, *Persuasion* is filled with a sense of the moment—both historical and personal—at which it was written.

It is not these particular signs of contemporaneity, however, but Jane Austen's powerful response to a changing relationship between society and the self that gives *Persuasion* its hold on the modern reader. In *Pride and Prejudice* the old order of Darcy and Pemberley can be accommodated to the new forces represented by the middle-class Gardiners; in *Persuasion* there seems little hope of accommodation between stasis and unpredictable change. 'The Musgroves, like their houses, were in a state of alteration, perhaps of improvement' (p. 40), and this tension between old ways and 'more modern minds and manners' divides the novel. Sir Walter has retreated into a wilderness of mirrors, the Baronetage his favorite looking-glass, and Jane Austen's sympathies are firmly on the side of the new natural aristocracy represented by the Navy; but in giving her allegiance to them Jane Austen knows that Anne must 'pay the tax of quick alarm' (p. 252). The ending of *Persuasion*, unlike that of the other novels, is open and problematic. One could glean from *Persuasion* a list of terms which would make it sound like a textbook in modern sociology: 'estrangement,' 'imprisonment,' 'alienations,' 'removals.' The heroine is 'only Anne' (pp. 5–6), and the word 'alone' echoes through the novel. *Persuasion* is filled with a sense of what time can do, with its 'changes, alienations, removals': it can lead to 'oblivion of the past' (p. 60) and even annihilation of the self. Anne has painfully learned 'the art of knowing our own nothingness beyond our own circle' (p. 42), and at the end of the novel that circle, so lovingly restored and enlarged, has no permanence beyond the moment. Virginia Woolf might have said that *Persuasion* is marked by a peculiar terror as well as a peculiar beauty.

NOTES

1. Jane Austen: *A Study of Her Artistic Development* (New York, 1965).
2. *Ibid.*, p. 153.
3. J. E. Austen-Leigh, *Memoir of Jane Austen*, ed. R. W. Chapman (Oxford, 1926), p. 157.

4. *Sense and Sensibility*, p. 38. All page references for the novels are to *The Novels of Jane Austen*, ed. R. W. Chapman (London: Oxford University Press; 3rd ed., 1933).

5. Angus Wilson, 'The Neighbourhood of Tombuctoo,' in *Critical Essays on Jane Austen*, ed. B. C. Southam (London, 1968), p. 191.

6. *Ibid.*

7. In *Jane Austen and Her Predecessors* (Cambridge, 1966), pp. 78 and 107–8, Frank W. Bradbrook points out the allusions to *The Merchant of Venice* and *The Mysteries of Udolpho*.

8. Norman Page, *The Language of Jane Austen* (Oxford, 1972), pp. 48–53 and 127–36.

9. *Ibid.*, p. 50.

10. *Ibid.*, pp. 51–2.

11. *Two Chapters of Persuasion*, ed. R. W. Chapman (Oxford, 1926), pp. 20–1.

12. See Alethea Hayter, 'Xanadu at Lyme Regis,' *Ariel*, 1 (1970), 61–4.

13. *Jane Austen: The Critical Heritage*, ed. B. C. Southam (London, 1968), p. 68. Jane Austen refers to Scott's review in a letter of 1 April 1816.

GENE W. RUOFF

Anne Elliot's Dowry: Reflections on the Ending of Persuasion

The endings of Jane Austen's novels present obstacles to anyone attempting to link her works to those of the other major writers of her age. The problems are not in those wholly fictive qualities which have preoccupied traditional Jane Austen criticism, such as the perfunctory cast of her endings or the parodistic tone which plays about them. In an era of unfinished masterworks, any ending at all may seem a technical accomplishment. Elemental issues are raised, though, by the way things turn out in Jane Austen's world—how the strength of human love is demonstrated and how, particularly, it is rewarded. Of Jane Austen's peers and contemporaries, Wordsworth would seem the most optimistic about the actual state of things in which man finds himself; yet when he celebrates the triumphs of the heart's affections, his most memorable victories tend to be wrenched from apparent defeats, as Michael, Margaret, Leonard Ewbank, and many others could bear witness. A pile of stones and an old dog are difficult to translate into Darcy, Pemberley, and ten thousand a year.

The simple fact that Jane Austen's heroines, heroes, and other characters of value invariably find their proper rewards suggests a belief that nothing is so radically wrong with the self or society that good sense, moderation, patience, and humor cannot finally make things work out. Few would claim that such a belief would be deeply Romantic. Jane Austen's

From *The Wordsworth Circle* 7, no. 4. © 1976 by Marilyn Gaull.

apparent optimism that man's constituted society offers a possible and even proper home for his aspirations leads invariably to the charge, which is perhaps felt more often than voiced these days, that she is an unreflectively conservative defender of the status quo, ignorant of or choosing to ignore the ills which grow from the social system into which she cheerfully integrates her heroines.[1] Why should the people be unhappy? Are there not landed gentry, country parsons, and even wealthy naval commanders for them to marry?

That Jane Austen's novels do affirm the value of a social order is undeniable; but how a proper society comes into being within them, how its values are grounded, and how its structure relates to commonplace hierarchies of wealth and rank are problematical. Of the five novels which come before *Persuasion*, *Pride and Prejudice* can serve as an illustrative model. The acute consciousness of social and economic status with which the novel begins—the respective layers of the social pile represented by Bingley and Darcy—prefigures a complex interplay of hierarchical motifs, quite similar to those traced so convincingly by L. J. Swingle's essay on *Emma* in this issue. Darcy, for example, is discovered to be "*above* being pleased" (p. 10); Lady Catherine's outstanding virtue is her *condescension*; and Elizabeth, on hearing Wickham's false revelations about Darcy, remarks that even she "did not suspect him of *descending* to such malicious revenge" (p. 80, all italics mine). The terms *above* and *below*, in all their variants, dominate the narrative complications of the work, assuming critical force in such lines as those in which Darcy angrily responds to the curt rejection of his first proposal of marriage: "Could you expect me to rejoice in the inferiority of your connections? To congratulate myself on the hope of relations, whose condition in life is so decidedly beneath my own?" (p. 192).

Given the prevalence of hierarchical patterning in the novel, one might reasonably expect at its conclusion some emphasis on the levels which characters ultimately find. Instead, the ending of *Pride and Prejudice* is governed by motifs of physical and psychological distance. In the reformed social order which closes the book, Pemberley has become the center of societal values, just as its inhabitants are at the center of human values. The worth of other characters is mapped in terms of their proximity and access to Pemberley. After Bingley buys an estate in a neighboring county, "Jane and Elizabeth, in addition to every other source of happiness, were within thirty miles of each other" (p. 385). The Gardiners are "always on the most intimate terms" (p. 388) with Elizabeth and Darcy. Mr. Bennet "delighted in going to Pemberley, especially when he was least expected" (p. 385), and Kitty improves greatly by spending "the chief of her time with her two elder sisters" (p. 385). Among the characters who have been obsessed with questions of degree and rank, Miss Bingley is forced to drop her resentment of the marriage in order to "retain the right of visiting" (p. 387), while Lady Catherine is seen in only one visit to Derbyshire, still condescending. Lydia and her Wickham are safely exiled in Newcastle, but while she is "occasionally a visitor" Darcy could, of course, "never receive him at Pemberley" (p. 387).

The concluding society of *Pride and Prejudice* is ordered schematically, but not in the way that had threatened to frustrate the most admirable of desires for happiness throughout the narrative. To a large extent, even the idea of society, in all its stratificational complexity, has been displaced by the idea of community. Consequently, the story of Elizabeth Bennet, an obvious enough rendering of the Cinderella myth, is less concerned with social mobility than social stability: she has not climbed a ladder; she has found and become a center. The novel indicates that a just and stable society cannot be formed by a shuffling and reshuffling of certificates of pedigree and statements of net worth, the respective fixations of Lady Catherine and Mrs. Bennet. A center is needed, a secure point from which civilized and humane values may emanate. For all their palpable differences, Pemberley has the same kind of meaning for Jane Austen that Grasmere has for Wordsworth: it is an organizing point for a society that has possessed only semblances of order. If it is a retreat, it is also a center for continuing moral regeneration.

Jane Austen's place endings move toward a point at which intimacy may be established and from which distance may be measured. That final location may, like Pemberley, have substantial value in and of itself; but its value is clearly subsidiary to its function as a place around which a community may form. "Elinor's marriage divided her as little from her family as could well be contrived, without rendering the cottage at Barton entirely useless" (*SS*, p. 378); she and Marianne finally live "almost within sight of each other" (p 380). The fortuitous death of Dr. Grant allows Fanny and Edmund to move into the Mansfield parsonage "just after they had been married long enough to begin to want an increase of income, and feel their distance from the paternal abode an inconvenience" (*MP*, p. 473). Mr. Knightley gives up his residence at Donwell Abbey in order to move in with Emma and Mr. Woodhouse.[2] The psychological and social benefits of a fixed and lasting home are treated eloquently in Wordsworth's well-known letter to Charles James Fox (14 January, 1801), where he proclaims the advantages of landed property. It provides, he says, "a kind of permanent rallying point for their domestic feelings, ... a tablet upon which they are written which makes them objects of memory in a thousand instances when they would otherwise be forgotten."[3] Good Burkean sentiments, we might nod, except that in both Wordsworth's and Jane Austen's presentations, disruption threatens the domestic feelings rather than the national security, and the home itself must be made safe before it can be confidently offered as an image of national order (in *The Improvement of the Estate*, Duckworth notes numerous parallels between Jane Austen and Burke. See esp. pp. 45–48). Given a rallying point, a sound community can form itself, and order can be established, at least on this small scale. Jane Austen's social views seem hardly optimistic from this perspective. As Professor Swingle has suggested her strong sense of place aligns her with the Romantic fascination with enclosures—bowers, caves, islands, and other enclaves of the elect. Such a habit of mind is not characteristic of those who feel that things can be made right by a little tinkering and fiddling with the existing social machine.

But if Romanticism's affirmations often involve the successful discovery of a center, its darker musings are concerned with what happens when the center does not hold—when the bower is destroyed, the island invaded, the longed-for return to the childhood home crushed by the death of a beloved brother, or, to borrow Alistair Duckworth's phrase, the estate abandoned. Without a fixed point, can there be any secure foundation for the individual or social existence? Cain and Asmodeus, we remember, are nightmare figures of the age. Duckworth has commented tellingly on some of the ways in which the conclusion of *Persuasion* differs from those of the preceding novels: "the final marriage of the novel is not a 'social' marriage in the way that previous marriages are in Jane Austen; Anne's union with Wentworth fails to guarantee a broader union of themes and attitudes in *Persuasion* as say, Elizabeth's union with Darcy does in *Pride and Prejudice*. Nor, uniquely among Jane Austen heroines, does Anne return to the stable and rooted existence of the land; she has 'no Uppercross-hall before her, no landed estate, no headship of a family'" (*The Improvement of the Estate*, pp. 180–81). With all this I would agree and add one further significant point of departure. The ending suggests no continuity of blood ties across generational lines: no visits from Mr. Bennet, no residence near Mrs. Dashwood or the Sir Thomas Bertrams, no living with Mr. Woodhouse. Here even the worthy Gardiners of *Pride and Prejudice*, the aunt and uncle who act as surrogate parents for Elizabeth, are replaced by the Musgroves, who are perhaps harmless enough but so lacking in stature as to be forgotten by the ending of the book. Anne feels her deprivation keenly: "The disproportion in their fortune was nothing; it did not give her a moment's regret; but to have no family to receive and estimate him properly; nothing of respectability, of harmony, of good-will to offer in return for all the worth and all the prompt welcome which met her in his brothers and sisters, was a source of as lively pain as her mind could well be sensible of under circumstances of otherwise strong felicity. She had but two friends in the world to add to his list, Lady Russell and Mrs. Smith. To these, however, he was very well disposed to attach himself" (p. 251).

Here are unmistakeable signs that we are in at the founding of a new "community," one considerably different from those which have drawn together at the ends of the preceding novels. Lady Russell, with her deeply ingrained "prejudices on the side of ancestry" (p. 11) and the impoverished Mrs. Smith, who is, as Sir Walter Elliot puts it, "one of the five thousand Mrs. Smiths whose names are to be met with every where" (p. 157), seem an unlikely combination just in themselves. Their being added to the secure cluster of friends already surrounding Wentworth, principally Admiral and Mrs. Croft and Captain Harville and his family, leads one to wonder just what the common bond might be which holds this assemblage together. Certainly it is not the land. With the possible exception of Lady Russell, all are tenters, with temporary accommodations ranging in scale from the grandeur of Kellynch-hall to cramped lodgings in Bath, "a noisy parlor, and a dark bedroom behind" (p. 154). Anne and Wentworth are themselves given no geographical destination. Some sense of the mobility of habitation in *Persuasion* may be caught in Mrs. Croft's comments about living aboard ship: "Women may be as comfortable on board, as in the best house in England. I believe I have lived as much on board as most women, and I know nothing superior to the accommodations of a man of war" (p. 69).

Although the perspective into which Mrs. Croft places country houses—albeit with a "kind bow to Anne" (p. 69)—suggests the significance of those portions of the novel praising the naval life, it does not really justify the haste with which critics have commonly aligned its society into two alien camps, the inert landed gentry and the rising professional class, an aristocracy and a meritocracy. According to such a view, Anne Elliot's progress is marked by her steadily detaching herself from the gentry, her class by birthright, and attaching herself to Wentworth and his fellow naval officers.[4] Anne cannot be said to leave her "feudal" past behind her as she rides the "revolutionary" currents, though, because she brings with her two of her oldest friends, neither of whom has shown the slightest predisposition toward the emerging professional class and one of whom is the most strenuous and—save Anne—the only genuine defender of the old order. That Anne should "bestow" Lady Russell and Mrs. Smith on Wentworth, and that he should accept them, creates an uncomfortable situation for readings which would pit professionalism against inheritance.

The ending of *Persuasion* is especially severe in its exclusions: it brushes aside all the Elliots except Anne, all the Musgroves, and even one naval officer, Captain Benwick, who has become engaged to Louisa Musgrove. We might, therefore, expect it to be equally exacting in its grounds for friendship, an issue which has commanded Jane Austen's attention since the juvenilia. Without a fixed geographical center, proximity can play no role in these newly formed relationships, nor to a large degree do a number of other familiar Austenian bonding agents—blood ties, cultural backgrounds, ages, and even dispositions. For all this, the figures who come together seem somehow solider than those who have closed the other novels. *Persuasion* embraces fewer charming eccentrics and tolerates fewer bores, and it proposes few startling reformations after the close of its dramatic action: no Kitty to be "improved," no Marianne to learn to love Colonel Brandon, no Sir Thomas Bertram to gain a rejuvenated sense of parental responsibility. At the end of both *Pride and Prejudice* and *Mansfield Park*, one is left with the feeling that the communities formed are stronger than either the individuals within them or the relationships among them would ordinarily allow. Problematical characters, weak and immature but not evil, are propped up by the related supports of generational continuity and landed property. In making do without these supports, *Persuasion* asks considerably more of its characters. The sort of parental incompetence tolerated in Mrs. Dashwood, the Bennets, and the Bertrams, for example, is not acceptable in the case of the elder Musgroves, even though they are generally pleasant and well meaning. Harmlessness is not on the novel's list of approved virtues.

In seeking the grounds of community in *Persuasion*, one might recall that a primary function of the estate in the earlier endings was to stimulate familial and cultural memory. The emotions engendered by the portrait gallery at Pemberley display this role at its most successful, just as the disarray into which Mansfield is thrown in Sir Thomas's absence shows its failure. Sir Thomas's response to the desecration of his billiard room dwells in a complicated way on the issue of family memory: "he felt it too much indeed for many words; and having shaken hands with Edmund, meant to try to lose the disagreeable impression, and forget how much he had been forgotten himself as soon as he could, after the house had been cleared of every object enforcing the remembrance, and restored to its proper state" (p. 187). This is the sort of word game through which Jane Austen often depicts the self-deluded. Upset by a failure of family memory, Sir Thomas tries to forget it by wiping out its visible signs.[5] Obliterating this "disagreeable impression," of course, leads ultimately to others even more disagreeable, which will be less easily forgotten. An excessive reliance on houses or objects in general for recollection can be a tricky business, as prone to generate the self-indulgent and wallowing joys of nostalgia—one vice from which Fanny Price herself is not quite free—as vital and effective memories. *Persuasion* is even more centrally concerned with the vagaries of remembering and forgetting than *Mansfield Park*, but along with the estate it does without the various keepsakes and tokens which are Fanny's treasures in the old schoolroom. *Persuasion* places its highest value on the power of the individual memory, which, in the absence of such mnemonic aids as a stable home and family, must itself provide the continuity essential to the formation of a new community.

The importance of the theme of memory in *Persuasion* is implied ironically at the outset of the book, where we are allowed to read with Sir Walter Elliot his favorite page of the Baronetage: "there, if every other leaf were powerless, he could read his own history with an interest which never failed" (p. 3). Put off by a snobbery even more exalted than Lady Catherine's, we may fail to pay sufficient heed to the precise nature of that history which he reads with evident satisfaction: "Walter Elliot, born March 1, 1760, married July 15, 1784, Elizabeth, daughter of James Stevenson, Esq. of South Park, in the county of Gloucester; by which lady (who died 1800) he has issue Elizabeth, born June 1, 1785; Anne, born August 9, 1787; a still-born son, Nov. 5, 1789; Mary, born Nov. 20, 1791" (p. 3). Sir Walter has "improved" the account by adding the date and consequence of his youngest daughter's marriage and "by inserting most accurately the day of the month on which he lost his wife" (p. 3). The entry in the Baronetage has all the makings of family tragedy: the untimely loss of a wife, the still-born male heir, who would have secured the succession of the estate and guaranteed the future well-being of his unmarried sisters who, as matters stand, have no adequate provision. Whatever sorrow Sir Walter may ever have felt, though, is lost in his euphoric "vanity of person and of situation" (p. 4). Even the succeeding account of the exertions of his forebears in the service of the nation fails to call forth an inkling of personal inadequacy. He traces endlessly the skeletal account of a personal and hereditary past which seems scarcely to have touched him.

It has long been recognized that Anne Elliot differs from other Jane Austen heroines in having had a "past," in the sense of a romantic disappointment, and that, as the book's central consciousness, her view of its present actions is deeply interpenetrated by recollections of her past experience.[6] At times, indeed, such as her first encounter with Wentworth at Uppercross, the present moment threatens to recede entirely, lost between her fearful anticipations of the event and her retrospective ponderings of its meaning. The key to Anne's character lies in a short reflection which follows the episode: "Alas! with all her reasonings, she found, that to retentive feelings eight years may be little more than nothing" (p. 60). On numerous occasions the retentive feelings of Anne are juxtaposed against the weak or faulty memories of those who surround her. Anne, for example, "could not hear that Captain Wentworth's sister was likely to live at Kellynch, without a revival of former pain" (p. 30). Whether her father, older sister, and Lady Russell make the same connection, though, is left to speculation: Anne is "assisted" in controlling her feelings "by that perfect indifference and apparent unconsciousness, among the only three of her friends in the secret of the past, which seemed to deny any recollection of it. She could do justice to the superiority of Lady Russell's motives in this, over those of her father and Elizabeth; she could honour all the better feelings of her calmness—but the general air of oblivion among them was highly important, from whatever it sprung" (p. 30). Anne must assume that Lady Russell remains silent in order to spare her feelings; her fidelity to the memory of Anne's mother and the hereditary responsibilities of the gentry would argue that she has not forgotten such an important crisis in Anne's life. Elizabeth and Sir Walter, however, may be either disdainful of or oblivious to the past: neither is ever to acknowledge a prior connection between Anne and Wentworth.

Sir Walter obliterates the past in his many looking glasses, anxious to think "himself and Elizabeth as blooming as ever amidst the wreck of good looks of everybody else" (p. 6). Elizabeth, who seems at first to be haunted by a memorable grudge against William Walter Elliot, the heir presumptive of Kellynch Hall, forgets it as soon as the scapegrace seems to make himself available to her again. Mrs. Musgrove's maudlin outburst over her dead son is described as an improbable occurrence: "that Mrs. Musgrove should have been suddenly struck, this very day, with a recollection of the name of Wentworth, as connected with her son, seemed one of those extraordinary bursts of mind that do sometimes occur" (p. 51). Anne's sister Mary, so proud that her husband Charles will some day inherit Uppercross, shows no signs of recollecting that he first proposed to Anne. Henrietta Musgrove forgets Charles Hayter in her pursuit of Wentworth, and Louisa, in the absence of Wentworth, turns abruptly to Captain Benwick, who himself forgets his lost Fanny, for whom he has been pining Byronically, repeating "with such tremulous feeling, the various lines which imaged a broken heart, or a mind destroyed by wretchedness" (p. 100). A representative sample of the kinds of memories possessed by Anne's Uppercross associates is provided by Louisa's breathless account of a recent conversation: the Crofts "happened to say, that her brother, Captain Wentworth, is just returned to England, or paid off, or something, and is coming to see them almost directly; and most unluckily it came into mamma's head, when they were gone, that Wentworth, or something very like it, was the name of poor Richard's captain, at one time, I do not know when or where, but a great while before he died, poor fellow!" (p. 50). In the midst of such fuzziness, it is little wonder that Jane Austen inserts her notoriously succinct and brutal account of the "real circumstances of this pathetic piece of family history" (p. 50).

Faulty memories make personal relationships treacherously inconstant in *Persuasion*, and the relative strength of memory becomes a primary basis for ethical judgment. In the novel's climactic chapter, Captain Harville has been entrusted with delivering a miniature portrait of Captain Benwick, intended for Harville's dead sister Fanny, to Louisa Musgrove. After carefully recalling the circumstances of its being painted, he bursts out, "Poor Fanny! she would not have forgotten him so soon!" (p. 232). His statement sets off the famous debate with Anne on male and female constancy which, while itself remaining unresolved, underlines the moral distinction drawn throughout the novel between those who remember and those who do not, between those who are true to their pasts and those who are oblivious to, or evade, or disguise them. Consider the basis on which Anne judges William Walter Elliot: "she would have been afraid to answer for his conduct. She distrusted the past if not the present.... Though he might now think very differently, who could answer for the true sentiments of a clever, cautious man, grown old enough to appreciate a fair character? How could it ever be ascertained that his mind was truly cleansed?" (p. 161). In attempts to reconcile the past and present of the heir presumptive, Anne receives no assistance from his own accounts of himself. She distrusts the apparent discontinuity of his character, a discontinuity echoed, on a different level, by Benwick's rapid movement from obsessive grief over Fanny to love for Louisa. In *Persuasion* character is judged less in terms of behavior in a present situation than in terms of how individuals relate and relate to their own past experiences.

In a society pervaded by both clever and unwitting amnesiacs, how much people remember becomes an overriding concern. When Wentworth reappears, such questions multiply rapidly, as Anne must read his conversations for small signs, gestures, glances, any evidence that he might remember her in the way that she remembers him. That he does remember is clear from his initial unguarded comment upon seeing Anne: "Henrietta asked him what he thought of you, when they went away; and he said, 'You were so altered he should not have known you again'" (p. 60). For change to be noted so vividly, the remembered image must be sharply etched. In general, though, it is Wentworth's conversations with his fellow officers which offer firm, if oblique, testimony to the strength of his memory. Much of the dialogue of *Persuasion* is anecdotal. Wentworth and Admiral and Mrs. Croft talk familiarly and lovingly of their various ships, encounters, and spoils while, in ironic counterpoint, the Misses Musgrove attempt to follow the conversation through their navy-list. The distinction between the summary knowledge provided by the list (another book of books, like the Baronetage) and the remembered personal history of the officers is made clear. The *Asp*, Wentworth's crucial first command, cannot be found in the list, because it has been taken from service. But above all, the stories of Wentworth and the admiral convey emotional knowledge, personal authenticity, a sense of having lived and experienced and remembered that is plainly lacking among the residents of both Kellynch Hall and Uppercross. One recalls that while Sir Walter is devoted to the Baronetage, Lady Russell and Anne remember the true meaning of the baronetcy; Mrs. Musgrove has to pillage her son's memorabilia, dragging forth his slender and illiterate correspondence, in order that her head, previously oblivious to his fate, should become "full of it, and of poor Richard!" (p. 50).

The anecdotal cast of the dialogue of *Persuasion* may, of course, be a sign of Jane Austen's deepening realism. Concerned as many novelists are with the dramatic analogue of scenic development, they sometimes overlook how much of our ordinary conversation—the best as well as the worst— consists of exchanged stories about ourselves. Sir Thomas Bertram, though, had serious motives for drawing Fanny's brother William out to talk about himself: "William was often called on by his uncle to be the talker. His recitals were amusing in themselves to Sir Thomas, but the chief object in seeking them, was to understand the recitor, to know the young man by his histories; and he listened to his clear, simple, spirited details with full satisfaction—seeing in them the proof of good principles, professional knowledge, energy, courage, and cheerfulness—every thing that could deserve or promise well" (*MP*, p. 236). Similar motives led Wordsworth to wander the public roads, and he made similar discoveries: "sounds in unison / With loftiest promises of good and fair" (*Prelude* [1850], XIII, 184–85). Equivalent roles are played in *Pride and Prejudice* and *Emma* by the letters in which Darcy and Frank Churchill, successfully and not so successfully, present their characters by giving an account of their actions, attempting to make themselves known by their histories. We may safely declare Jane Austen innocent of any knowledge of Wordsworth's unpublished masterpiece, but her tendency toward embedded narratives, so marked in *Persuasion*, would seem to proceed from similar considerations of the ways in which character should be presented.

Characters in *Persuasion* must render accounts of themselves. Some, like Sir Walter, Elizabeth, and the Musgroves, having experienced little and registered and retained even less, have precious little to tell. Others, like William Walter Elliot and Mrs. Clay, are thoroughly creatures of the present moment, vague or deceptive about their past lives. And still others, like Anne and Wentworth, the Crofts and Harvilles, and Lady Russell and Mrs. Smith, ultimately acquit themselves admirably, if not always painlessly. In their reconciliation scenes, Anne and Wentworth must retrace the past to come to terms with how things went wrong originally, how they might have been made right without the passage of eight lonely years, and how they very nearly misfired again. Mrs. Smith's account of the earlier life of Mr. Elliot does not spare her own youthful follies. When Lady Russell is faced with the truth about Mr. Elliot and with Anne's renewed attachment to Wentworth, "There was nothing less for [her] to do, than to admit that she had been pretty completely wrong, and to take up a new set of opinions and hopes" (p. 249). She is able to accomplish this confrontation with her past errors in judgment because "She loved Anne better than she loved her own abilities; and when the awkwardness of the beginning was over, found little hardship in attaching herself as a mother to the man who was securing the happiness of her other child" (p. 249). Anne's place in Lady Russell's life guarantees Wentworth's, just as Lady Russell's place in Anne's demands that he come to love her equally. The group which comes together at the end of the novel finds its bond in interlocking personal memories. Austen seems to suggest that a party of individuals with a firm sense of the integrity and continuity of the self will be able to overcome the fragmentation of society at large, which is so clearly imaged by the loss of the Kellynch estate and the near dissolution of the extended family as a social institution. In thinking of *Persuasion*'s principle for social unity, lines from *The Prelude* would again seem appropriate: "what we have loved, / Others will love, and we will teach them how" (1850; XIV, 446–47).

Jane Austen's earlier emphases on the discovery of a secure center and the maintenance of familial bonds, however inadequate the parents, are signs of her intense interest in cultural continuity. Her giving over these issues at the conclusion of *Persuasion*, accepting a world of fluidity of habitation, in which worthy older individuals must act, as Lady Russell explicitly does, in the place of parents, suggests a profound change in her attitudes on the possible foundations of a viable society. Controversy about the ending of the novel, most of which hinges in one way or other on the roles of Lady Russell and Mrs. Smith, may indicate that for many readers its vision of social continuity secured through the individual memory seems somehow inadequate. Old dreams die hard, and those of a secure place and generational continuity die harder than most. William A. Walling remarks of *Persuasion* that "Austen's art conveys to us a peculiarly modern terror: that our only recourse amid the accelerations of history is to commit our deepest energies to an intense personal relationship, but that an intense personal relationship is inevitably subject to its own kind of terrible precariousness." On the response of the modern reader, Professor Walling is undoubtedly correct; as far as Jane Austen herself is concerned, though, the terrors of her ending remain firmly circumstantial: "the dread of future war" and "the tax of quick alarm" (p. 252) paid by the sailor's wife are factors extrinsic to their personal relationship, which has already overcome obstacles equally threatening. An indication of Jane Austen's feelings about the adequacy of the grounds both of that relationship and of the small community which closes the novel may be found in the scene in which Anne and Wentworth find themselves alone and finally able to share their thoughts and feelings of the past moments and past years. "Soon words enough had passed between them," she writes, "to decide their direction towards the comparatively quiet and retired gravel walk, where the power of conversation would make the present hour a blessing indeed; and prepare it for all the immortality which the happiest recollections of their own future life could bestow" (p. 240). Such a belief in the power of memory—its ability to uphold and cherish and its power to make our noisy years seem moments in the being of the eternal silence—we have met with before, and in a writer whose central position in English Romanticism is uncontested.

NOTES

1. An encouraging sign in Jane Austen studies is the desynonymization of such terms as *conservative* and *unreflective*. Both Alistair M. Duckworth, The *Improvement of the Estate* (1971), and Marilyn Butler, *Jane Austen and the War of Ideas* (1975), pay close attention to the intellectual backgrounds of Jane Austen's social thought.

2. Here, at least, I am tempted to agree with Mr. Elton: "Rather he than I!" (*E*, p. 469).

3. *Letters of William and Dorothy Wordsworth: The Early Years 1787–1805*, ed. Ernest de Selincourt, 2nd. ed rev. by Chester L. Shaver (1967), pp. 314–15.

4. With varying interpretative emphases, the following find revolutionary implications in the treatment of class structure in *Persuasion*: Malcolm Bradbury, "*Persuasion* Again," *EiC*, 18 (1968), 383–96; Joseph Wiesenfarth, "*Persuasion*: History and Myth," *TWC*, 2 (1971), 160–68; Nina Auerbach, "O Brave New World: Evolution and Revolution in *Persuasion*," *ELH*, 39 (1972), 112–28.

5. Stuart M. Tave, *Some Words of Jane Austen* (1973), pp. 194–204, and Barbara Hardy, "The Objects in *Mansfield Park*," *Jane Austen: Bicentenary Essays*, ed. John Halperin (1975), pp. 180–96, explore the interrelationship of objects and memory in *Mansfield Park*.

6. Thomas P. Wolfe, "The Achievement of *Persuasion*," *SEL*, 11 (1971), 687–700, and Karl Kroeber, *Styles in Fictional Structure* (1971), pp. 79–84, offer interesting commentaries on the retrospective emphasis of Jane Austen's narrative method in the novel.

JULIA PREWITT BROWN

The Radical Pessimism of Persuasion

A gentleman and a lady are traveling in a hired coach up a rough lane in Sussex, around the year 1817. Their destination is a place called Willingden. The driver grumbles and shakes his shoulders at having to pursue so difficult a side-road, and—as if to justify his complaints—the carriage overturns. After scrambling out, the gentleman discovers that he has sprained his foot. The laborers from a nearby hayfield gather around to watch, and a gentleman approaches, introduces himself, and offers assistance. In the course of their conversation, it is discovered that the travelers have reached a parish called Willingden, but that it is not the Willingden they are seeking. After much confusion, they learn that there are two places by that name in the same county.

Whatever we associate with the novels of Jane Austen, we do not expect them to begin like this, yet the above is a summary of the opening of Austen's last, unfinished novel, *Sanditon*. The gentleman who sprains his foot is a capitalist speculator traveling with his wife, and the ensuing chapters are filled with restless dialogue concerning his efforts to turn his home village, Sanditon, into a profitable seaside resort. This alone would strike us as uncharacteristic of the author's concerns, but the opening itself is even more so. The scene opens in the homeless universe of travel and ends in an atmosphere of almost complete geographic disorientation—a disorientation

From *Jane Austen's Novels: Social Change and Literary Form.* © 1979 by The President and Fellows of Harvard College.

made even more uncomfortable by the experience of physical injury. The main characters appear to be placed in an open social frame, for the carriage driver and field workers are not shadows (as in Austen's earlier novels) but distinct presences. The manuscript looks curiously like the beginning of a Victorian novel, and not just because of the Dickensian carriage driver and the roving capitalist. The discovery of the two Willingdens is ominous. The world had grown just large enough to contain two parishes of the same name; between 1801 and 1831 the population of England increased from roughly eleven to sixteen and a half million; new towns were built, and old localities grew and split and doubled. Austen's scene of human, humorous confusion may be one of the first expressions in English fiction of the modern anxiety of displacement. Just as science fiction writers play on our fear of infinity by creating other worlds, modern novelists use mistaken locations and identities to convey the dread of endless anonymity. Later in *Sanditon*, the possibility of another coincidence is entertained: that two families, of the same size and means and taste in remote resorts, might bear the same name.

Sanditon may seem an oblique entrance into a discussion of *Persuasion*, but it is a telling one. If *Sanditon* had been finished, the common belief in Jane Austen's separation from the Victorians would never have taken hold; and no other novel has suffered more from this notion than *Persuasion*. The traditional assumption that all the novels are essentially the same in their unambitious, un-Victorian concern with domesticity is highly questionable without *Sanditon*, but a completed *Sanditon* would have precluded its formation. The social frame of *Sanditon* is sufficiently precarious. The heroine herself is a stranger in a foreign county, introduced to strangers; and the world she finds herself in would have rivaled Thackeray in its exposure of what society is like "when Rich People are Sordid" (*Sanditon*, p. 402). The story even includes a tender, half mulatto heiress who is to be forced on an impoverished baronet. And this is the novel that was begun only a few months after the completion of *Persuasion*.

A closer look at *Persuasion* will prove that the difference is not extreme, for many of the conceptual changes apparent in the unfinished work also exist in the finished one. *Persuasion* is Jane Austen's most "modern" work— perhaps the only novel that fully justifies F. R. Leavis's placing its author at the beginning of the modern tradition. In narrative mode, social view, and character conception, it marks a radical change from all that has gone before. Its debilitating ambiguities and hatreds, its conception of society, its surrender to disgust, take us through George Eliot and Henry James to, finally, the theories of Georg Lukács. For *Persuasion* is a novel as Lukács defined the novel: the epic of a failed world, or of the failure of the self to fulfill itself in the world.

The change in narrative style is immediately felt:

> Vanity was the beginning and the end of Sir Walter Elliot's character; vanity of person and of situation. He had been remarkably handsome in his youth; and, at fifty-four, was still a very fine man. Few women could think more of their personal appearance than he did; nor could the valet of any new made lord be more delighted with the place he held in society. He considered the blessing of beauty as inferior only to the blessing of a baronetcy; and the Sir Walter Elliot, who united these gifts, was the constant object of his warmest respect and devotion. (*Per*, pp. 8–4)

The prose is direct; definitive, and unambiguous to a degree that we have never before witnessed in Jane Austen. In the earlier novels, in descriptions of General Tilney, Mrs. Bennet, and Mr. Elton, the language shifts around the character; when definition occurs, it appears, as John Bayley suggests, as a form of exasperated sympathy, of humorous chastisement; it is never a substitute for personality, and further uncertainties of character are allowed and expected. Here the language closes in completely; the judgment is implacable and unchanging.

The ironic exuberance of former narrations is absent; there is no uncertainty, no sense of being occasionally surprised and generally appalled by the character. The narrator of the other novels provided these emotions and acted as an intermediary between the character and the reader's emotions about the character; the narrator's role was both to stimulate and to check these emotions. Hence the element of ironic challenge in all the novels up to *Persuasion*, an element that strongly characterizes the ironic comedies but also makes itself felt in harsher ways in the other novels. Recall one of the opening remarks of *Mansfield Park*: "But there certainly are not so many men of large fortune in the world, as there are pretty women to deserve them" (*MP*, p. 3). Like the openings of the earlier works of satiric realism, *Sense and Sensibility* and *Mansfield Park*, the opening of *Persuasion* possesses a great intensity of scorn; yet unlike the others, its assault is unrelieved by such interjections. No ironic narrator intercedes to modify or objectify the disgust. Sir Walter is viewed from the perspective of one who lives with him, whose very intimacy, like Gulliver's view of the Brobdingnagians' skin, makes derogation inevitable. The description and Judgment are simultaneous and the reader has nothing to do but accept them.

We see now that a major function of the ironic narrator was to involve the reader in the moral difficulties of the story. The above sentence from *Mansfield Park* is wholly characteristic of the crude slyness of the narrator, of her unceremonious ambition to draw the reader in by trifling with him—in this case by teasing his intelligence with a cliché. Such efforts always succeed in Jane Austen, in a way that George Eliot's narrative intrusions never can, because of their element of self-irony. There is something irresistible about irony directed against oneself; James Thurber, for example, may not be a great writer but he is an irresistible one. Jane Austen's narrator never calls on the reader with the majesty of compassion one finds in George Eliot; she never pretends to enlist the better part of ourselves. Her method is to provoke us into participation by stimulating our judgment in a variety of ways: challenging, withholding, encouraging, and satirizing it. The result is an exuberance of interchange between reader and narrator that serves to counteract the corrosiveness of many of the insights contained in the story. The absence of this exuberance is conspicuous in *Persuasion*; the narrator no longer cares what the reader thinks.

This coolness to the reader contrasts with an intensity of feeling for the characters in the story, particularly for the heroine. The reason for this contradiction is that Anne Elliot is the central intelligence of the novel. Sir Walter is seen as Anne sees him, with resigned contempt. For the first time Jane Austen gives over the narrator's authority to a character almost completely. In *Emma*, many events and situations are seen from Emma's point of view, but the central intelligence lies somewhere between the narrator and the reader, who together see that Emma sees wrongly. In *Persuasion*, Anne Elliot's feelings and evaluations correspond to those of the narrator in almost every situation, although there are several significant lapses, which I will take up later. It seems that this transfer of authority placed a strain on Jane Austen's accustomed narrative tendencies and that she could not maintain it completely.

Because Anne Elliot is fatigued and despondent, the mood of the narrative is one of resignation and exhausted care. A sense of things ended, things spent, powerfully characterizes the beginning of the novel. It appears in images of finished movement. Sir Walter slowly pages through the entire Baronetage and then closes it; his character is illuminated from "beginning" to "end"; Elizabeth Elliot cannot find a baronet "from A to Z" who suits her as much as her cousin. The exhaustion implied in these metaphors is intensified by the opening conviction that we have hit the rock bottom of moral life in Sir Walter. The often-praised mood of disappointment in the opening chapters is a result of this conviction, for the reader intuitively expects things to move upward since they cannot move downward. Yet this upward movement does not occur for some time, and so the narrative seems to become even heavier. Even the heroine participates in the oppression, because she has given up hope of influencing or changing her environment. Anne's revenge upon her father and sister is that she does not try to change them. She has been disappointed in love and is unable to get beyond the experience.

The heroine's failure to fulfill herself in the world, then, is as much a result of the feebleness of her soul as it is of the inessentiality of the world.[1] A minor dialogue later in the story seems to me to be especially illustrative of Anne's state of mind, and hence of the novel's. On the morning of Louisa Musgrove's accident, Anne and Henrietta stroll down to the sea before breakfast. Henrietta intends to marry Charles Hayter, who she hopes will become resident curate of Dr. Shirley's parish at Uppercross. They praise the morning and the breeze, then are silent until Henrietta suddenly begins:

> Oh! yes,—I am quite convinced that, with very few exceptions, the sea-air always does one good. There can be no doubt of its having been of the greatest service to Dr. Shirley, after his illness, last spring twelvemonth. He declares himself, that coming to Lyme for a month, did him more good than all the medicine he took; and, that being by the sea, always makes him feel young again. Now, I cannot help thinking it a pity that he does not live entirely by the sea. I do think he had better leave Uppercross entirely, and fix at Lyme.—Do not you, Anne?—Do not you agree with me, that it is the best thing he could do, both for himself and Mrs. Shirley? (*Per*, p. 102)

In any of the earlier novels, the heroine's reply to such a speech would be a difficult compromise. Like Elizabeth Bennet's words to Mr. Collins, the response must unite civility and truth, must acknowledge the reasonable without acquiescing to the selfish. Anne Elliot, however, senses no difficulty; to her it is a matter of "general acquiescence." "She said all that was reasonable and proper on the business; felt the claims of Dr. Shirley to repose, as she ought; saw how very desirable it was that he should have some active, respectable young man, as a resident curate, and was even courteous enough to hint at the advantage of such resident curate's being married" (*Per*, p. 102). "Very well pleased with her companion," Henrietta chatters on until the others approach, giving Anne only time to offer a "general answer" once again, "and a wish that such another woman were at Uppercross, before all subjects suddenly ceased."

Anne does not simply comply with the innocent egotism of Henrietta; she actually encourages it. It is not her courtesy but her apathy that lends the seaside conversation its curiously soft emptiness. In *Pride and Prejudice* or *Emma* the same scene would have been tightened with a more emphatic irony and heightened with comedy, and therefore would have conveyed at the very least a commitment to the character. In *Sense and Sensibility* or *Mansfield Park* Henrietta's speech would have been treated with greater scorn, but only in *Persuasion* could it be treated with indifference. I am reminded of Hamlet's encounter with the court fop Osric in the last act of the play. Earlier Osric would have aroused Hamlet's loathing and brought on his scathing abuse; now Hamlet is mocking and detached and accepts Osric out of a fundamental moral indifference that is far more disturbing, and seems far more perverse, than his earlier madness. A similar atmosphere of controlled apathy, of resigned indifference, characterizes the first half of *Persuasion*. Even the unrelenting judgments of the opening page amount to a kind of indifference in their surrender to disgust. Like Anne herself, *Persuasion* walks a thin line between wisdom and apathy, between resignation and despair.

One of the remarkable aspects of the famous passage about Dick Musgrove is that it breaks through the shield of indifference into anger:

> The real circumstances of this pathetic piece of family history were, that the Musgroves had had the ill fortune of a very troublesome, hopeless son; and the good fortune to lose him before he reached his twentieth year; that he had been sent to sea, because he was stupid and unmanageable on shore; that he had been very little cared for at any time by his family, though quite as much as he deserved; seldom heard of, and scarcely at all regretted, when the intelligence of his death abroad had worked its way to Uppercross, two years before.
>
> He had, in fact, though his sisters were now doing all they could for him, by calling him "poor Richard," been nothing better than a thick-headed, unfeeling, unprofitable Dick Musgrove, who had never done any thing to entitle himself to more than the abbreviation of his name, living or dead. (*Per*, pp. 50–51)

This passage is one of the few instances in Jane Austen in which we sense a loss of control, perhaps because the exact source of the statement is confused. The sentiment of the passage comes both from a narrator (in some ways the old Jane Austen narrator appearing suddenly) and from the central consciousness of Anne. Like Sir Walter in the opening scene, Dick Musgrove is seen as the frustrated Anne might see him. He was a sailor on Captain Wentworth's vessel and enjoyed Wentworth's company when Anne was denied it. The jealous feelings that might be evoked under these circumstances would be greatly intensified by the anxiety Anne feels for rejecting Wentworth. In the judgmental description of Dick Musgrove, the intolerable blame is transferred or displaced to the foolish boy.

On the other hand, the passage contains the less neurotic, and more ironic, impulses of the standard Austen narrator. Whenever this narrator treats the subject of death, attention always focuses on how people respond to it. In *Persuasion*, the question of one's response to loss is of particular interest; many of the characters are widows, and the heroine herself is figuratively widowed. Austen's contempt for the Musgroves' self-serving grief, and for their coarse foolishness in choosing to like their son *after* he is dead, is consistent with her treatment of human evasions in general, and of the persuasions and evasions of *Persuasion* in particular.[2]

Yet Austen's attitude toward evasion does not explain the extraordinary vehemence of the passage and the hatred of the dead boy that is revealed in it. The statement is aberrant and uncontrolled; it suggests, perhaps above all, the pathology of disillusion. The novel of disillusion is always in danger of losing its irony and of simply demanding meaning in outright form. I have discussed the opening despair of *Persuasion*, which is felt in the debilitating emotions of the heroine herself. The Dick Musgrove passage reads like a terrible and irrational outburst against this despair: an exasperated attempt to force meaning—even negative meaning—onto the despondent world. In the insincerity of their grief, the Musgroves exemplify the Sartrean condition of "nothingness": like the French waiter who plays the role of the French waiter, the Musgroves play the role of grieving parents. For the first time in Jane Austen the narrative irony cannot sustain the insincerity, and in a burst of frustration the narrator makes some claim for the diabolical truth.

The animus behind the statement ("and the good fortune to lose him") is as anarchic as a modern conception of truth usually is. The narrator is saying that some lives really are worthless. This is the dark, unfamiliar side of the narrator's characteristically didactic insistence that some lives really are worth something.

The judgment on life is not confined to the Musgroves and their dead son but is applied even to the heroine herself. It is often said that Anne, unlike previous heroines, has nothing to learn. But unsettling suggestions in the narrative imply that the author felt Anne has much to learn. Her friendship with Mrs. Smith constitutes an education, particularly with regard to the information about Mr. Elliot's character. On her walk to Mrs. Smith's the morning after the concert at which Wentworth has betrayed his jealousy of Mr. Elliot, Anne thinks about Mr. Elliot's suit and magnanimously regrets that she will have to discourage him: "There was much to regret. How she might have felt, had there been no Captain Wentworth in the case, was not worth enquiry; for there was a Captain Wentworth: and be the conclusion of the present suspense good or bad, her affection would be his for ever. Their union, she believed, could not divide her more from other men, than their final separation" (*Per*, p. 192). Had the passage ended here, we would not question her sentiment, but it is followed by a harrowing interjection: "Prettier musings of high-wrought love and eternal constancy, could never have passed along the streets of Bath, than Anne was sporting with from Camden-place to Westgate-buildings. It was almost enough to spread purification and perfume all the way" (*Per*, p. 192). The variety of interpretation of this passage indicates how individual each reader's understanding of Austen's tone can be. Marvin Mudrick, in general so stringent an interpreter of Austen's irony, sees this passage as a sincere "burst of affection" from Jane Austen herself. "We share the author's overt sympathy," he writes, in an instance of "unalloyed joy."[3] I confess to bafflement at such an interpretation. The passage seems to me directly and passionately hostile in its irony; nothing could be more antithetical to Austen's conception of love than the image of purification and perfume. The statement is another example of the sudden, uncontrolled outburst of the authorial mind. As in the Dick Musgrove passage, the hostility is pathological but understandable. Anne is on her way to visit Mrs. Smith, who has no suitors to choose from, no money, and few friends. It seems a grotesque luxury for Anne to insist that, given her choice of suitors, she would only choose Wentworth and love him eternally. The passage is an angry defense of those who have to make do with what they have.

Jane Austen wrote *Persuasion* during her illness under circumstances similar to those of Mrs. Smith. In a curious way, she seems to blame Anne for feeling the isolation and sadness that Mrs. Smith would be justified in feeling. A poverty-stricken invalid possesses a cheerful fortitude, while Anne Elliot indulges in tender sonnets of declining happiness and, unlike the farmer, does not mean "to have spring again."

During the visit with Mrs. Smith Anne learns of Mr. Elliot's true character and of instances of inhumanity that make Sir Walter seem harmless. The confrontation of her own worldly ignorance makes her humble; and, at the close of the chapter, her assurance of the invulnerability of her love for Wentworth has disappeared: "Anne could just acknowledge within herself such a possibility of having been induced to marry him, as made her shudder at the idea of the misery which must have followed. It was just possible that she might have been persuaded by Lady Russell!" (*Per*, p. 211). If this humility survived to an admission that she was wrong to take Lady Russell's advice in the first place, *Persuasion* would be a novel of education, like the ironic comedies. But Anne eventually decides that she was right, and her refusal to learn from her mistake is one reason why *Persuasion* is not a novel of education but one of disillusion—the characteristic nineteenth-century form. Anne Elliot has something to learn but does not quite learn it. As in her insistence on unrequited constancy to Wentworth, it is as if Anne must have everything, must be right even in the past. She never confronts the issue of persuasion, as Wentworth confronts his own stubbornness. (He admits he stayed away too long out of angry pride.) Anne's main failing is that she is too "tender," as the closing lines suggest, too excessively "feminine." Wentworth admits his stubbornness, and he even mocks the masculine pieties when he says, "'I have been used to the gratification of believing myself to earn every blessing that I enjoyed. I have valued myself on honourable toils and just rewards. Like other great men under reverses,' he added with a smile, 'I must endeavor to subdue my mind to my fortune. I must learn to brook being happier than I deserve'" (*Per*, p. 247). In *Persuasion*, the feminine pieties are never mocked, although they are occasionally undermined. Anne's maternal longings and her desire to be needed, for example, make her grateful when people are hurt or unwell and she can care for them. But because Anne herself is the central consciousness of the novel, the author's reservations about her disposition or preferences remain ambiguous and faint.

Either because of Austen's inexperience in working within a central consciousness or because of her inability to revise the novel completely before her death, the transference of perception is never fully controlled. Despite occasional judgments against her, too much power is given to Anne Elliot—too much power, one may say, over the other characters in the story. In one respect, Louisa Musgrove's accident is an act of revenge, a symbolic murder of Anne's rival. And the story becomes the imaginative fulfillment of Anne's fantasies. Had Jane Austen lived to write more novels, she would have mastered the technique (had she chosen to) and been able to center her intelligence inside a character without either violating the actuality of circumstance or destroying the moral realism that the old narrator had so responsibly maintained. Or, as for example in *Middlemarch* or *Washington Square*, she would have perceived and exploited the connection between fantasy and circumstance, and shown the mind's ability to impose its fantasies on the world.[4] The fact that Jane Austen was making these changes in narrative method, however, and that, for example, *Persuasion* strongly influenced *Washington Square*, justifies Leavis's placing Austen at the head of his tradition. Austen attempts to transfer the narrator's authority to the isolated consciousness of Anne Elliot in order to conform to a new conception of society and of the individual's place in that society. The changes in English society that were to separate the world of *Emma* from that of *Portrait of a Lady* were well underway at the end of Austen's life, and she recorded them in *Persuasion*.

Persuasion is the first novel by Jane Austen, for example, in which society is conceived of no longer as a meaningful whole, but as a series of disparate parts. Both *Mansfield Park* and *Emma* rely on an ethos of place for their sense of society; the organized propriety of Mansfield and the cooperative energy of Highbury provide each novel, and the characters in them, with a clear sense of context. But *Persuasion* is made up of a meaningless variety of places and the conflicting minor identities that attend them: Sir Walter's Kellynch Hall, Uppercross Cottage, Uppercross Great House, the Hayters' farm, the Crofts' Kellynch Hall, the various habitations of Lyme and Bath, and so on. It is perhaps for this reason that in *Persuasion* social structures are contemplated with almost systematic dissatisfaction. The society of *Mansfield Park* is an infected whole, but a whole nonetheless; its only virtue lies in its ability to provide some context for the individual. In *Persuasion* this last consolation has disappeared. The heroine moves from place to place, disoriented, isolated. Almost every community and form within which she functions is made meaningless by sheer disparity, or by the inevitable necessity of removal.

For this reason, Anne Elliot may be said to be"alienated"—certainly the first heroine in Jane Austen to be so, and perhaps, the first in English fiction. She passes beyond the mere loneliness of Fanny Price and the magisterial conceit of Emma, into an egocentric isolation very similar to that experienced by Dorothea Brooke or Isabel Archer. For Anne is genuinely estranged—overcome and enfeebled—by her homeless condition. Her fate will never flow into the communities through which she passes, and her marriage signifies a movement out of the communities she has known. The navy represents the only adequate community in the novel, and Anne's final association with it provides the only antidote to what would otherwise be a completely private resolution or an exclusively lyrical finish. But the special status accorded to the navy is qualified by its precarious military destiny, as the last page of the novel suggests.

The robust security of *Emma*, written a few years before *Persuasion*, comes precisely from this safety from alienation, from its implicit confidence that a reconciliation between interiority and reality, between Emma and Highbury, is possible. The same may be said of *Mansfield Park*, whose reconciliation is actually enhanced by its joylessness. Its population purged and reshuffled, Mansfield finally opens itself to meaning, and the piteous integrity of Fanny Price is at last rewarded. Fanny had always struggled to maintain the connection between interiority and reality. (Compared to her, the Crawfords seem "free," as indeed they are, because they have released themselves from the struggle.) Self-deceiving as she sometimes is, only Fanny probes continually: how much of what I feel or know to be true can I perform? For both Fanny Price and Emma Woodhouse the way is open to salvation, and through various comic and tragic struggles and sacrifices, salvation is attained: the embracing of an outside order that corresponds to interiority, and that therefore includes love. For the modern soul who seeks fulfillment in this correspondence with reality, as Lukács has said, irony must be the texture and form of his experience, but this irony does not compromise the ideal itself, which is the lived experience of meaning in the world. When the ideal is attained, as it is at the close of all Jane Austen's novels except the last, it is experienced to some degree by more than just the main characters; it is, or was, potentially accessible to all.

This belief in the possibility of common meaning and common destiny is greatly weakened in *Persuasion*. Unlike the conclusions of the earlier novels, that of *Persuasion* does not resound with other marriages, but rather with a series of failed unions. We do not feel that others will follow Anne into paradise. Even the marriage between hero and heroine has far less communal significance than those of earlier novels, for the navy is an accidental home for Anne, as Kellynch Hall is for the Crofts. The sense of impermanence felt in *Persuasion* anticipates the anxieties of many nineteenth-century novels.

The moral and aesthetic order sustained by Austen's earlier narrators, then, is no longer possible in the dislocated world of *Persuasion*. As a result, Anne Elliot—whose social circumstances make her a passive observer— almost becomes the central consciousness of the novel. Yet the transference of moral perception is never complete, because Anne is still too dependent on the various communities she visits. She can judge the Musgrove girls, for example, but not completely or absolutely (the way the authorial voice judges Mrs. Bennet in the first chapter of *Pride and Prejudice*); Anne lives among the Musgroves and knows she lives among them. She is in a position to resist them in certain ways but not to decide against them. She is more isolated than the earlier heroines but still she must participate; she does not have the choices, say, of Jane Eyre, Dorothea Brooke, or Isabel Archer.

The opening portrait of Sir Walter is perhaps the best example of what Austen could do within the new mode of perception produced by the loss of a narrative frame. Sir Walter is inelastic, implacable, conceptualized. There is no air between him and the author's conception of him. He is a fixed image in the book, and Austen's genius makes him so. In *Emma* Austen explored questions of human nature in a Shakespearean way; in *Persuasion* her sense of the social world she wrote about had changed so as to make this approach impossible. The description of Sir Walter paging through the Baronetage in search of his own name and lineage, or contemplating his reflection in his mirror-filled room, is a psychological portrait of the dissociation of the self. Sir Walter is a man in search of an existence, in search of some exterior proof of his existence in the world. He derives his existence from the volume, and he bestows in it the existences of others. Birth, death, and "heir presumptive" are recorded there. One of the novel's closing ironies is Wentworth's acquisition of an existence in Sir Walter's eyes: Sir Walter inscribes his name in the Baronetage.

The portrayal of Sir Walter is a social portrait of the dislocation of role. Role is the self's "job," the self's direction, and Sir Walter fails in his role as the baronet of an estate. *Persuasion* deals with the crisis of separation between self and role in society. In an increasingly democratic society, such separations are inevitable as individuals assume roles they were not born to (the Crofts move into Kellynch) and lose roles they were born to (Sir Walter is forced to leave). The basic uncertainties in the novel separate it markedly from Austen's earlier works.

Persuasion is the only one of the novels that ends with a vague ignorance of where the hero and heroine are going to live, and even of what the years will bring for them. Wentworth does not have an estate, and the novel's close acknowledges the possibility of another separation to come (another war). The nature of society in *Persuasion* makes assurance about the future impossible, and therefore causes a loss of personal assurance. (Uncertainty about the future is what leads Anne to reject Wentworth in the first place.) Unlike the earlier heroines and their lovers, Anne and Wentworth, or the love between them, lack the simplicity of will to overcome illusions and obstacles; they fail before the novel opens. Nowhere is Austen's irony more emphatic than in the beginning of her denouement: "Who can be in doubt of what follows? When any two young people take it into their heads to marry, they are pretty sure by perseverance to carry their point" (*Per*, p. 248).

Let us now take a closer look at the social world of *Persuasion*. Actually the term "social world" is slightly misleading. We can speak of the social world of *Pride and Prejudice*, of the Mansfield estate, of Highbury, but the world of *Persuasion* is made up of separate and divided communities, of opinion and idea, of imagination and memory: "Anne had not wanted this visit to Uppercross, to learn that a removal from one set of people to another, though at a distance of only three miles, will often include a total change of conversation, opinion and idea" (*Per*, p. 42). From Uppercross she moves to Kellynch-Lodge, Lady Russell's house: "When they came to converse, she was soon sensible of some mental change. The subjects of which her heart had been full on leaving Kellynch, and which she had felt slighted, and been compelled to smother among the Musgroves, were now become but of secondary interest. She had lately lost sight even of her father and sister and Bath. Their concerns had been sunk under those of Uppercross" (*Per*, p. 124). And from Kellynch-Lodge she moves to her family's house at Bath: "Uppercross excited no interest, Kellynch very little, it was all Bath" (*Per*, p. 137). The only continuity among these worlds is Anne's consciousness: "It was highly incumbent on her to clothe her imagination, her memory, and all her ideas in as much of Uppercross as possible" (*Per*, p. 43). Only Anne is aware of the mental distance among the different locales she inhabits. This awareness above all sets Anne apart from the closed consciousnesses of other persons.

In the first part of *Persuasion*, until Anne's arrival at Bath, the separation of mind is primarily perceived as a separation of place. As Anne visits one house after another, she encounters different states of mind: Kellynch-Hall, Uppercross cottage and Uppercross Great House, Lyme, Kellynch-Lodge, and Kellynch-Hall again with the Crofts inhabiting it. At Bath all worlds seem to converge: the Crofts, Elliots, Musgroves, and Harvilles, and Lady Russell, Anne, and Wentworth all join there, and two figures out of the past, Mrs. Smith and Mr. Elliot, appear to make the convergence total. Yet the convergence is deceptive, and the geographical unity only serves to set off the actual disunity of the society. Distinctions of estate now become distinctions of street, as Sir Walter keeps reminding us. And the closer social milieu of Bath only seems to emphasize class distinctions in the minds of the people who live there. Elizabeth Elliot's unexpected invitation to Wentworth only confirms our consciousness of her conceit, for she is convinced that he will be flattered and grateful to receive it, just as she and her father are grateful to receive an invitation from the Dalrymples. Class snobbery is always criticized in Jane Austen, yet only in *Persuasion* is it presented with unrelieved seriousness and simplified disapproval. The Price family's relative poverty in *Mansfield Park* was clearly linked to their insensitivity. In *Persuasion*, Mrs. Smith's poverty is more genteel that the Elliots' wealth; the snobbery that ostracizes her is a destructive illusion. Similarly, Lady Dalrymple and her daughter, latter versions of Lady Catherine de Bourgh and her daughter, have an emptiness that is too offensive to Jane Austen to tempt her to treat them humorously, to allow them any eccentricity that could redeem their self-important mediocrity.

The sense of individuality gathers intensity throughout the novel, until at Bath all the characters are life so many autonomous beings, encountering one another with haphazard regularity, each expecting and seeing something unique to his or her self, each oblivious of the others. The reconciliation of Anne and Wentworth takes place gradually through a series of accidental encounters; that the proposal itself is spurred by an overheard conversation and realized in a note increases our sense of the tenuousness of human interchange. Even characters who pride themselves on their shrewd awareness, like Mr. Elliot in his understanding of Mrs. Clay, are always blind at some crucial point. Preoccupied with Mrs. Clay's ambitions with Sir Walter, Mr. Elliot overlooks her ambitions with himself. These disparities of view and personality are seen to originate in the disparities of age, experience, physical appearance, and family with which the novel is preoccupied. The narrative is saturated with allusions to differences between persons: Lady Russell's manners are old-fashioned and Elizabeth Elliot's are not; those who are in the navy see things differently from those who are not (even down to the painting of the ship that irritates Admiral Croft); those who are young and attractive are different from those who are not; Mrs. Musgrove is fat and Anne, we are told several times, is slender. These details give *Persuasion* a dimension that is not felt in the other novels. *Pride and Prejudice*, for example, underplays all differences but those of mind; it opens with the disembodied voices of the Bennets. Physical differences, class differences, and so on are realized only in differences of state of mind. The same is true, though to a lesser degree, of *Emma*, in which communal interaction encompasses individual difference. In *Persuasion*, the individual is at once independent and estranged, looming and yet powerless.

The confidence of *Emma* in a stable, cooperative community is lost in the social and personal fragmentation of *Persuasion*. As a result, the heroine is far more uncertain. The ever changing egotism of the environment is too much for Anne to resist; hence her compliance with whatever environment or situation she is in. This compliance ranges from apathy (with Henrietta) to sympathy (with Benwick) to resignation (with her family)—all passive responses.

In discussing *Emma* I stressed the importance of the idea of cooperation in Jane Austen, and I pointed out that Austen saw a distinction between cooperation and compromise, restraint and repression, that we no longer see. This changes in *Persuasion*. Social cooperation assumes a stable community in which individual cooperation ultimately benefits the individual: Emma and Highbury go together. *Persuasion* does not have a Highbury at its base, a communal form with its own memory and imagination in which an Emma could participate and thrive. Its heroine is the more uncertain Anne Elliot, who moves from community to community, and who can only comply rather than cooperate. She is happy to be "of use," which is to say that in the different environments she enters, she is being used. The personal damage such a posture incurs is fully realized later in the century by Henry James in the character of Madame Merle. Madame Merle is another woman whose life is a series of visits to other people's houses, and who by necessity cultivates an ability to comply while preserving a secret will. Anne Elliot's secret intelligence is far from the indomitable and uncooperative will of Madame Merle, yet she too must live with secret consolations: "Anne always contemplated [the Musgrove sisters] as some of the happiest creatures of her acquaintance; but still, saved as we all are by some comfortable feeling of superiority from wishing for the possibility of exchange, she would not have given up her own more elegant and cultivated mind for all their enjoyments" (*Per*, p. 41). In statements like these Anne Elliot reminds us of many nineteenth-century heroines. We think of her in these instances almost as a "case": an unmarried, unoccupied women, superior in mind and character to all about her, yet unrecognized, unnoticed, and even shunned among them. In a reversal of the case of Emma Woodhouse, Anne's situation defines her more than her personality does. And that, of course, is her problem, and the problem of so many other Victorian heroines.

Anne's consolation represents the Victorian (and modern) variation of stoicism. It is not the consolation we are asked to accept in *King Lear*: that Cordelia's goodness is its own reward. Anne's protective conviction of her own rare "cultivated mind" seems to state that the burden of intelligence is its own reward: that the estranged consciousness is better than the communal stupidity. This awareness of the enforced isolation of the sensitive and thinking person appears in the complaints of Victorian intellectuals. John Henry Newman, who admired Jane Austen's novels, complained that the age was becoming "the paradise of little men, and the purgatory of great ones," and Matthew Arnold complained in a letter to A. H. Clough that the society was becoming "more comfortable for the mass, and more uncomfortable for those of any natural gift or distinction." Although both had in mind the decline in "great careers" of men, their sentiment is fundamentally analogous to Austen's intuition of the burden that both the mediocrity and the discontinuity of social life place on the intelligent and sensitive person.

This resentment of social life takes us back to the first half of *Sense and Sensibility*, to Marianne's Blakean exasperation with the insincerity of society. In the earlier novel, however, the burden is ultimately shown to have its source in the illiberal illusions of its sufferer, for several of the seemingly unfeeling supporters of society (from Mrs. Jennings to Elinor) turn out to be sincere, while the romantic lover is actually shallow and worldly. In *Persuasion* suffering is also rooted in a particular weakness of the heroine, yet social life remains intolerable to the end. In its general structure, *Persuasion* registers a fundamental, almost Weberian crisis of belief in the legitimacy of social structures. Certainly one of the most radical statements in all of Jane Austen is Anne's subversive sentiment concerning her father's departure from Kellynch-Hall; that "they were gone who deserved not to stay, and that Kellynch-Hall had passed into better hands than its owners" (*Per*, p. 125). As Weber has said, established power is sustained only through a subjective belief in its legitimacy; through people believing it is legitimate and allowing themselves to be so dominated. Revolutions begin with a crisis of legitimacy.

In *Persuasion* we see the beginning of a failure to support traditions, a failure that led to nineteenth-century reforms. The positive feeling toward the navy lies in its widespread invigoration of domestic life. In the words of Sir Walter, the navy was "the means of bringing persons of obscure birth into undue distinction, and raising men to honours which their fathers and grandfathers never dreamt of" (*Per*, p. 19). As the closing lines of the novel suggest, Austen rated the domestic advantages of this revitalization as equal to the military achievements of the navy. "Anne gloried in being a sailor's wife, but she must pay the tax of quick alarm for belonging to that profession which is, if possible, more distinguished in its domestic virtues than in its national importance" (*Per*, p. 252).

These alterations in social life are perceived as transformations within and among families. As "always in Jane Austen, the basic instrument of both division and unity is the family, of which marriage is the origin. Class feeling is an extension of family feeling, or pride of ancestry, as the opening of the novel makes clear. Jane Austen originally entitled her work *The Elliots*; her brother Henry changed it after her death to perhaps the more ingenious title. Yet the first title may hint at what Austen meant to explore: a family's mind and future. The culmination of Sir Walter's ancestral account is "Heir presumptive, William Walter Elliot, Esq., great grandson of the second Sir Walter" (*Per*, p. 4). The question of inheritance is central to many English novels and crucial to those of Jane Austen. Because she centered on the destinies of women, this question has been overlooked, together with her concern for establishing the difference between legal and rightful, between material and moral, inheritance. In their concern with the passage of generations, all the Austen novels pose the question that Lionel Trilling perceives in Forster's *Howards End*: "Who shall inherit England?"[5] In the opening pages we learn that William Elliot is the heir presumptive, but Mr. Elliot's part in the plot is relatively insignificant; like all the novels, *Persuasion* focuses on the actual inheritors. Anne and Wentworth inherit the England of *Persuasion*, if only because they see it, and will experience it, as it really is: fragmented and uncertain. For the first time in Jane Austen, the future is not linked with the land, and the social order is completely dissociated from the moral order. William Elliot will inherit the impoverished Kellynch, but that does not matter. The future is in the hands of Anne and Wentworth, as the present is in the hands of the Crofts, that almost comic national couple whose defense of England abroad makes them the rightful inhabiters of Kellynch. It is significant that to Anne the only temptation to marry Mr. Elliot is that she would inherit her mother's position at Kellynch. Her rejection of him makes clear a distinction between familial and moral inheritance.

Anne's marriage to Wentworth represents an act of will to replace, through marriage, the old inadequate family with the new adequate family, an act that is at the core of the generational concept of every Jane Austen novel. The feminine conception of marriage, unlike the masculine one, traditionally assumes loss as well as gain, because until well into the nineteenth century only the woman left her family when she married; the woman also, of course, lost her name and assumed a new one. A basic movement in all Jane Austen's mature novels is the heroine's struggle to create a new "family" for herself, to replace with a new relationship the unsatisfactory family in which she is unappreciated or unfulfilled. In *Persuasion* the sense of the pains of the original family is particularly keen. Sir Walter and Elizabeth's most serious failing is their lack of feeling for Anne. And Lady Russell's concern to see Anne married is analogous, in its awareness of the need for escape, to the concern felt for all the heroines after *Sense and Sensibility*. "[Lady Russell] would have rejoiced to see her at twenty-two, so respectably removed from the partialities and injustice of her father's house [through marriage to Charles Musgrove]" (*Per*, p. 29).

In Jane Austen marriage represents a reorganization of social life. Anne sees her marriage in part as the formation of a new social group, and regrets that in that respect she can offer so little: "[Anne] had no other alloy to the happiness of her prospects, than what arose from the consciousness of having no relations to bestow on him which a man of sense could value. There she felt her own inferiority keenly" (*Per*, p. 251). The marriage that ends *Persuasion* is viewed as part of the general revitalizing of English society that took place upon the navy's return from the war.

The revitalizing power of marriage is suggested in all the Austen novels, but most urgently, most despairingly, in *Persuasion*. In the earlier novels, marriage is linked to the general functioning of the society and to the land; marriage is a form of participation in society. In *Persuasion*, society no longer offers the couple a defined context for their adult identities; compared to Elizabeth and Darcy, Anne and Wentworth are directionless after their marriage. For this reason, the individuals themselves and the relationship they embark on carry a great burden. Marriage is no longer sustained by a larger framework; Anne Elliot will not receive the spontaneous social support and identity that Marianne Dashwood receives when, upon her marriage to Colonel Brandon, she finds herself "placed in a new home, a wife, the mistress of a family, and the patroness of a village" (*SS*, p. 379). Mary Musgrove "would not change situations with Anne," for "Anne had no Uppercross Hall before her, no landed estate, no headship of a family" (*Per*, p. 250). Whatever social strength Anne and Wentworth's marriage possesses will be created and sustained by themselves. For this reason, the singular existence and quality of the marriage itself becomes vitally important.

It is the individual's lonely responsibility for his entire future that perhaps gives *Persuasion* its powerfully ambiguous mood. The closing marriages of the earlier novels seem to represent possibility more than necessity, a stage in the moral growth of the heroine, the nexus of generational change. In *Persuasion*, marriage between Anne and Wentworth is a matter of sheer need, the last hope for the individuals themselves and for the dissolving society around them. In the closing felicities of *Emma*, as I have said, we understand the different marriages through comparison. This statement holds true with a vengeance in *Persuasion*. Most of the major characters are literally or figuratively widowed; and among the complete pairs, only Admiral and Mrs. Croft possess a moral existence. The only hope of the novel rests almost entirely upon two characters, Anne and Wentworth, who are alike in their superiority of mind and sensibility and yet are alienated from each other.

For this reason, the progress of Anne and Wentworth's reconciliation is fraught with tension and significance. All the novels are imbued with a tension between the pains of the present and the hopes of the future; and all implicitly contrast the lovers with the lesser world around them. The emotional intensity of *Persuasion* is heightened by the addition of another dimension: the past. Together with a sense of the isolation of the heroine, the use of the past is responsible for the intensity of feeling contained in the reconciliation of Anne and Wentworth.

Like *David Copperfield*, *Persuasion* poses the question: is the past a pain or a pleasure?[6] The pains of the present are rooted in Anne's past mistake, but so are the hopes for the future. The past seems to envelop the whole; we feel the hero and heroine are moving forward and backward in time simultaneously. This paradox lends the novel an urgency that is at once painful and hopeful. The exquisiteness of the novel's emotion, like that of Shelley's poem to the West Wind, lies in the consciousness that spring will come. Also as in the poem, this consciousness is held in check; it is realized only momentarily in Anne's feelings of fearful happiness. The dominant experience of the novel is one of loss; the movement, though urgent, is downward.

The mood and feelings imparted in the beginning of *Persuasion*—the sense of resignation and regret, the feeling of the inalterable circularity of time expressed in the seasonal imagery, and the inescapable redundancy of life expressed in allusions to the eventless years preceding the opening of the novel—gather intensity when Anne learns of Wentworth's return. Then very gradually Anne's despair is replaced by a desire to act; like the farmer plowing the field, Anne finally "means to have Spring again." As this feeling grows, the sense of time lost and wasted becomes more intense. The hope for spring only makes the winter more acute.

Even though we know that Anne and Wentworth will be reconciled (either from previous reading or from romantic expectation) the novel seems to swirl downward to this conclusion. In the compression of events at Bath, there is a sense of rushing toward the reconciliation as though it were a last chance, as indeed it is. The grace of the language gives the novel an eerie quality because it contrasts so sharply with the separateness of events, the dislocation of characters. This grace may be why the novel is so frequently called "elegiac"; it possesses the grace of despair, the grace of giving way to despair.

Perhaps because of this weight of despair, *Persuasion* is Jane Austen's finest expression of her view of time and personality as ambiguous movement, as continual reorganization that has both progressive and regressive tendencies. There are no apocalyptic endings in Jane Austen; there is never a revolution, only a regeneration of attitudes. The heroine is never completely enlightened—that is to say, she is never as enlightened as the author or as the reader potentially is about her situation. Anne Elliot cannot take the final step in self-awareness by admitting that she was weak to take Lady Russell's advice, the step that would make the close of the novel a totally new beginning. Complete transcendence is not to be expected. That Anne and Wentworth are reconciled must satisfy us. In Jane Austen, social and personal changes are never absolute. That Austen could not conceive of a total revolution of consciousness is apparent in one of the most interesting minor incidents in all of her novels, Anne's response to Mr. Elliot's insulting letter about her father. He calls Sir Walter a fool, which Anne and the reader and the narrator know him to be. The issue at hand is one of filial respect, but still Anne's response intrigues us: "Anne could not immediately get over the shock and mortification of finding such words applied to her father" (*Per*, p. 204). The significance of Anne's indignation is that it shows us she has some family feeling after all; and who among us has not experienced the same thing, the same surprise of feeling an involuntary allegiance toward those one has ceased to care for? Anne cannot be fully conscious of her past any more than she can transcend all ties, to her family or to Lady Russell. Personal and social change in Jane Austen comes about through the ceaseless reorganization of persons through marriage; in the words of her contemporary Erasmus Darwin, it consists of the power of "delivering down those improvements by generation to its posterity, world without end."[7] In her earlier novels, Jane Austen showed that right marriages are socially and morally vital to the worlds in which they are realized. In the environment of *Persuasion*, in which the individual's social identity is in a state of collapse, the marriage of "intelligent love" becomes, for the well-being of the individuals involved, a stark necessity. And when we consider the peculiar, intense concern and suppressed hope with which later novelists were to invest the marriages of their heroes and heroines—the marriages, for example, of David Copperfield, Dorothea Brooke, and Isabel Archer—we see that the ambiguous, autumnal mood of *Persuasion* comes from neither sentimentality nor sickness nor oncoming death, but from a full consciousness of the fate of marriage in the century to come.

NOTES

1. Lukács's description of novels that are halfway between "education" and "disillusionment."

2. That *Persuasion* is concerned with the nature of death as it is experienced by the living is revealed not only in passages concerning the dead or injured (Dick Musgrove, Fanny Harville, the young Musgrove whose collarbone is broken, Louisa Musgrove) but in the sheer quantity of widows and widowers in the novel: Sir Walter Elliot, Lady Russell, Mrs. Clay, Mr. Shepherd (we assume), Captain Benwick, Mr. Elliot, Mrs. Smith, Lady Dalrymple. Add to these those who are figuratively widowed: Anne, Elizabeth, and Captain Wentworth. How people bear up under loss is therefore a consistent concern in *Persuasion*—and the loss can be of any kind; the novel opens with portraits of Sir Walter and Elizabeth trying to cope with their financial loss.

The sense of a human winter is persistent in *Persuasion*. The novel has an "end of life" feeling; it was written, of course, at the end of the author's life. There is in general a preoccupation with aging. Sir Walter continually comments on physical appearance; Lady Russell keeps her shades drawn when he visits to hide the crow's-feet around her eyes. In the fifteen or so years' absence from Anne, Mrs. Smith seems to have aged from girlhood to middle-aged convalescence. Anne's sense of aging is particularly keen, especially after Wentworth's mortifying comment that she was "so altered he should not have known her again." Anne possesses "every beauty excepting bloom"—a curious description in its association of beauty and death.

In *Persuasion*, the connection between evasion and persuasion is consistently examined. Everyone in the novel persuades himself in the face of misfortune, and the question arises (the question of a moralist, as Gilbert Ryle correctly insists): "When is persuasion evasion and when is it fortitude?" Sir Walter persuades himself for several years that he is financially secure; this is evasion, as is the Musgroves' grief over the son they did not care about when he was alive. Mrs. Smith's self-persuading cheerfulness is a form of fortitude, as Anne readily sees.

3. Marvin Mudrick, *Jane Austen: Irony as Defense and Discovery* (Berkeley and Los Angeles: University of California Press, 1968), p. 226.

4. At moments, this modern kind of ambiguity is finely achieved in *Persuasion*, such as the moment when Anne thinks Lady Russell has seen Wentworth from her carriage window at Bath. Lady Russell says instead that she has been looking at some curtains, and it is left up to the reader to decide whether Anne has fantasized it (*Per*, p. 179).

5. Lionel Trilling, *E. M. Forster* (Norfolk, Conn.: New Directions Books, 1943), p. 118.

6. Austen's language often turns on this paradox: "She was deep in the happiness of such misery, or the misery of such happiness" (*Per*, p. 229).

7. Quoted in Eiseley, *Darwin's Century*, p. 48.

SUSAN MORGAN

The Nature of Character in Persuasion

> I am certain of nothing but the holiness of the Heart's affections and the truth o' Imagination.
>
> —Keats

From the opening declaration of *Northanger Abbey*, that "No one who had ever seen Catherine Morland in her infancy, would have supposed her born to be a heroine" (13), the concern of Austen's fiction has included the question of what we can suppose women to be. And if Austen's novels shine, at least part of the light comes from the brilliant characters she creates in answer to that question. *Persuasion* is no exception. Anne Elliot, though nobody with her own family and lacking Emma Woodhouse's desire to be so "always first and always right," dominates her story and charms us all. Mr. Woodhouse, speaking to another of Austen's dark and elegant women, one also doomed to watch while the man she loves flirts with someone else, to play while others dance, tells Jane Fairfax that "Young ladies are delicate plants" (*E294*). In what must be one of Mr. Woodhouses most appealing moments, the "kind-hearted, polite old man" (295) goes on to express his concern at Jane's having been out in the rain: "My dear, did you change your stockings?" (294). But in spite of Mr. Woodhouse's kindliness, in spite of Jane's having, indeed, changed her stockings, young ladies are not delicate

From *In the Meantime: Character and Perception in Jane Austen's Fiction.* © 1980 by The University of Chicago.

plants. And that kind of old-fashioned gallantry, when it reappears in *Persuasion* in Captain Wentworth's reluctance to have women aboard ship because of the inadequacy of the accommodations, is answered with effective directness by his sister: "I hate to hear you talking so, like a fine gentleman, and as if women were all fine ladies, instead of rational creatures" (70). Neither conventional heroine nor delicate plant nor even young lady, Anne Elliot is one of those rational creatures Sophia Croft invokes. Through Anne, Austen takes up once again the problem of how we see and know other people.

Austen's last completed book, published—and, possibly, titled—posthumously, is the third in which the main action is not a process of education. Austen returns in *Sanditon* to a character whose lively observations remind us more of Elizabeth Bennet than of Anne Elliot. But we cannot know how that plot would have developed. Captain Wentworth receives "lessons of more than one sort" (242) and has a crisis of self-revelation, but *Persuasion* is not his story. Not only is Anne the center of our interest: as Mary Lascelles long ago noted, the narrative point of view is almost entirely Anne's.[1] We see Anne watching and listening to everyone else. We have seen other Austen women similarly engaged. The sense of distance and the struggle to understand produced by not knowing another's feelings is experienced at least as intensely by Elizabeth Bennet, as she pours the coffee at the Longbourn dinner and hopes for an opportunity to talk to Mr. Darcy, as it is by Anne Elliot as she waits in her seat at the concert for Captain Wentworth to speak to her again. Given the continuing problem of understanding character, the particular focus of *Persuasion* is on how the very process of understanding can itself shape character. That is why we see through Anne's eyes. Our perceptions shape our judgments and our actions, shape what we become. Austen's interest in persuasion, part of her constant interest in the issues of teaching and influence, proceeds inevitably from her belief that character is not fixed. *Persuasion* means involvement with other people and it implies the power to change.

Anne Elliot, a faded twenty-seven, the accompanist while others dance, is yet a passionate heroine. Austen tells us in a famous sentence that Anne "had been forced into prudence in her youth, she learned romance as she grew older" (30). From the initial moments of the novel when Anne walks in her favorite grove at Kellynch and says "with a gentle sigh, 'a few months more, and *he*, perhaps, may be walking here'" (25), to that first personal attention in the drawing room at Uppercross Cottage when Captain Wentworth silently removes little Walter from around Anne's neck, to his written declaration in the Musgrove apartment at the White Hart that "I offer myself to you again with a heart even more your own, than when you almost broke it eight years and a half ago" (237), the action of *Persuasion* is the course of renewing love with Captain Wentworth and renewing hope with Anne. And no reader can fail to share the "delightful emotions" (184) produced by that conversation in the octagon room before the concert when Anne first concludes that "all, all declared that he had a heart returning to her at least" (185). *Persuasion* is above all a love story, one in which love reawakens love in a reciprocal cycle of feeling.

All of Austen's novels are love stories. But perhaps the explicit importance of Anne Elliot's emotions, along with the natural temptation to discover a chronological development in any writer's career, accounts for *Persuasion*'s unique reputation. Readers have generally preferred the brightness of *Pride and Prejudice* or *Emma*, and lately many have praised the difficult beauty of *Mansfield Park*. But *Persuasion* is often described as a departure from the rest of the novels, a turning away from the brilliant and public play of the mind for the deep and private truths of the heart. Many of the accounts of *Persuasion*'s difference at least imply its superiority—in insight if not in technique. The beginning of such a view may be Virginia Woolf's influential comment that in *Persuasion* Austen "is beginning to discover that the world is larger, more mysterious, and more romantic than she had supposed."[2] Litz's discussion of Austen's awakening to nature, Duckworth's analysis of the estate defeated yet internalized, Auerbach's argument for revolutionary feelings; all assume a knowledge or point of view which modern readers have and which Austen does not recognize or express until this last completed work.[3] Many of the qualities seen as new in *Persuasion* are associated with the concerns of romantic poetry, as if Austen suddenly, in her final novel, caught up with her own age and so moved closer to ours.

The view of *Persuasion* as an innovative departure is, I think, wrong for many reasons. And those reasons are worth noting not so much in particular cases but because they point to a general misapprehension in our reading of Austen's fiction. I do not mean that there are no changes or development in Austen's work, but that these changes can be understood within the context of interests which remain constant throughout her career. To view *Persuasion* as more emotional, more private, more in tune with nature than the other novels, is to presume what I have been arguing against all along: that the previous novels were committed to reason and social order, and were old-fashioned in the age in which they were written. It is to presume that prior to *Persuasion* Austen had subordinated feeling to reason and control. It is to misread *Persuasion* because we have misread her earlier work.

In the essay on Austen Virginia Woolf had taken up *Persuasion* in order to "look by its light at the books she might have written had she lived."[4] But the charm of her speculations about Austen's future, with *Persuasion* pointing the new direction, shrinks the previous novels. Let us recall them now. Can we read *Emma* and yet believe that *Persuasion* has a truer sense of the largeness of the world, though Emma herself never leaves the boundaries of Highbury? Can we recall Emma's tears on the ride home from Box Hill or her acceptance of the pain anticipated in taking one more turn around the grounds with Mr. Knightley or the joy we are allowed to share with the "small band of true friends" (*E*484) at the "perfect happiness" of Emma's marriage, and yet assert that *Persuasion* has more depth of emotion? Can we recollect Elizabeth Bennet's continuing imperceptiveness in the second half of *Pride and Prejudice* and still believe that *Persuasion* has a new or increased sense of the mystery and elusiveness of other people? And if we wish to say that the tone of *Persuasion* is somehow more serious, more "autumnal" and sad, then what are we to do with *Sense and Sensibility*?

Singling out *Persuasion* as the novel which shows Austen's assimilation of the new romantic poetry brings more difficulties. Litz, commenting on "the deeply physical impact of *Persuasion*," remarks that "*Mansfield Park* is about the loss and return of principles, *Emma* about the loss and return of reason, *Persuasion* about the loss and return of 'bloom.'"[5] Litz acknowledges the crudeness of these formulations and we recognize that he is attempting to discuss a quality of the novel which is hard to describe. But such summaries, even tentatively offered, only distort. The few brief nature scenes in *Persuasion* (and they are brief out of all proportion to the commentary on them), the walk to Winthrop and the environs of Pinny and Lyme, are certainly described with sensibility and appreciation. And in Anne's mind they are just as certainly bound up with "the sweets of poetical despondence" (85). Moreover, the interdependence of the rhythm of the seasons and the rhythm of characters' lives is at least as suggestively depicted in *Pride and Prejudice* as in *Persuasion*. The round of autumn parties in Hertfordshire, the lonely winter with Jane away in London, spring in the lanes of Hunsford, midsummer at Pemberley and the return of autumn marked by the return of Mr. Darcy and Mr. Bingley—all take for granted the connections between our hearts and the natural landscape, the physical cycles of our lives. It is as difficult to show that Austen's sense of nature is new in *Persuasion* as it is to say that *Emma* is about reason or to base Austen's connections to the new poetry on the issue of a sense of nature.

Austen's connections to her contemporaries in poetry are to be found throughout her work, although readers have only begun the attempt to describe them. Such descriptions are still perilous not only because of the difference in genres but, I believe, because Austen has been read as a defender of society while her concern with problems of perception has been neglected. The split between reason and felt or emotional truths is denied throughout Austen's fiction. And we must take that denial seriously. At least from the writing of *Sense and Sensibility*, Austen had explicitly defended strong feelings directed outside the self against those weaker emotions which do not see their objects because they turn inward. Mary Musgrove's depressions and fancied illnesses are related to Marianne Dashwood's hysterics, while Anne Elliot's deeper feelings must recall Elinor Dashwood's suffering and silence. Anne's "joy, senseless joy" (168) upon hearing that Captain Wentworth is free is a direct echo of Elinor's "tears of joy" (360) when she realizes that Edward has not married Lucy Steele. *Persuasion* is a great novel, but not because it is an emotional release or an awakening to a felt physical life or the truths of the heart. At their best, all of Austen's "rational creatures" honor the truths of the heart.

The relations between Austen's completed novels need to be expressed in language more innocent than differences as departures or improvements. The idea that *Persuasion* is an exception, like the ideas that *Sense and Sensibility* or *Mansfield Park* are exceptions, is based on a view of Austen's work which, finally, is too exclusive. *Persuasion* is not a novel of moral education. In this sense it clearly differs from the novels of crisis: *Northanger Abbey*, *Pride and Prejudice*, and *Emma*. But if we consider *Persuasion* in the ways in which I have been discussing the other two novels of passage, then its essential relation to all the novels becomes clear. Like *Sense and Sensibility* and *Mansfield Park*, *Persuasion* addresses itself to the more fundamental form of difficulty inherent in the nature of character and the nature of reality. And *Persuasion*'s particular resolution to that difficulty accounts for the emotional quality of the book.

As in all of Austen's novels, reality in *Persuasion* consists primarily of other people's characters and actions. These are the outside which we and Anne attempt to understand. But reality also includes the natural landscape; the groves of Kellynch and the environs of Pinny and Lyme. In Austen's work the meaning of nature, like the meaning of any experience, is intertwined with our feelings about it. And no response, not Marianne's love of dead leaves, Elizabeth Bennet's delight in the river winding through the valley at Pemberley, Fanny's appreciation of the stars, or Anne's pleasure in the autumn walk to Winthrop, is purified of the emotional state of the observer. As Mary Lascelles wrote, "There is indeed little, if any, landscape in her novels, hardly a field or hedgerow, but is presented through the eyes of a character."[6] There are people in Austen's fiction, like Mary Crawford, who do not have feelings toward nature. But Mary is not open toward the people around her either. The responsiveness to nature, with its inevitable tone of an emotional perspective not objectively part of the view, is a useful paradigm for Austen's idea of perception, be it of leaves or of people. The means to see the world outside the self can be hampered or even destroyed by the emotions we bring to it. But without emotions we will probably not see at all.

Austen's commitment to feeling is clear enough in *Persuasion*, a novel which, in Howard Babb's words, vindicates "a mode of apprehension essentially emotional and intensely subjective."[7] But Babb's phrase needs to be qualified. Anne's mode of emotional apprehension is the mode of an intelligent and thoughtful woman whose emotions have a range and continuity far beyond any simple definitions of passionate love. Moreover, in Austen's work intelligence is always a matter of the heart. There is no sense without sensibility or, to recall my transformation of Andrew Wright's terms in discussing *Pride and Prejudice*, there is no clarity without involvement. This also means that Anne's feelings are better guides than, say, Catherine Morland's, because Anne has more sense. Her sensibilities are highly wrought. Further, for all Austen's heroines right feeling is a matter of time. To use the language of Wordsworth, feeling is a matter of contemplation, of emotion recollected in tranquillity.

The realists in Austen's novels, the people who believe that their modes of apprehension are rational and objective, are self-deceived. People like Lucy Steele or Charlotte Lucas or Mary Crawford or Mr. Elliot are guided by selfish feelings which they disguise to themselves as well as to others as simply being clear-eyed and practical. And these feelings, like the more literal vanities of Sir Walter Elliot, blind them to their world. One cannot properly make a distinction in Austen's work between those characters with feelings and those without. The distinction is simply between those whose feelings are focused on promoting themselves and those whose feelings move outward to people around them. That move is an imaginative act which makes clarity possible. As *Emma* so joyously reminds us, Austen argues for neither reason nor self-abnegation. What she argues for is generosity of heart.

Persuasion, then, cannot be explained as a turn toward feeling or individualism in Austen's work. But this is not to deny that the novel is distinctive in the character of its heroine. Anne Elliot is a rare medium of fortitude and gentleness. We see Anne, at Kellynch, at Uppercross, at Lyme and Bath, living among people less perceptive and less self-controlled than she. And through her efforts, through her energy and persuasiveness and insights, she helps them to live together better and promotes a more general comfort if not a more general happiness. We see Anne making the proper arrangements for leaving Kellynch, sorting the garden plants and taking leave of the tenants, brightening Mary's life at Uppercross Cottage by her forced cheerfulness and mediating persuasions, nursing little Charles and taking charge when Louisa Musgrove falls. In other words, we see Anne leading a useful life of duty and kindness, helping her small circle of relations and friends to overcome the small and large difficulties in their lives. As Captain Wentworth says in the Harvilles' parlor, "no one so proper, so capable as Anne!" (114).

But at the same time we also know what Anne is feeling. In the midst of this calm and serviceable existence, "glad to be thought of some use, glad to have any thing marked out as a duty" (33), Anne experiences the passions, the mortifications and sadnesses and hopes, of deep and serious love. Captain Wentworth lifts a child from her shoulders and she is too overcome to remain in the room. She meets his friends and must struggle "against a great tendency to lowness" (98). He passes on the street in Bath while she is in a shop and she must go to the door, "to see if it rained. Why was she to suspect herself of another motive?" (175). His proposal letter leaves her in such "overpowering happiness" that she cannot control herself to sustain a conversation and must plead indisposition and struggle up to be escorted home.

What is the connection between a capable life and overpowering happiness? *Persuasion* is a love story, marked particularly by our direct insight into the intense feelings of its heroine. But that insight is possible because Anne is a rational creature. Her passion is part of a nature distinguished by feeling not only as romantic love but as the desire to make sense of her own life and to be a force for understanding and good in the lives of those around her. In *Sense and Sensibility* Elinor Dashwood, explaining to the mystified Marianne why she never mentioned Edward's engagement to Lucy Steele, says, "I did not love only him" (*SS*263). It is a remark beautiful in its simplicity and in what it tells us about Austen's idea of intelligence. Elinor can control her own feelings. But that strength of mind comes, as she tells Marianne, from a depth of heart. She is not overcome by despair at losing Edward because she loves many people. This involvement enables Elinor to comfort herself in her own distresses while comforting others as well. And the very range of her feelings allows her to understand Willoughby as well as Marianne.

Anne Elliot's involvement in life expresses itself not only in her love for Captain Wentworth but in her memory, which connects past and present, in her hope, which connects present and future, and in her consciousness, which connects the disparate circles of people in her life. Anne's usefulness proceeds from a concern with those around her which is strong enough to connect her to different times, places and people, and strong enough to connect them to each other through her in some kind of harmony. At the end of *Persuasion* not only is past reunited with present, Captain Wentworth with Anne, but all—the Musgroves, the Elliots, the Crofts, even the Wallises and Mr. Elliot—meet together at that evening party at Camden Place. "It was but a card-party, it was but a mixture of those who had never met before, and those who met too often—a common-place business, too numerous for intimacy, too small for variety; but Anne had never found an evening shorter" (245). This commonplace card party is the public bringing together of those who had formerly been connected only by the solitary power of Anne's consciousness. They will soon disperse. But for this evening at least, for Anne's sake, in her author's celebration of Anne's "sensibility and happiness," they are brought together.

Elinor Dashwood has "strong feelings" which inform her sense. Fanny Price, for all her timidity, has the acute feelings to struggle toward understanding. But it is in *Persuasion*, in the character of Anne Elliot, that the interdependence of lucid vision and deep emotion is most thoroughly and most intensely sustained. For Anne's character—and through Anne, the warts of seeing others' characters—is the subject of *Persuasion*. What are people like and how can we come to know them? This simple question has been present from the beginning of Austen's writing. Answering it led to brilliantly innovative novels which present ideas about the nature of perception and often connect Austen to her contemporaries in poetry. Instead of delicate plants, taking "care of their health and their complexion" (*E*294), Austen offers us all her characters, ranging from the unheroic Catherine Morland to Anne Elliot, one of the most sensitive and intelligent creations in English fiction. Austen's rational creatures are recognized by their engaged emotions and by minds which, however isolated or unappreciated, bring together the people and the passing stages of their lives. The fascinating point about persuasion is that the themes both of involvement and of time are comprehended in the power to persuade. These two themes connect *Persuasion* to all of Austen's other novels, most directly to *Sense and Sensibility* and *Mansfield Park*. In Anne Elliot the separation of self and world which is the continuing problem of all Austen's characters is most successfully overcome.

We can reach Austen's idea of character in *Persuasion* through the attitudes she rejects. Mrs. Smith and, more important, Captain Wentworth, share an idea of character as a center to be revealed. The implications of their view are perhaps most easily seen with Mrs. Smith. This "poor, infirm, helpless widow" (153), offers dark revelations about Mr. Elliot which, in their conventional indecency, have put off many readers. They remind us of Colonel Brandon's poor Eliza story or Mr. Wickham's shady past or Henry

Crawford's affair with Maria Bertram Rushworth. These are all discoveries of villainy which are uncomfortably conspicuous among the mixed characters of Austen's fiction. But the very familiarity of Mrs. Smith's jarring information serves to highlight its irrelevance. Marianne had been taken in by Willoughby, but not by his machinations. Hers was the fault. Elizabeth was never in danger from Mr. Wickham, and Henry would only have got Fanny if he had truly been good. Anne, we know, was not in danger from any feeling stronger than pity. In *Persuasion* villainy is about as threatening as those gypsies which pass through Highbury and frighten Harriet Smith. Both have wandered out of their way.

Mrs. Smith's disclosure, as Anne says, tells "me nothing which does not accord with what I have known, or could imagine" (201). The reader must agree. How could we take seriously the gentleman introduced into the novel as a mysterious stranger dressed in mourning who casts admiring glances at Anne on the steps of the Cobb and in the hall of the inn at Lyme? Anne moves around Bath for days meaning to inform Lady Russell of what she has learned about Mr. Elliot, but never quite getting around to it. The very obtrusiveness of Mrs. Smith's exposé, the anticipation of it by "the charm of such a mystery" (187) as Mr. Elliot's somehow having known about Anne for years, and its expression in such language as "black at heart, hollow and black" (199), all make it out of place in Anne's world. She is "so little touched by Mr. Elliot's conduct" (229) that it becomes virtually a joke, and we are told that "Mr. Elliot's character, like the Sultaness Scheherazade's head, must live another day" (229). Austen then disposes of the villain, along with the views of human nature and of literary convention he represents, by banishing him from her novel in company with a freckled villainess.

Mrs. Smith's revelation, like Mr. Elliot's wicked character, is a conscious fictional cliché. Mrs. Smith, though crippled and with natural cheerfulness, has been irresponsible. She married for love, married "poor Charles, who had the finest, most generous spirit in the world" (200). Yet she saw nothing wrong that Mr. Elliot, whom she was "excessively pleased with," who was "like a brother" (199), married for money. This is language which exaggerates the claims of feeling, which is at worst hypocrisy and at best a self-indulgent blindness. We recall Marianne Dashwood; or Isabella Thorpe claiming that Catherine Morland was dearer to her than her own relations, "a pitch of friendship beyond Catherine" (*NA*118). Mrs. Smith has improved in principles since that thoughtless time of her youth. Yet she can still praise Mr. Elliot, a man "without heart or conscience; a designing, wary, cold-blooded being, who thinks only of himself" (199), as long as she believes Anne will marry him. Mrs. Smith tells Anne the truth about Mr. Elliot. But she is, nonetheless, an unreliable narrator.

In a novel intensely and almost solely focused on the ways we can see into other hearts, Mrs. Smith offers the wrong way. For her the ways of knowing are those in which the "Facts shall speak" (199). She believes that Anne "ought to have proof" and "shall have proof" (202), in spite of Anne's claim that she has no need of it. At the same time Mrs. Smith's narrative style is distinctly gothic. Her method is as exaggeratedly scientific as it is sentimental. For there is really no distinction between the two. Science and sentiment merge in that wonderful moment when Mrs. Smith produces her "proof," preserved in that "small inlaid box" (202), which she sighs over as she unlocks. She offers Anne the kind of knowledge which can be put in a box, with its trust in "objectivity" overlaid by stylized emotions, as if truth were outside our perception of it. Can any reader help recalling another box, the one containing Harriet Smith's "Most Precious Treasures"? Mrs. Smith, certainly, is not a comic figure. She is neither silly nor seventeen. But she is, we would guess, a distant relation of Harriet's in more than just name.

For all Mrs. Smith's cheerfulness, her experience and her goodwill, she does not see the truth. Mr. Elliot may be "totally beyond the reach of any sentiment of justice or compassion" (199), or, if he is not, he may have been. But it was not he who ruined her. It was poor Charles. It was herself. Her self-presentation as outraged victim of a villain obscures the truth of her own complicity and mistakes. We do not need to condemn Mrs. Smith. We do need, even while acknowledging that her function in the book may not be a complete success, to see that the inappropriateness of Mrs. Smith's revelation is itself appropriate. The irrelevance of her information to the plot or to Anne's happiness is exactly its point. Mrs. Smith is about as useful to the lovers as Lady Catherine de Bourgh was to Elizabeth Bennet and Mr. Darcy. The awful revelation is an empty convention of romance.

What Mrs. Smith had offered Anne was "to be made acquainted with Mr. Elliot's real character" (199). For her Mr. Elliot had pretended to be a friend and then, suddenly, with her husband's financial distresses and death, had shown his real character as a conventional villain. But of course, Mr. Elliot had been a selfish and irresponsible man all along. People's secrets are frequently unreachable, and Austen's novels are characteristically full of surprises. Many facts and feelings are mysterious and unknown. For Austen character is never simply a matter of sudden revelations. The appearance of goodness, if it consists of good deeds, is good. We often cannot know the truth. But we can know that there is more to the truth than we know. Judgment need not be final because character need not be final. For character is not some center to be uncovered, some proof in a box. That is why Anne, knowing nothing of Mr. Elliot's "real character" but feeling his charm, had still not grown fond of him.

The negative definition of character which Mrs. Smith offers to Anne in the form of a revelation is similar to Captain Wentworth's ideas of character. And if Mrs. Smith was ineffectual, Captain Wentworth's attitude had caused Anne years of sadness. He too thinks of people in layers. In the pain of the broken engagement, he chose to understand Anne's decision as a revelation of her true character, as if there were a truth which somehow underlay the woman he fell in love with, as if that truth erased what he had come to know of her. Captain Wentworth does not renew his proposal, as he might have, when he is posted to the *Laconia*. He returns almost eight years later believing he does not love Anne. He has chosen to see what happened between them as an instance of being deceived in her character, and suddenly discovering the fatal flaw.

Mrs. Smith and Captain Wentworth, by denying continuity of character, deny their own responsibility in forming opinions about others. For the truth is that a revelation about someone else, if it is a revelation, is a revelation about oneself. Mr. Elliot's cold selfishness was visible even while he was Mrs. Smith's friend. But it is easier to call him a villain than to acknowledge her own wrong values. It is one of the constancies of Austen's fiction that her worst characters, while they can and often do hide their deeds, continuously give themselves away. Isabella Thorpe's protestations of eternal friendship, Wickham's story about Mr. Darcy, Willoughby's evasions, Henry Crawford's delight in flirtations—all reveal their characters at least in part to those who care to see. And those who do not see have preferred not to.

During the walk to Winthrop Captain Wentworth tells Louisa Musgrove, "My first wish for all, whom I am interested in, is that they should be firm" (88). This is a simple enough prescription for happiness, so simple as to be inadequate for understanding anyone. Captain Wentworth says that Louisa's "is the character of decision and firmness." And he thinks that Anne Elliot lacks the firmness of that "beautiful glossy nut, which, blessed with original strength, has outlived all the storms of autumn" (88). Certainly, this view is wrong in its particulars. What Admiral Croft has to say about both Louisa and Henrietta when the Crofts drive Anne home at the end of that walk is a truer picture: "Very nice young ladies they both are; I hardly know one from the other" (92). Moreover, Anne's breaking the engagement involved being firm as well as soft, as her resistance to his persuasions to continue the engagement should have taught him. Anne was misled in what she believed she should do. But her decision showed "the steadiness of principle" (242).

Captain Wentworth is wrong in his theory of character as much as in its applications. What he had taken to be a revelation about Anne's weakness has actually been "the pride, the folly, the madness of resentment" (242). It took Louisa's knock in the head to set the circumstances for another revelation about Anne, one which this time concerned him. For "only at Lyme had he begun to understand himself," and, therefore, to understand "the perfect excellence of the mind with which Louisa's could so ill bear a comparison" (242). What Captain Wentworth comes to see is that revelations of character are not a means of understanding others and that, when one is engaged in trying to understand people, revelations are no real help. Instead, they are simply forms of self-deception, conveniences substituted for the risks of responsible judgment. How much more painful it would have been for Captain Wentworth to release Anne without the easy consolation of "feeling himself ill-used by so forced a relinquishment" (28). How much more painful, but more generous and more honest as well.

People are not hazelnuts, though the metaphor is a telling one. That firmness which does not change has as its greatest virtue the quality of resistance, of not being affected by what happens. It implies a relation to life which is fundamentally hostile, a matter of holding out against experience. And within a gothic or Richardsonian world, a world where inns can turn out to be prisons and saviors would-be rapists, where wicked relatives block the course of love, such an attitude is a proper measure of strength of character. But life in Austen's fiction is not "the storms of autumn" which buffet hazelnuts. Captain Wentworth, we know, comes from a life of adventure, of captured French frigates and gales at sea. He moves from a life which does not call Bermuda or Bahama the West Indies to the drawing room at Uppercross, where Mrs. Musgrove "could not accuse herself of having ever called them any thing in the whole course of her life" (70). None of Captain Wentworth's adventures change the fact that when "any two young people take it into their heads to marry, they are pretty sure by perseverance to carry their point" (248). We forgive Captain Wentworth as we have Mrs. Smith, but only when he has remembered his own heart.[8]

In a framework where receptivity to experience points the only way to understanding and goodness, to be firm to the point of being unpersuadable is at worst to be hard of heart. It is, in Elizabeth's words to Mr. Darcy, "to allow nothing for the influence of friendship and affection" (*PP*50). Austen's comic view of the usefulness of such an attitude is clear from the fate of Louisa, in whom the folly of being headstrong leads literally to a fall on the head. Her willfulness was a pose rather than a reality. And many a reader may join in the pleasure of those who were collected on the Cobb "to enjoy the sight of a dead young lady, nay, two dead young ladies, for it proved twice as fine as the first report" (111). It is a moment of burlesque reminiscent of the comedy of the juvenilia.

Mrs. Smith's gothic sentiments and Captain Wentworth's heroic metaphor are both fictions. These fictions are designed to hide from themselves the true feelings of this pair. It may be that all ideas of character are fictions, created forms by which we attempt to shape and make sense of other people. Many of these forms, such as "the too-common idea of spirit and gentleness being incompatible with each other" (172), can only limit our insights. Character is more profound than our definitions of it. But there are fictions about the nature of character which tend to open rather than obscure the feelings of others and ourselves. These fictions, as methods of understanding, are useful in novels and in life.

The problem with revelations is that they contradict what has previously been thought. Revelations also have a quality of finality. They don't allow for the possibility of getting to know someone. Revelations are endings. They deny time. Alternative forms of perceiving and presenting character include recognizing that character is mixed, that perception is based in part on the emotional perspective of the viewer and that people have the power to change. Understanding is not the revelation of a moment, nor is truth a matter of facts. People are more interesting than the boxes we put them in. Against Mrs. Smith's crude and familiar fictions, against Captain Wentworth's killing decisiveness, Austen offers a way to understand others which depends upon a proper sense of time. She offers Anne.

Marianne Dashwood had claimed that "a woman of seven and twenty ... can never hope to feel or inspire affection again" (*SS* 38). In the novel which followed *Sense and Sensibility* Austen created Charlotte Lucas, who, at twenty-seven, seems to have accepted Marianne's view of the possibilities for a woman of that age. Charlotte's marriage to Mr. Collins fits Marianne's description of "a compact of convenience" (38). Whatever twenty-seven may have meant in Austen's life, in her work it represents that time which both sentimentalists and realists see as too late for love. We should notice that Austen's interest in the romantic possibilities of a woman past conventional marrying age is established as early as her first published novel. Also established is her commitment to the possibilities of passion at any age. Charlotte may never have been romantic, but both Charlotte and Marianne are wrong. It must surely have been with these two in mind that Austen made Anne Elliot twenty-seven. A fair description of Anne's story is that she both feels and inspires affection again.

On first hearing Mrs. Croft mention a brother with whom Anne had been acquainted, "Anne hoped she had outlived the age of blushing; but the age of emotion she certainly had not" (49). The distinction calls attention to one of the central narrative facts about *Persuasion*. Readers have long noticed that the novel is set eight years after what has been the happy ending and the beginning of perfect happiness for the rest of Austen's heroines. As I have discussed in relation to *Sense and Sensibility* and *Mansfield Park*. a fiction which explores questions of perception must include ideas of time (most simply because understanding so often precedes choice and action). Elinor Dashwood had maintained that good judgment is partly a matter of giving oneself time. Austen gave Fanny Price a time which began in her childhood. And if Fanny's progress was slow, it was marked by continuity and memory and all the advantages in generosity and involvement which the pure affections of childhood can bring.

Austen gives Anne Elliot a different kind of time, one unique in her fiction yet perfectly in keeping with that "age of emotion" which is the time of all her heroines, no matter what their age. Anne's time is not only much later than that of any other Austen heroine. It is explicitly the time long after which her story should have been concluded, almost eight years after the expected happy ending. Yet the ending had been canceled, and by Anne's own act. All of Austen's heroines accept, at least for a moment, that the ending will not work out as they want, that they will not be able to marry the person they love. Anne is Austen's study of what might happen if that loss were realized. What is traditionally a convention preceding the ending of a comedy is here actually made to occur. The girl does not get the boy. But what then? *Persuasion* is a move into the future, as *Mansfield Park* began with a move into the past. Austen most frequently studies her characters during a significant period of choice. But she is also interested in them before and after. Moreover, those significant periods need not occur only once. Particular choices may be irretrievable, but the act of choosing goes on. If *Mansfield Park* shows us that growing up does not necessarily presume a crisis of revelation, *Persuasion* shows us that it also does not imply a conclusive state of grace. Whatever we pass into when we learn to understand ourselves, the passage is never complete. When that happens, we have stopped being properly alive.

Like Fanny Price, Anne is conscious of a continuing personal history which connects her future with her past. And also like Fanny, Anne has an excellent memory. Gene Ruoff has beautifully pointed out the tie to Wordsworth, that "such a belief in the power of memory—its ability to uphold and cherish and its power to make our noisy years seem moments in the being of eternal silence—we have met with before."[9] Certainly, it is Anne's memory which connects her period of happiness at nineteen with the present events of her story. Austen makes the point that, apart from Anne, there was a "perfect indifference and apparent unconsciousness, among the only three of her own friends in the secret of the past, which seemed almost to deny any recollection of it" (30). This "general air of oblivion" (30), whatever its motives, means that only Anne shapes for us the contextual meaning of events. Through her memory Anne establishes the significance of the time of her story—that it is a present which continues, relives, and reshapes the past.

When Anne first meets Captain Wentworth again that morning at Uppercross Cottage she begins "to reason with herself, and try to be feeling less." Those reasonings take the form of a denial of memory: "What might not eight years do? Events of every description, changes, alienations, removals,—all, all must be comprised in it; and oblivion of the past—how natural, how certain too!" (60). Duckworth cites this passage as a sign of the novel's "sense of temporal uncertainty."[10] But the point, rather, is that Anne's reasonings are wrong. Oblivion is neither natural nor certain. And Anne finds that "to retentive feelings eight years might be little more than nothing" (60). Feeling and memory merge in that power to retain. Anne's story, then, cannot stand by itself but is explicitly a revision of another story, a present only comprehensible, only possible, through its past. All presents presume a past. But what happens to Anne is in its essence a realization of that past, a coming true at last of what should have happened eight years and a half ago. The result is that Anne's and the reader's attentions are simultaneously focused on continuity and on change. The present in *Persuasion* is frequently compared to the past, from Anne's opening feelings of "Once so much to each other! Now nothing!" (63), to Captain Wentworth's claim that he had been "most fervent, most undeviating" in his "true attachment and constancy" (237). The woman he has first thought to be "wretchedly altered" (61) he comes to believe "could never alter" (243). The juxtaposition of past and present in the novel moves from a sense of difference and radical change to a sense of identity. The power of memory as retentive feelings is a power which brings the past to life again and re-creates it as the present. And the re-creation is something of a miracle because it is a second chance. The original meeting, which did not end in marriage, is allowed to recur. And the second time it ends as it should.

The narrative controlling hand is perfectly visible in all this. One of the most delightful moments in *Persuasion* is the matter of Captain Wentworth's coming to Bath. Admiral Croft, mouthpiece at this moment for conventional novelistic arrangements, announces to Anne that Captain Wentworth, no longer able to think of Louisa, must "begin all over again with somebody else. I think we must get him to Bath. Sophy must write, and beg him to come to Bath" (173). But having provided this perfectly plausible means, the narrator immediately uses a more direct method: "While Admiral Croft was taking this walk with Anne, and expressing his wish of getting Captain

Wentworth to Bath, Captain Wentworth was already on his way thither. Before Mrs. Croft had written, he was arrived, and the very next time Anne walked out, she saw him" (174). Captain Wentworth will later explain his speed. For the moment we can only notice and admire the de facto ease with which the narrator puts her two lovers in the same vicinity and, by then invoking some rain, has them meet. Although, near the end of the story, Anne's "heart prophesied some mischance, to dampen the perfection of her felicity" (239), our hearts do not. Not only do we agree with her rational argument, "We are not boy and girl, to be captiously irritable, misled by every moment's inadvertence" (221). Beyond any powers of chance or of reason, we know that the author will not allow this second time for Anne to end in any feeling but joy.

Presenting the growth of love and hope in *Persuasion* as a repetition with differences of a past process which originally did not succeed, means that the whole matter of falling in love is understood as a revival of already existing feelings. Austen has used a similar method in *Emma*, where the two lovers are neighbors who had known each other all Emma's life. The progress of their love, though not a matter of revival, also involved a bringing to consciousness of feelings which were already there. What these patterns— and probably also the relations of Fanny and Edmund in *Mansfield Park*— share is an appreciation of the forms of passion which are also forms of familiarity. It is Mrs. Norris who believes that "the only sure way of providing against the connection" (*MP*6–7) between a Bertram son and Fanny is to bring them up together. Mrs. Norris can only imagine falling in love with someone she does not know, not because she fancies herself to be romantic but because she is hard of heart and so little loves the people she does know.

Generally, Austen does not believe that true lovers suddenly appear in our daily lives in some romantic fashion. To think they do is to imply an injustice to the charms of those around us. That is what Henrietta Musgrove does when she allows her head to be turned away from her loving cousin by the man she and Louisa decide at first meeting is "infinitely more agreeable ... than any individual among their male acquaintance" (54). But the case is different with Anne. Both making Anne's story a second chance and describing Anne's first falling in love with a touch of irony come from Austen's lack of interest in the situation of lovers who are newly met. The love affairs which stimulate Austen's imagination are those between people who are already familiar to each other. Mr. Darcy, it is true, is a glamorous stranger. But the first movement of his feelings is a failure and he must return to propose again. The exception is Henry Tilney, but even in this early novel Austen points the direction of her interest by having Henry introduced in a

properly mundane way by the master of ceremonies in the pump room at
Bath. *Persuasion* offers a developed form of the repeated proposal in *Pride and
Prejudice*. The device of a previous engagement allows Austen to create a
hero who is both glamorously heroic and at the same time an old
acquaintance, one first loved before he had all those successful adventures at
sea. Then he was merely the younger brother of the gentleman at Monkford,
a captain without a ship, "not immediately employed" (26). Captain
Wentworth, handsome, dashing and rich, is a highly romantic hero. But for
Anne Elliot he is also the man she has long known and long loved.

Austen has so arranged the story of Anne and Captain Wentworth that
its meaning depends upon the mutual values of familiarity and of difference.
What Litz has called Anne's loss and return of bloom is possible because she
has feelings which, by retaining the past, can transform it. And it is almost
impossible to distinguish between Captain Wentworth's renewing his
feelings and his recalling them. Cognition is recognition. Or perhaps we
should simply say that what is most surprising and beautiful about other
people is what has been there all along.

Such recognitions, as against the revelations of Mrs. Smith, do not
introduce new truths about others which suddenly negate all that we have
known. Mrs. Smith had gone from thinking of Mr. Elliot as a beloved friend
to thinking of him as a villain. Whatever the continuity of his character, it
lies in neither of her opinions, and she does indeed come to see her own past
indulgences for what they were. Proper revelations, like that of Elizabeth
Bennet about the characters of Mr. Darcy and Mr. Wickham, are revelations
about oneself. Captain Wentworth believed that eight years ago he had
discovered the truth about Anne. He comes to recognize at Lyme what he
had known before and chosen to forget, that Anne is the sort of woman he
wants to marry: "A strong mind, with sweetness of manner" (62). What he
remembers are his own feelings, both his affections and the anger through
which he convinced himself he had forgotten her. Recognizing those feelings
connects him again to the past and enables him to renew that attachment he
can truly describe as constant and undeviating. As he and Anne slowly paced
the gravel walk, "they returned again into the past, more exquisitely happy,
perhaps, in their reunion, than when it had first been projected" (240).

Time is a promise of change, and particularly change as something
other than metamorphosis. One of the explicit topics of *Persuasion* is that the
people one knows do not turn into strangers. The "perpetual estrangement"
(64) Anne describes between herself and Captain Wentworth cannot be
sustained. Even Elizabeth and Sir Walter are made at last to acknowledge
that Captain Wentworth is not unknown to them, is at the least "a bowing
acquaintance" (188). Poor as their motives are, they must be brought to

recognize him. And one measure of Anne's power to attach present and past and maintain the continuities of her life is her willingness to visit Mrs. Smith. Mrs. Smith has radically changed. "Twelve years were gone since they had parted, and each presented a somewhat different person from what the other had imagined" (153). But even the transformations of time and circumstance have not made Mrs. Smith a stranger. The "strong claims" (152) of acquaintance remain. And there also remains, with all her differences, something of the person Anne has known. With Mrs. Smith, as with Captain Wentworth, the attractions of the present are intertwined with "the interesting charm of remembering" (153).

Anne's "age of emotion" is bounded, not only by the reach of memory but also by the reach of hope. Those retentive feelings which connect her to the past and continually involve her with different circles of friends also lead Anne toward the future. Anne begins the novel without much hope for renewing her relations with Captain Wentworth. After watching him flirt with the Musgrove sisters and upon receiving his cold civilities, she can compare her state with Captain Benwick's and decide that Benwick is better off, that "he has not, perhaps, a more sorrowing heart than I have. I cannot believe his prospects so blighted for ever" (97). But Anne has other feelings as well, feelings which counteract grief and acknowledge the self-indulgence of sustaining a sorrowing heart. The hope of inspiring Captain Wentworth's affections again is not the only hope for Anne. Like Elinor Dashwood, she did not love only him.

In spite of her sadness watching the November rain and her early loss of spirits and her tendencies to lowness, Anne is like her mother. And surely the point of Austen's description of Mrs. Elliot, a woman "of very superior character" (4) to Sir Walter, is that in spite of romantic disappointment she found enough in her duties and her friends "to attach her to life" (4). Not the least source of Anne's attachment to life is her self-love. Even without an Emma's desire to be first, she has pride enough to want not good company but the best. Although Anne feels her own lack of the "mutual affection" of the Musgrove sisters, she is saved from envy by a "comfortable feeling of superiority" and "would not have given up her own more elegant and cultivated mind for all their enjoyments" (41) or, we might add, for all their happiness.

Anne's retentive feelings for Captain Wentworth again and again cause her to feel overcome. But she does not long remain overcome because she exerts herself. And her exertions are our most powerful proof of her hope. Anne frequently exerts herself for other people or for her own self-control. But her most intense exertions are to understand and live with her own feelings. Often when Anne argues against what she is feeling, the particular reasons turn out to be wrong. When Anne begins "to reason with herself" (60) or when she hopes "to be wise and reasonable in time" (178), reason means not being in love with Captain Wentworth. But this is not a novel where feelings are wrong and reasonings the truth. Those reasonings are a process of giving herself time. Another way of putting this is that Anne's aim in these exertions is to feel. Her "senseless joy" (168) is to be transformed not into sense but into sensible joy.

When Captain Wentworth's careless comment is repeated to Anne, that he found her terribly altered, his "words could not but dwell with her." Yet their dwelling with her Anne sees as an eventual good: "She soon began to rejoice that she had heard them. They were of sobering tendency; they allayed agitation; they composed, and consequently must make her happier" (61). The process is clear. Anne, giving herself up to the pain Captain Wentworth's words cause, will come to feel differently, will, most importantly, come to feel happier. Anne's very struggle implies hope, implies a better day. For feelings are not simply those spontaneous responses which occasionally overwhelm. As Wordsworth knew, there are also those feelings which require the sober coloring of reflection, which require time. Whatever might happen with Captain Wentworth, Anne means "to have spring again" (85).

Like Elinor Dashwood, Anne's forms of self-control emerge from strength of feelings which cannot remain overcome or subdued by loss. In her sweetness and her strength, in the exertions of her own feelings, in her efforts to see he world fairly and affectionately, Anne must find sources of happiness. That is her hope for the future on which her strength depends. That is her self-love. Loving herself and most of the people and places she is surrounded by, Anne cannot long remain unhappy. As she says of Lyme, "One does not love a place the less for having suffered in it" and "altogether my impressions of the place are very agreeable" (184). Anne's range of feelings is the basis of that thoughtfulness out of which emerges both her perceptiveness and her sense of duty. For Anne, as for Elinor Dashwood and Fanny Price, the powers of understanding and control are directly related to the power to feel. Anne Elliot is not a heroine of romance. Hers are the complex and changing emotions of "an elegant little woman of seven and twenty, with every beauty except bloom, and with manners as consciously right as they were invariably gentle" (153).

Anne's most characteristic act is exertion, because there is no immediate rightness in feeling any more than there is in knowledge. Judgment requires giving oneself time. As Marianne Dashwood came to realize and as the action of *Persuasion* again demonstrates, so too does feeling.

We recall Henry Tilney's advice to Catherine Morland that her feelings should be investigated, that they may know themselves. Anne's most interesting exertions are those investigations into feelings, her own and those of the people around her. And Henry's advice explains why so many of our insights into ourselves and others turn out to be recognitions of what we have already been feeling. Those investigations, Anne's active struggles to understand and live with others and herself, are the action of *Persuasion*. The period of those investigations is the age of emotion, its only temporal boundaries being those flexible ones of memory and of hope.

One of the fascinations of Austen's fiction is that she distinguishes the problem of perception from that of individual fallibility and moral improvement. This separation guarantees the complexity and charm of what is passing around us. And it requires a proper sense of time. The heroines who undergo education—Catherine, Elizabeth, and Emma—all find after their moments of revelation that their experiences are more interesting and less immediately comprehended than they had fancied them. But to say that experience is complex is also to say that character is complex, since much of the reality we experience is composed of other people. And certainly, in our everyday lives most of the confusion and doubts which are not self-inflicted have to do with not being able to see into other people. Anne Elliot is Austen's portrayal of the best means of seeing into others and, thereby, of the best that character can be.

Anne's powers of feeling and understanding are special. It is a long way from Catherine Morland's blunt spontaneity to Anne's conscious delicacy, and the distance is more than a matter of age. Near the end of *Persuasion* Austen explains Lady Russell's "opposition of feeling" to Captain Wentworth and her preference for Mr. Elliot on the simple grounds that she is "less gifted in this part of understanding" than Anne. "There is a quickness of perception in some, a nicety in the discernment of character, a natural penetration, in short, which no experience in others can equal" (249). Anne is gifted by nature, more gifted than most, with a quickness of perception. And we have watched her quickness throughout the novel. Lady Russell misjudged because "Captain Wentworth's manners had not suited her ideas" and "Mr. Elliot's manners had precisely pleased her in their propriety and correctness" (249). Anne's gift of discernment comes from her gentle warmth and the resultant openness which does not prefer her preconceptions to life.

But if Anne has the acuity to discern that there "was never any burst of feeling, any warmth of indignation or delight, at the evil or good of others," in Mr. Elliot and, like Mr. Knightley, to prefer "the open-hearted, the eager character" (161), she is not offered to us as a model of perfect understanding.

Anne knows that Mr. Elliot is reserved but not that he can control his feelings so well because he has so few that are not selfish. Anne's knowledge of her father is such "as she often wished less" (34). Yet we are told that "her knowledge of her father and Elizabeth, inclined her to think that the sacrifice of one pair of horses would be hardly less painful than of both" (13). In this instance at least, Anne's own warmth in wishing to be free of debt misleads her. Anne's feelings frequently direct her in ways she does not acknowledge. When the Crofts call at Kellynch, Anne "found it most natural" (32) to be out walking. And when Captain Wentworth assists her into the Crofts' carriage at the end of the walk to Winthrop, Anne tells herself that "she understood him," that "though perfectly careless of her, and though becoming attached to another" (91), Captain Wentworth was acting from the pure impulse of his amiable heart. The reader may suspect that Captain Wentworth's impulses are more complex than purely benevolent. We recall Jane Bennet's plea to Elizabeth about how she wishes to judge Mr. Bingley's departure: "Let me take it in the best light, in the light in which it may be understood" (*PP*137). The light in which others may be understood is often the light reflected by Anne's heart.

One of the early pleasures of *Persuasion* is the discrepancy between Anne's projections and actual events. Anne's first gentle speculation that "a few months more, and *he*, perhaps, may be walking here" (25) is not a perhaps that comes true in the way she foresees at all. Indeed, the whole "interesting question" (93) of what it will be like to have Captain Wentworth at Kellynch, Anne anticipates with careful solicitude. But it never happens. And at last she can only smile "over the many anxious feelings she had wasted on the subject" (128). From the moment Anne learns of the Crofts renting Kellynch she begins to prepare for seeing Captain Wentworth there. Instead, she sees him everywhere else. Anne's insights are special but not infallible, not only because she sees through her own feelings but because events and people are always more varied than our predictions for them.

Anne is often wrong, and charmingly so. But the greatness of *Persuasion* is that Anne's fallible moments express Austen's notions of the nature of character and are not to be seen in moral terms. A memorable instance is that morning in Bath after the concert and before Mrs. Smith's disclosure when Anne is thinking about Mr. Elliot. She begins simply and reasonably enough by acknowledging her goodwill toward him, her "gratitude and regard." But she soon moves from her flattering regrets to the fact that there was a "Captain Wentworth in the case" and from there to "her affection would be his for ever. Their union, she believed, could not divide her more from other men, than their final separation" (192). At this climactic point Austen offers her commentary: "Prettier musings of high-wrought love and eternal constancy, could never have passed along the streets of Bath, than Anne was sporting with from Camden-place to Westgate-buildings. It was almost enough to spread purification and perfume all the way."

Austen is once again turning to a subject which interested her throughout her fiction—loving only once in life. We know Austen's opinion of such an attitude; we know it from Marianne Dashwood and Edmund Bertram explicitly, but also from the whole orientation of Austen's thought. From Isabella Thorpe to Anne Elliot, Austen has always presented sentiments about one true love as, at worst, hypocritical and, at best, self-deceived. But whether false or sincere, such sentiments are always limiting. Anne's perfumed thoughts may be sincere. But they are nonetheless sentimental and need to be distinguished from her opinions in that conversation with Captain Harville at the White Hart. Not only does Anne have too much delicacy to allow herself to state what she allows herself to think on that walk. The privilege "of loving longest, when existence or when hope is gone" (235) is not the same as "eternal constancy," a pitch of romance beyond people with real attachments. This is surely why Austen tells us at the beginning of *Persuasion* that what any "final separation" needs is a "second attachment, the only thoroughly natural, happy, and sufficient cure" (28). There is no question but that Anne's author is at an amused distance from those pretty musings.

Yet, while Anne is being laughed at, she is not being condemned. We need only consider the difference between her treatment and Marianne Dashwood's. Marianne's defense of loving once in life is understood to be a serious character flaw. It is an opinion essential to her sense of feelings as absolute, as unaffected by time. But Anne's very exertions presume that her feelings are open to modification and change. One of the beauties of *Persuasion* is that the heroine who feels so much and who speaks so persuasively to Captain Harville in defense of lasting feelings is the character most capable of having new feelings. Captain Benwick's feelings are short-lived because, we suspect, his feelings are not deep. This is not true of Anne. She is long constant. But the very depth of her heart would protect her from an abstraction like "eternal constancy." If there had been no Captain Wentworth in the case, there might never have been a "second attachment." But there would always have been other attachments, for there always was Anne's attachment to life.

Anne's pretty musings, then, are not the object of our moral judgment for the very reason that we know they are not fixed opinions. They are the musings of a particular moment, indulgences only possible in the context of that morning's joy. To say that people are "wise and reasonable in time" (178) is also to say that it is in time that people are reasonable and wise. Anne is not obliged, no one is obliged, always or immediately to think correctly. And the process of feeling aright includes all those feelings, such as eternal constancy, which we experience and count on not to endure. By the time Anne takes that walk her author has made certain that we trust her to be wise and reasonable in time. The reader and the narrator, laughing at Anne, recognize a distance from her. But the distance is not one of superiority or of judgment. It is simply the distance of not being Anne.

Particularity of character is the premise of *Persuasion*. Character is character in the process of being formed, and those for whom change is not possible have given up their lives. Our understanding of character must include both how the self is shaped in relation to an impinging reality and how that reality, itself composed of people in the process of changing, may be understood. Anne's thoughts on the walk from Camden Place to Westgate Buildings are part of a continuing pattern of involvement which is different for each of us. The scene highlights the connection between ways of seeing character— gradual relativistic ways—which we see Anne using and the way we see Anne, that is, through the explicit importance of her feelings. Thus, as there is no moment of revelation about other people's characters, no sudden opening of a little box, so there is no sudden or immediate seeing into Anne's character through a particular feeling. In other words, pretty musings offer no more important or revealing a moment than others. It is through the constant play and replay of feelings, through modifications over time, that Anne comes to understand her feelings and we, like Anne, can know another's character.

The particularity of character is assumed in all Austen's work. This is most often forgotten in interpreting *Mansfield Park*, when the reader's sense of distance from Fanny Price becomes a means of disliking her. But we are not Fanny, any more than we are Anne. Between *Mansfield Park* and *Persuasion* Austen wrote *Emma*. And if *Mansfield Park* looks at the good that can grow out of small beginnings and limited means, Emma is a celebration of abundance, of the riches of character and the riches of life. Emma, loved by us all, is a reminder that Austen does not claim anything spiritually better or more beautiful in a quiet heroine with "soft light eyes" (*MP*470). After *Emma* Austen returns to a quiet heroine, with "delicate features and mild dark eyes" (6). Anne Elliot, like Elinor Dashwood, begins her story with "an elegance of mind and sweetness of character" which assures her the approval of "any people of real understanding" (5), including readers of the novel. But Anne does not represent perfection in Austen's canon of heroines, not because we find fault with her but because perfection implies an end—of change, of difference, of the chance to persuade.

Austen had established in *Northanger Abbey* that character is mixed, and the point includes not only people's weaknesses but their peculiarities as well. Human relations are often a matter of complementary peculiarities, differences between people made amenable by the smoothing influence of affection. This is most often true of Austen's minor characters. We need only think of Admiral and Mrs. Croft, whose style of driving was "no bad representation of the general guidance of their affairs" (92). The Crofts' influence on each other is the basis of their happiness. People may have fixed natures, like Elizabeth Elliot and Sir Walter, neither of whom can be persuaded on a point "against previous inclination" (16). Mr. Woodhouse, too, is fixed in his opinions. But he is a comic character, endeared to us, at least in part, by his willingness to be counseled by those he loves. Some people, such as Louisa Musgrove, are so easily persuaded as to change entirely their habits and pursuits. Nonetheless, the openness to influence is essential to right thinking and right feeling in Austen's fiction. It is the ability to be moved by a landscape, by a person, by an event.

Austen's attention to the problems of perception leads naturally, even predictably, to the issue of persuasion. An active relation between self and others, persuasion implies the changing aspect of truth. Austen can make a heaven in this world for her favorites because she offers a temporal paradise, not one where ripe fruit never falls. The eternity she offers on this side of the grave is the infinite abundance of a reality as interesting as the forms by which we understand it. A sense of continuity, of time, is essential to a moral consciousness. *Persuasion*, then, is a moral imperative. For it is a receptiveness to others which depends upon feeling. Elizabeth Elliot cannot be persuaded of the danger of Mrs. Clay, Anne cannot "make it perceptible to her sister" (34), because Elizabeth doesn't care about Anne. The power to understand is inseparable from the power to feel. We remember Mr. Bingley, perhaps too easily persuaded, but with a heart open to his friend. *Persuasion* allows for the future. It allows for the return of love and the return of bloom.

During the evening card party at Camden Place, while admiring a display of plants, Anne speaks to Captain Wentworth about Lady Russell's advice to her eight years and a half ago to break the engagement: "It was, perhaps, one of those cases in which advice is good or bad only as the event decides" (246). The event decided the advice was bad. And yet Anne's point remains. The characters in Austen's fiction must perceive and judge and act in circumstances which are not clear and which often will not be clear except in the course of time. There are many moments, such as Anne's decision to accept Lady Russell's advice, in which duty is discernible. But the outcome lies in the future, beyond anyone's wisdom to predict. Anne is not a perfect heroine. She is a character who does at least as well as any of us in the effort to perceive and act. She is persuaded and the result is years of unhappiness.

But even when time belies our best guesses, the advantages of being persuadable remain. They are the advantages of a warm and receptive heart. It is in that receptivity, however faulty, that our best chances of happiness lie. The danger of persuasion is, essentially, the danger of change. But change, for all its risks, is more natural than any of the structures we can create. Austen's optimism brings Captain Wentworth back to Anne, to exchange "again those feelings and those promises which had once before seemed to secure every thing, but which had been followed by so many, many years of division and estrangement" (240). It is a return which we may feel the future is not often likely to provide. It is the gift of a second chance. But that gift is Austen's fictional representation of the possibilities of all our futures, possibilities which, though risk, and unpredictable, are worth all our care and our time.

NOTES

1. Mary Lascelles, *Jane Austen and her Art* (1939: reprint ed. Oxford: Oxford University Press, 1974), p. 203.

2. Virginia Woolf, *The Common Reader* (1925: reprint ed., New York: Harcourt. Brace & World. 1953). p. 147.

3. Walton Litz. *Jane Austen: A Study of Her Artistic Development* (London: Chatto & Windus. 1965): Alistair Duckworth, *The Improvement of the Estate* (Baltimore: The Johns Hopkins Press, 1971): Nina Auerbach. "O Brave New World: Evolution and Resolution in *Persuasion.*" *English Literary History* 39 (1972).

4. Woolf, *Common Reader*, p. 147.

5. Walton Litz. "*Persuasion*: Forms of Estrangement," in *Jane Austen: Bicentenary Essays*. ed. John Halperin (London. Cambridge University Press, 1975), p. 223.

6. Lascelles, *Jane Austen*, p. 1.

7. Howard Babb. *Jane Austen's Novels: The Fabric of Dialogue* (Columbus: Ohio University Press. 1962). p. 203.

8. Susan Kneedler has pointed out in an unpublished paper, dated May 1, 1978, that we can measure Captain Wentworth's change by his no longer being "governed by the traditionally heroic vocabulary of willfulness: 'ever,' 'never,' 'always,' and 'must.' which creates brittle fragile people like Louisa."

9. Gene Ruoff. "Anne Elliot's Dowry: Reflections on the Ending of *Persuasion,*" *The Wordsworth Circle* 7 (1976): 350. I am indebted to this discussion for the idea of Wordsworthian associations in *Persuasion*.

10. Alistair Duckworth, *The Improvement of the Estate*, p. 181.

TONY TANNER

In Between: Persuasion

Persuasion. Not '*Persuasion* and ...'—Resistance, Refusal, Rebellion, for instance. Just *Persuasion.* In previous titles using abstract nouns Jane Austen had deployed pairs. This time the debate, the struggle, the contestation, the contrarieties and ambiguities are all in the one word. As they are all in, or concentrated on, the one girl. Anne Elliot is the loneliest of Jane Austen's heroines. Persuaded by others, she has to repersuade herself.

> Sir Walter Elliot, of Kellynch-hall, in Somersetshire, was a man who, for his own amusement, never took up any book but the Baronetage; there he found occupation for an idle hour, and consolation in a distressed one; there his faculties were roused into admiration and respect, by contemplating the limited remnant of earliest patents; there any unwelcome sensations, arising from domestic affairs, changed naturally into pity and contempt, as he turned over the almost endless creations of the last century—and there, if every other leaf were powerless, he could read his own history with an interest which never failed— this was the page at which the favourite volume was always opened:

From *Jane Austen.* © 1986 by Tony Tanner.

'ELLIOT OF KELLYNCH HALL'

Jane Austen opens her book with the description of a man looking at a book in which he reads the same words as her book opens with—'Elliot, of Kellynch-hall'. This is the kind of teasing regression which we have become accustomed to in contemporary writers but which no one associates with the work of Jane Austen. It alerts us to at least two important considerations: the dangers involved in seeking validation and self-justification in book as opposed to life, in record rather than in action, in name as opposed to function; and the absolutely negative 'vanity' (her key word for Sir Walter) in looking for and finding one's familial and social position, one's reality, in an inscription rather than in a pattern of behaviour, in a sign rather than the range of responsibilities which it implicitly signifies. We learn how fond Sir Walter is of mirrors and how hopelessly and hurtfully unaware of the real needs and feelings of his dependents he is. This opening situation poses someone fixed in an ultimate solipsism gazing with inexhaustible pleasure into the textual mirror which simply gives him back his name. The opening of Jane Austen's text—a title, a name, a domicile, a geographic location—implies a whole series of unwritten obligations and responsibilities related to rank, family, society and the very land itself, none of which Sir Walter, book-bound and self-mesmerised, either keeps or recognises. He is only interested in himself and what reflects him—mirrors or daughters. Thus he likes Elizabeth because she is 'very like himself'—this is parenthood as narcissism—and Mary has 'acquired a little artificial importance' because she has married into a tolerably respectable family; 'but Anne, with an elegance of mind and sweetness of character, which must have placed her high with any people of real understanding, was nobody with either father or sister: her word had no weight; her convenience was always to give way;—she was only Anne'. Only Anne—no rank, no effective surname, no house, no location; her words are weightless, and physically speaking she always has to 'give way'—that is, accept perpetual displacement. Anne we may call the girl on the threshold, existing in that limboid space between the house of the father which has to be left and the house of the husband which has yet to be found. No longer a child and not yet a wife, Anne is, precisely, in between, and she lives in in-betweenness. She is a speaker who is unheard; she is a body who is a 'nobody'. I emphasise this because the problems of the body who is, socially speaking, a nobody were to engage many of the great nineteenth-century writers. We might recall here that in one of the seminal eighteenth-century novels, *La Nouvelle Héloïse*, Julie's father refuses even to listen to the idea of her marrying Saint-Preux, because Saint-Preux is what he calls 'un quidam', which means an unnamed individual or, in dictionary terms,

'Person (name unknown)'. This is to say that, as far as the father is concerned, Saint-Preux exists in a state of 'quidamity'. As far as her father is concerned, Anne also exists in that state of quidamity—she was nobody, she was only Anne: 'He had never indulged much hope, he had now none, of ever reading her name in any other page of his favourite work.' Until she is, as it were, reborn in terms of writing in the Baronetage, she does not exist—not to be in the book is thus not to *be*. We may laugh at Sir Walter but Jane Austen makes it very clear what kind of perversity is involved in such a radical confusion or inversion of values whereby script and name take absolute precedence over offspring and dependents; or, to put it another way, when you cannot see the body for the book.

Anne Elliot, then, is perpetually displaced, always 'giving way' as opposed to having her *own* way—it is worth emphasising the metaphor. The story of her life consists precisely in having had her own way blocked, refused, negated. One might almost think of the book as being about dissuasion, for she is urged or forced not into doing something which she does not want to do, but into not doing something which her whole emotional self tells her is the right thing (that is, marry Captain Wentworth at a time when he had no fortune). Her words carry no weight. The word 'persuasion' echoes throughout the novel of that title just as it is constantly haunting Anne Elliot (it occurs at least fourteen times). It is as if she cannot get away from what she has done in allowing herself to be persuaded not to marry Frederick Wentworth—or dissuaded from marrying him. Yet 'persuasion' implies some sort and source of 'authority'—preferably moral authority; mere power can work by simple imperatives or prohibitions backed up by force. But what is striking about the world of *Persuasion* is the absence of any real centre or principle of authority. Among the possible traditional sources of authority we might include the family, parents, the clergy, social rank and respected names, familiar and revered places, codes of manners and propriety, codes of duty and prudence, the care and concern of friendship, or true love so certain of itself that it becomes self-authorising. But in this novel all such potential sources of authority have gone awry, gone away, gone wrong; they are absent, dispersed or impotent; they have become ossified, stagnant or—worse—totally unreliable and misleading. Everything is in a condition of change in this novel, and as often as not it is change as deterioration or diminution. In such a world it becomes a real question, what can and should remain 'constant'? To retain an uncritical allegiance to certain decaying inert social hierarchies and practices means dehumanising the self for the sake of rigidifying deathly formulae; to abandon oneself to the new might be to opt for a giddy dissolution. Just about all the previous stabilities of Jane Austen's world are called into question in this novel—in which things really are 'changed utterly', with no terrible beauty being born. It is a novel of great poignancy and sadness; as well as one of real bitterness and astringency, for it is deeply shadowed by the passing of things, and the remembrance of things past.

It is hardly surprising, then, that time plays a larger part in this novel than in any other of Jane Austen's works. It is the only one of her novels which gives a specific date for the opening action—'summer 1814'—as *Emma* is the only novel to use a single name as a title. The significance of that date (the end of the Napoleonic wars—apart from 'the hundred days' of Napoleon's abortive return, concluded by the battle of Waterloo in 1815), becomes increasingly obvious: it marks a big change in English history and society. But in the novel the crucial passage of time is that which has elapsed since Anne was 'persuaded' to give up Wentworth and he disappeared into the navy—'more than seven years were gone since this little history of sorrowful interest had reached its close.' Indeed *Persuasion* is in effect a second novel. (Part of its rare autumnal magic—not unlike that of one of Shakespeare's last plays—is that it satisfies that dream of a 'second chance' which must appeal to anyone who has experienced the sense of an irreparably ruined life owing to an irrevocable, mistaken decision.) The 'first novel' is what might be called (warily) a typical Jane Austen novel and is told in telescopic brevity in a few lines in chapter 4:

> He [Wentworth] was, at that time, a remarkably fine young man, with a great deal of intelligence, spirit and brilliancy; and Anne an extremely pretty girl, with gentleness, modest taste and feeling.— Half the sum of attraction, on either side, might have been enough, for he had nothing to do, and she had hardly any body to love; but the encounter of such lavish expectations could not fail. They were gradually acquainted, and when acquainted, rapidly and deeply in love. It would be difficult to say which had seen the highest perfection in the other, or which had been the happiest; she, in receiving his declarations and proposals, or he in having them accepted.

End of story. To get there could have taken the younger Jane Austen some hundreds of pages. But times and things have changed. That was a happy novel of yesteryear, here no more than a distant trace, a radiant but receding, summarisable memory in this second novel. 'More than seven years were gone since this little history of sorrowful interest had reached its close.' The first novel ended when the totally vain, egotistical anti-father (he is even described as womanly in his vanity) Sir Walter Elliot 'gave it all the negative of great astonishment, great coldness, great silence'. His 'negative' blocked the marriage and the novel alike. It is a 'negative' which is against generational and narrative continuity and renewal and it has far-reaching social implications.

Here it is enough to point out that it provides the starting-point for a new kind of novel for Jane Austen; a novel which arises precisely out of the thwarting and 'negating' of her first (earlier type of) novel. Hence the stress on time past. What has happened in between then and now? And what can happen next? It must be something quite different from the action and resolution of any previous Jane Austen novel, because something—history, society or whatever it is that is embodied in the sterile, life-denying figure of Sir Walter—has given that kind of novel 'all the negative'. What Jane Austen does say is this: 'She [Anne] had been forced into prudence in her youth, she learned romance as she grew older—the natural sequence of an unnatural beginning.' Most of Jane Austen's heroines have to learn some kind of prudence (not Fanny Price, who has suffered for her undeviating dedication to prudentiality). Anne, born into repression and non-recognition, has to learn romance—a deliberate oxymoron surely, for romance is associated with spontaneous feelings. But in Anne's case these had been blocked; her father gave them all the negative. To find her own positive she has, as it were, to diseducate herself from the authorities who, whether by silence or disapproval or forceful opposition, dominated that early part of her life when she was—in relation to Captain Wentworth—becoming somebody. Anne has to start on a long and arduous second life, which is based on loss, denial, deprivation. This is the 'unnatural beginning' to her life, and to Jane Austen's novel, which differs quite radically from her previous works in that there, as I said, her heroines tend to graduate from romance to prudence. And because of what she has lost and regretted losing (again an unusual condition for the Jane Austen heroine, who has usually not yet had any significant romance when the book opens) Anne undergoes a new kind of ordeal and tribulation, since any reference to Captain Wentworth offers 'a new sort of trial to Anne's nerves' so that she has to 'teach herself to be insensible on such points'. Among other things, Anne Elliot has to combine sense and insensibility— again, a marked change from Jane Austen's earlier work.

The novel starts, then, with Sir Walter contemplating 'the limited remnants of the earliest patents' in a volume which records 'the history and rise of the ancient and respectable family'. 'Limited remnants' are indeed all that now remain, and *this* volume will complete the work by recording the 'fall' and self-destruction of this 'respectable family'—if not the traditional family in general. Around the unnaturally well-preserved appearance of Sir Walter he can only see the 'wreck of good looks of everybody else'. Did he but realise it, the 'wreckage' goes a good deal deeper than that. What is irremediably wrecked and what might yet remain to generate new life from among the 'remnants' becomes a key question of the book. Anne has to live with the regret for what she has lost, while her one friend and mother-substitute, Lady Russell, while feeling sorry for Anne, 'never wishes the past undone'. As a result 'they knew not each other's opinion, either its constancy or its change'. When Sir Walter decides to move with his daughters out of the family home, Kellynch Hall, Anne is aware of 'the general air of oblivion among them'. It is an air which partially pervades the book. When Anne does finally meet Wentworth again, her concern is very much with the possible effects of time:

> How absurd to be resuming the agitation which such an interval had banished into distance and indistinctness! What might not eight years do? Events of every description—changes, alienations, removals,—all, all must be compromised in it; and oblivion of the past—how natural, how certain too!

In the event Anne finds that 'to retentive feelings eight years may be little more than nothing'. Time can obviously mean one thing to a couple in love—and something quite different to the society around them. Anne is a lonely figure of emotional constancy living in a society of 'changes, alienations, removals'. She hears that Wentworth finds her 'altered beyond his knowledge', but his enlightened knowledge will find her essentially unaltered. There is of course much emphasis on the past and the pastness of the past: 'That was in the year six'; 'There had been a time'; 'those rooms had witnessed former meetings'; and so on. The pluperfect tense is poignantly present. Even painful memories are precious; indeed even precious because painful.

> Scenes had passed at Uppercross, which made it precious. It stood the record of many sensations of pain, once severe but now softened; and of some instances of relenting feeling, some breathings of friendship and reconciliation, which could never be looked for again, and which could never cease to be dear. She left it all behind her; all but the recollection that such things had been.

The dominant mood before the end is autumnal, nostalgic, a sense of the most significant period of experience being in the past, recollectable but irretrievable and unrepeatable. 'One does not love a place the less for having suffered in it.' There are moments when Wentworth speaks to Anne 'which seemed almost restoring the past'. 'Restoration' on this personal level does prove to be joyfully—miraculously—possible. But on the social and familial level no such restoration is possible. This is made clear when the heir to Kellynch, Mr Elliot, enters the novel and is not only keen to marry Anne but *seems* a correct and suitable figure to assist at such restoration after the gross and ruinous derelictions of Sir Walter. Lady Russell, characteristically, would like to forward this marriage and see Anne 'occupying your dear mother's place, succeeding to all her rights ... presiding and blessing in the same spot'. To Anne herself the idea of 'being restored to Kellynch, calling it her home again, her home forever, was a charm which she could not immediately resist'. But love is stronger than even the most precious property. Anne really has 'left it all behind her'. Whatever else it might be, this is not a 'restoration' age.

The question of 'what lasts' obviously figures most largely in this novel in connection with human feelings—even leading to a recurring debate as to whether man or woman is capable of the greater constancy, of loving longer. Captain Benwick is slightly reproached by Wentworth for having put aside his devotion to the dead Fanny Harville (whom he apparently worshipped) to marry Louisa Musgrove. 'A man does not recover from such a devotion of the heart to such a woman!—He ought not—he does not.' Wentworth obviously has his own motives for such an assertion: he is both indirectly signalling his own unbroken devotion to Anne, and questioning hers. And indeed such pointed exchanges proliferate towards the end of the book: 'You did not like to use cards; but time makes many changes.' Wentworth's statement is of course also a question. To which Anne replies, 'I am not yet so much changed'—'and stopped, fearing she hardly knew what misconstruction'. In the crucial 'recognition' scene—in the revised chapter 23—the central debate is between Captain Harville and Anne while Wentworth apparently writes a letter. Harville argues that men love longer, that women have a legendary reputation for inconstancy. Anne maintains that 'We certainly do not forget you, so soon as you forget us', and 'All the privilege I claim for my own sex ... is that of loving longest, when existence or hope is gone.' This is all said for the benefit of the apparently preoccupied but all-attentive Wentworth. I shall return to the indirect mode of communication in this crucial scene. Here the point to note is that, as Lady Russell says, 'Time will explain'—certainly in this novel, in which time is so central, and 'explanations' (making intelligible, laying things out clearly) are both crucial and difficult to come by. And the novel itself is an inquiry into—an explanation of—the effects of time. As I have said, this is the 'second' novel, made necessary by the rude 'negation' of the first one, which remains as an aborted embryo in chapter 4.

I shall return to the relationship between Anne and Wentworth. First we should consider the general state of society as it is represented in this book. The normal sources of stability and order in Jane Austen's world would include social position, property, place, family, manners and propriety, as generating a web of duties and responsibilities which together should serve to maintain the moral fabric and coherence of society. In this novel all these institutions and codes and related values have undergone a radical transformation or devaluation. There *are* values, but many of them are new; and they are relocated or resited. Instead of a heedful regard for position and property and family, we have a new obsession with 'rank', 'connexions', money and private relationships—Lady Russell esteems Sir Walter not as a man or father (he is a wretched example of both) but as a baronet: 'she had prejudices on the side of ancestry; she had a value for rank and consequence'. There are discussions of 'rank, people of rank, jealousy of rank'. Mary, the most insufferable snob (she is not comic—she is unbearable), looks not at Mr Elliot but at 'the horses ... the arms ... the livery'; she regards only the insignia of rank, empty signifiers of another empty series of signifiers. For 'rank' in this book does not betoken a responsible authoritative position in society: it signifies only itself. It is rigidifying self-reifying system—signifying nothing. It is symptomatic of a 'state of stagnation' existing in the class which should be exemplary and active if it is to serve as, and deserve to be, a ruling class. Mr Elliot at one time of his life despises 'the honour of the family' and declared that 'if baronetcies were saleable, anybody should have his for fifty pounds, arms and motto, name and livery included'. 'Rank' is degraded into a mere commodity. On the other hand, when it seems that it would be more profitable for him to become the serious heir to baronetcy, he speaks seriously in favour of 'the value of rank and connexion'. This is a mark not of his conversion but of his ruthlessly selfish opportunism and hypocrisy. The discourse and ideology of 'rank' happen to be available to disguise or 'embellish' his crudely egotistical aspirations. The new realm where rank *does* have a genuine significance and is related to a hierarchy of real functions and obligations is the navy—but I shall come back to the navy. The emphasis on the 'value' of 'connexions', which Lady Russell upholds in an apparently rational way, as the unspeakably foolish Mary does in the crudest possible way ('It is very unpleasant having such connexions', she declares of the respectable Hayters), is a relatively new one in Jane Austen. It emphasises a merely titular or 'nominal' and fortuitous relationship rather than any true bonding or sense of reciprocal human relatedness. An extreme example of the meaninglessness and folly of this stress on 'rank' and 'connexions' is offered by Sir Walter's and Elizabeth's frantic anxiety and eagerness to cultivate the acquaintance of their titled cousins, Lady Dalrymple and her daughter. As people they are not even 'agreeable'; 'they were nothing'. Mr Elliot asserts that 'rank is rank'. The book confirms this as a meaningless tautology and counterasserts that rank is 'nothing'.

More than one person is said to be 'nothing' or 'nobody'. Anne 'was nobody' because unmarried; Mr Wentworth (Frederick's brother) 'was nobody ... quite unconnected', because he was a curate and not 'a man of property'; Charles Hayter is 'nothing but a country curate'; Captain Wentworth, when he reappears as rich 'and as high in his profession as merit and activity could place him' was 'no longer nobody'. These are mainly the verdicts of Sir Walter, a 'foolish spendthrift baronet' who has neither money nor profession nor merit nor activity. He is also no longer married and has rented his property. If anybody is now 'nobody', it is he. It is indirectly Jane Austen's verdict—through Anne's silent assessment—that the Dalrymples 'were nothing'. But who then is somebody and something—and by what social criteria? It would seem that there are no longer any agreed-on standards, no authoritative modes of assessment, to discriminate the somebodies from the nobodies, to tell a something from a nothing. This in itself is a symptom of a crisis of values—a chaos if not a total absence and loss of 'common' (i.e. communal) standards of modes of identification and evaluation. There seems to be no correlation or connection between social title and social role, between rank and merit.

The honorific term 'gentleman'—always somewhat vague—now means different things to different people (Sir Walter is 'misled' when his agent Mr Shepherd refers to Mr Wentworth as a 'gentleman'), or it is meaningless (as applied to Captain Wallis) or worse it conceals heartless and ruthless anti-social egotism (Mr Elliott passes as 'completely a gentleman'). The true 'gentlemen' are now to be found in the navy, but they are neither recognised nor addressed as such. A whole social system of categorisation and terminology is slipping into meaningless or perverse misapplication, dangerously so when the label 'gentleman' is confidently affixed to a man who is the complete opposite (or inversion) of everything a true gentleman should be. Society's very taxonomy seems to have collapsed, being at best misleading and at worst totally corrupt. Names themselves seem to have lost any social significance—at least from the perverse and anachronistic point of view of Sir Walter, who laments thus: 'One wonders how the names of many of our nobility became so common.' One explanation may involve the dilution of aristocratic families with the wealthier members of other classes; another could simply point to the behaviour of Sir Walter himself, who effectively does just about everything he could to bring his family name into disrepute. It is he who, on hearing that Anne is going to visit her crippled and impoverished friend Mrs Smith, says disdainfully, 'Mrs Smith, such a name!'

'Smith' is indeed the archetypal anonymous English name, a name which is in effect no 'name' at all. But, here again, this novel forces us to question all kinds of social assumptions. What really is in a name? In the case of Sir Walter Elliot, an impoverished and fatuous vanity; in the case of Mrs Smith, a wealth of misfortune and misery; in the case of Lady Dalrymple, 'nothing'. Like 'rank' and 'connexions', names also no longer serve to facilitate any kind of social orientation. They now manifest themselves as truly arbitrary signifiers—designations unrelated to any coherent social design or structure.

Let us now consider property and places, houses and homes and families. We can note immediately that the action of the novel is dispersed among an unusually large number of different places (unusual for Jane Austen). Fanny Price visits her 'home' in Portsmouth; Emma goes to Box Hill. But Anne is variously 'removed' or 'transplanted' from Kellynch Hall to Uppercross cottage; to the Great House (of the Musgroves) to Bath; with a glimpse of Winthrop and a crucial visit to Lyme. This topographical diffusion and 'transplanting' is itself both a symptom and a part of a more far-reaching social fragmentation and mobility. One important scene takes place in an hotel in Bath. 'A morning of thorough confusion was to be expected. A large party in an hotel ensured a quick-changing, unsettled scene.' An hotel is the appropriate edifice for a transient, increasingly uprooted or unrooted society, and that 'quick-changing, unsettled scene' is—in little—the scene of the whole book. The 'thorough confusion' experienced in the hotel pervades society at large. This topographical dispersal and social scattering also have their effect on the style and vocabulary of the novel. Of the incident on the Cobb we are told parenthetically that '(it was all done in rapid moments)'. In a way that is true of the book as a whole, which is more episodic, more fragmentary, and more marked by quick and sudden changes and abrupt transitions and jerks of the plot than any of the previous novels. Related to that is a perceptibly new note of emotional volatility and irruptiveness, even excess. After the incident on the Cobb there is, not a cool discussion, but an 'interchange of perplexity and terror'—a significant dissolution of coherent speech in feeling. The word 'burst' appears a number of times in relation to sudden mental and emotional eruptions—'extraordinary burst of mind', 'bursts of feeling'; phrases such as 'a thousand feelings rushed on Anne', 'overpowering happiness' contribute to the increased presence of sudden unanticipated and unpredictable inward intensities. And such 'bursts', 'rushes of feeling', emotional 'overpowerings' are not always the signs of a potentially dangerous and disorderly (or 'improper') lack of control, as they often are in Jane Austen's earlier work. On the contrary, they can now be the desirable manifestations of a capacity for authentic and spontaneous feeling. This means that there is a much more ruffled 'choppy' surface to the narrative. 'Tranquillity' is often 'interrupted'; 'restraint' gives way to 'disturbance'. 'Every moment rather brought fresh agitation.' This refers to Anne near the end, but in a way it is true of the novel as a whole.

There are further lessons to be learned from Anne's constant 'transplantation'. The following is crucial:

> Anne had not wanted this visit to Uppercross, to learn that a removal from one set of people to another, though at a distance of only three miles, will often include a total change of conversation, opinion, and idea ... she acknowledged it to be very fitting, that every little social commonwealth should dictate its own matters of discourse; and hoped, ere long, to become a not unworthy member of the one she was now transplanted to ... she believed she must now submit to feel that another lesson, in the art of knowing our own nothingness beyond our own circle, was becoming necessary for her.

This awareness that within the one common language—English—there can be innumerable discourses according to group, place, and so on, is a very crucial one. It is not the same thing as a dialect but what Roland Barthes calls a 'sociolect'—'the language of a linguistic community, that is of a group of persons who all interpret in the same way all linguistic statements.' It is of course simply a general truth, and one well known to Jane Austen, that people speaking the same language can very often not 'hear' each other because they are operating within different discourses or sociolects It is characteristic of many of Jane Austen's heroines that they are aware when people are operating within different discourses—an awareness which is an aspect of their sense and linguistic 'conscience' and very often a consequence of their detachment and isolation. And Anne learns another lesson; just as one language is in fact made up of many discourses, so society is made up of many 'circles' and in many of these circles one may be a 'nothing' just as in some discourses one is inaudible. Anne's 'word' initially 'had no weight' precisely because she was regarded as a 'no-body' within the first circle of her family—'negatived' from the beginning. Her speech can only take on its full value when she is truly regarded as a 'somebody'—a person in her own right, not according to rank or status, and taken permanently into a new circle—the navy. In between she is, well, in between. But notice two things. Anne does not fight this state of affairs or lament the plurality of discourses. On the contrary, she is willing to try and adapt herself (within the limits of her unchanging sense of propriety). Yet her speech—like her love—is 'constant' in a society apparently given over to change. Having to negotiate a plurality of partial discourses, Anne comes to embody what we might call the conscience of language. She, and she alone, always speaks truly, and truly speaks. Indeed, Jane Austen may well be intending to depict Anne as in some ways old-fashioned—or, rather, out of fashion (which is by nature ephemeral and fickle). Not all change is regarded as unmitigatedly bad in this book— indeed, given the 'stagnation' and moral paralysis (if not something worse) which seems to prevail among the upper ruling classes, then some change may be not only unavoidable but positively necessary and welcome. But Anne's 'lessons' do point to the fact (glimpsed at the end of *Emma*) that society is breaking up into smaller and smaller 'circles' and units. This implies—indeed involves—the loss of any sense of a true, authoritative 'centre', and the possible disappearance of any 'common' language (and with that, a shared sense of 'common' values). Add to this the fact that even within the small separate 'sociolects' there are people who tend towards speaking an 'idiolect' (i.e. a language which is really private to themselves and not properly heard or understood by anyone else). This could portend a society which is no longer truly a society in any meaningful sense but rather an aggregate of contiguous but non-communicating groups or just families (or even just individuals), with no *real* connections, no overall coherence, no single structure binding them together. Separate 'commonwealths' with neither 'wealth' nor anything much else held in 'common': 'Dictate-orships' perhaps (Jane Austen's words carry a weight of possible irony) of one kind or another. To a large extent this is our 'society' today. It is not 'society' as Jane Austen had thought it should or could be. But she saw that the change was coming and was inevitable. To a large extent she could see why. It is all there in this unique novel.

In this prevailing atmosphere of change it is not surprising that 'property' no longer plays the assured and essential role it did in earlier novels. Mary, for instance, 'had merely connected herself with an old country family and respectability and large fortune'. That 'merely' is Sir Walter's thought, Jane Austen's irony. The advantage for people 'living on their own property', according to the insinuating Mrs Clay, is that they 'are not obliged to follow any ... profession' but can just 'follow their own pursuits'. Just what Sir Walter likes to hear, of course, but not at all what Jane Austen believed, since for her the owning of 'property' necessarily involved the recognition of obligations and duties to the community. If it is merely an arena for self-indulgence and hedonism, it is less than useless as a part of the maintained and maintaining order of society. It is still desirable to have property of course; but as a symbol of certain social values it is undervalued as Mary undervalues Charles Hayter s 'good, freehold property' because it confers no rank (adding, in her incomparably selfish way, 'it would be shocking to have Henrietta marry Charles Hayter; a very bad thing for *her*, and a still worse for *me*'), or as Sir Walter feels 'no degradation in his changes', seeing 'nothing to regret in the duties and dignity of the resident landholder' and finding 'much to be vain of in the littleness of a town'. His is the quintessential abdication and dereliction of the ruling-class landowner. When he rents Kellynch Hall he causes a 'break-up of the family', and leaves behind 'deserted grounds' and 'so altered a village'. (There is quite possibly here a barely ironic allusion to Goldsmith's *The Deserted Village*.) He is an agent of 'desolation', helping both to precipitate and to accelerate the destruction of the old order of society. (Anne will be the first Jane Austen heroine who will not found her marriage on the once-necessary basis of 'property'.) Society in the form of Sir Walter Elliot has become all empty self-regarding form and display: he has no sense of responsibility to his position, to the land, and it is significant that he rents his house to go and participate in the meaningless frivolities in Bath.

This matter of renting his house is worth pausing over for a moment. The notion 'quit Kellynch-hall' is initially horrendous to Sir Walter. But he would, as he says, 'sooner quit Kellynch-hall' than undertake any economies or constraints on his unrestricted pursuit of pleasure. His relation to his house is not a responsible one: he does not see his house as part of a larger context, an interrelated rural society, an ecology, if you will; it is more like a pleasure-dome or a three-dimensional mirror which flatters his vanity. So he agrees to quit if he cannot have those pleasures. But note that 'Sir Walter could not have borne the degradation of being known to design letting his house—Mr Shepherd had once mentioned the word "advertise"—but never dared approach it again.' I shall come back to 'advertising' in the last chapter, but here again we note that Sir Walter wants the profits of 'renting' while still pretending to belong to an aristocracy which did not contaminate itself with contact with any kind of 'trade' or commerce. This is the self-deception of a figure no longer sensible of the significance of his social rank. When he does consider renting it he thinks of it in terms of 'a prize' for the fortunate tenants—'a prize'; he has no appreciation of the real value of his inherited house. And I shall just note the areas to which he does not really want the new tenant to have access: 'The park would be open to him of course ..., but what restrictions I might impose on the use of the pleasure-grounds, is another thing. I am not fond of the idea of my shrubberies being always approachable.' Funny of course—but again there is no sense of the importance and significance of the house of his fathers, the house in which he so signally fails in his paternal duties. To abandon it in exchange for money, for mere pleasure, rather than 'economise' is a very notable dereliction of his duties. This is an alteration which is most definitely not 'perhaps an improvement' but indisputably a degradation.

Even before Sir Walter decided to 'quit Kellynch-hall' we are told of 'the prosperity and the nothingness' of the life there, with nothing to fill 'the vacancies'—'no habits of utility abroad, no talents or accomplishments for home.' Lady Elliot, the true upholder of domesticity, is dead. Anne would carry on her work—but of course is not allowed to. Rather than practise the slightest economy or curtail any of his indulgences, Sir Walter prefers to rent his landed house, which is indeed nothing of a home and merely parasitic on the community it should help to maintain and preserve. (We might note in passing that we are told that, if Sir Walter follows Anne's sensible suggestions, Lady Russell estimates that 'in seven years he will be clear'. Of course he cannot deprive himself of any of his private gratifications for any length of time at all. It is Anne, who can wait and economise scrupulously on her emotional expenditure, who after 'seven years'—when Wentworth returns—will finally 'be clear'. 'Clear', one might say, of the whole rotten pack of her family; as well as 'clear' of the obstacles, negatives and disuasions which had blocked the growth and consummation of her true love seven years previously.) Seeing the Crofts in Kellynch Hall after they have rented it, Anne feels that 'they were gone who deserved not to stay, and that Kellynch-hall had passed into better hands than its owners.' Unlike the 'improvements' suggested in *Mansfield Park*, the 'few alterations' the Crofts make to Kellynch Hall are 'all very much for the better'. It is almost as if Jane Austen was passing a verdict on the defection of a whole class in whom she had once invested so much hope. Initially Anne is sad at the thought of 'a beloved home made over to others'—but that home was no longer home. Her loyalties shift and are displaced or realigned elsewhere. For instance: 'how much more interesting to her was the home and the friendship of the Harvilles and Captain Benwick, than her own father's house in Camden Place'. The Harvilles and Benwick are naval officers of course, and, just as there is a shift of significant, active 'rank' from society to the navy, so it is the navy who—apparently paradoxically—reconstitute a meaningful domesticity, re-create the idea of home, ultimately redefine the notion of society itself. It is Mrs Croft who asserts that 'Woman may be as comfortable on board, as in the best house in England', and clearly her ship was more of a 'home' than Kellynch Hall. But even the house of the Harvilles and Captain Benwick— rather like a ship on shore—in all its apparent oddity and somewhat cramped idiosyncrasy offers to Anne 'the picture of repose and domestic happiness'. Note that the rooms are extremely small and the very limited space is crowded. This was one of the major deficiencies of Fanny's home in Portsmouth which contributed to its 'impropriety'. Nothing of that now. The small space is turned into 'the best possible account' and instead of the chaos of excessive proximity and discord there is the snugness of hospitable ease and intimacy. The 'hospitality' of the navy is emphasised—and usual 'forms' of etiquette are at the same time devalued. There was such a 'bewitching charm in a degree of hospitality so uncommon, so unlike the usual style of give-and-take invitations and dinners of formality and display'. A whole system of socially prescribed 'formal' reciprocities is here effectively displaced by an informal spontaneity. It is not prompted by custom but by 'the heart'—the rooms are so small as none but those who 'invite from the heart' would think of asking people to share their living-space. The shift of emphasis from socially prescribed 'invitations' to those which come from 'the heart' is part of a larger change from a socially based to an emotionally justified code of behaviour. It has quite radical implications. As already intimated, I shall have more to say about the navy, but I want to return to land matters.

There is an example of a relatively happy home unrelated to the navy: the home of the Musgroves, the Great House. But it is 'happy' in a new way. For a start, it is characterised by an 'air of confusion' owing to the accumulating objects belonging to the lively children. The originals of the ancestral portraits would have been 'astonished' at the general 'overthrow of all order and neatness'. So surmises Anne. But, again, though these were characteristics of Fanny's Portsmouth home, the Great House is in no way another version of that horrific non-home. The tone of the description is worth noting with some care:

> The Musgroves, like their house, were in a state of alteration, perhaps of improvement. The father and mother were in the old English style and the young people in the new. Mr and Mrs Musgrove were a very good sort of people; friendly and hospitable, not much educated, and not at all elegant. Their children had more modern minds and manners ... and were now, like thousands of other young ladies, living to be fashionable, happy, and merry. Their dress had every advantage, their faces were rather pretty, their spirits extremely good, their manners unembarrassed and pleasant; they were of consequence at home, and favourites abroad.

Alteration, *perhaps of improvement*: the qualification is not barbed. There is no biting irony, no malice in the text. Jane Austen is genuinely open and uncommitted. The gay hedonism of the children is not seen as dangerous or disruptive. The older generation lack education and elegance. Once that would have been a serious defect in Jane Austen's eyes. Now it doesn't matter. Because other values, such as friendship and hospitality, are coming to seem more important. 'There is so little real friendship in the world!' laments poor

Mrs Smith later in the book, and it is now becoming for Jane Austen a cardinal virtue. The children's 'modern minds and manners' are not mocked. They may be somewhat giddy, perhaps a little shallow or frivolous. They are lively and good-spirited (*they* are not 'stagnant') and their 'manners' are at least 'unembarrassed and pleasant'—quite unlike the ludicrous snobbery, chilly hauteur, unpleasant seeming-politeness, and mean-spirited psuedo-etiquette of the upper classes. Jane Austen cannot whole-heartedly identify with these 'modern minds and manners', just as Anne 'would not have given up her own more elegant and cultivated mind for all their enjoyments'. But both Anne and her author can recognise their genuine happiness and applaud their 'good-humoured mutual affection'. Society—England itself—is altering, perhaps improving. Jane Austen does not take sides; she neither mocks the old style nor reprobates the new. Her stance is Anne's. But she is clearly undertaking a radical reassessment and revision of her system of values. She can be gently ironic about the domestic arrangements of the Great House, as when, later, she describes a tolerably confused and noisy scene there with everyone doing something different and contributing to a general disharmony, and comments, 'It was a fine family-piece.' But it is not Portsmouth. A new tolerance and relativism has entered Jane Austen's tone. What for Anne is a rather nerve-racking 'domestic hurricane' is for Mrs Musgrove 'a little quiet cheerfulness at home'. Jane Austen is amused but not censorious: 'Everybody has their tastes in noises as well as in other matters; and sounds are quite innoxious, or most distressing, by their sort rather than their quantity.' (Lady Russell would hear the street noises of Bath as signalling her 'winter pleasures' and would, says Jane Austen, have probably regarded them as part of 'a little quiet cheerfulness' after the deprivations of the country.) I do not believe that Jane Austen could have written that sentence at the time of *Mansfield Park*.

Having mentioned 'manners' I want to point to another major reversal or change in Jane Austen's habitual mode of assessment. We have seen how important manners were to her—as to Burke—and how crucial she made it seem to distinguish (if possible) between Lockean good manners and Chesterfield's type of good manners (alternatively, between English and 'French' manners). Again, this careful distinction—indeed the whole signifying role of manners—has become useless if not treacherously misleading. On Mr Elliot's first appearance he 'proves' by his 'propriety' that 'he was a man of exceedingly good manners'. By contrast, Admiral Croft's 'manners were not quite of the tone to suit Lady Russell'. Mr Elliot indeed serves single-handedly to undermine utterly any code of values attached to manners. 'His manners were so exactly what they ought to be, so polished, so easy, so particularly agreeable' that—as manners—Anne herself finds them as good as Wentworth's! His conversation leaves 'no doubt of his being a sensible man'. And it is not merely the cultivated appearance of manners. Lady Russell finds 'the solid ... so fully supporting the superficial' that she perceives him as an embodiment of all the virtues. 'Everything united in him.' He even seems to have 'a value for all the felicities of domestic life'. True, Anne begins to have her suspicions and reservations, and Lady Russell is capable of erroneous judgements. But nothing in Mr Elliot's manners could have prepared anyone for the revelation of the 'true' man.

> Mr Elliot is a man without heart or conscience; a designing, wary, cold-blooded being, who thinks only of himself; who, for his own interest or ease, would be guilty of any cruelty, or any treachery, that could be perpetrated without risk of his general character. He has no feeling for others. Those whom he has been the chief cause of leading into ruin, he can neglect and desert without the smallest compunction. He is totally beyond the reach of any sentiment of justice or compassion. Oh! he is black at heart, hollow and black!

Mrs Smith's description of the true Mr Elliot is never challenged or controverted. It is the most unqualified summary of unmitigated evil in all Jane Austen's work. Yet his manners are so perfect that even Anne can scarcely differentiate them from her true, beloved, Wentworth's. Anne's own manners are 'as consciously right as they were invariably gentle', but as usual, in her constancy and genuine 'invariability', she is an exception. With the vivid example of the absolute non-correlation between 'manners' and character presented by Mr Elliot we have to accept that 'good manners' in the socially accepted and prescribed sense are simply no longer of any use in estimating or inferring the inner qualities of anyone. Perhaps a new code of manners altogether is necessary—manners which, however 'incorrect' or even crude according to established social notions of decorum and propriety, do nevertheless reveal the true qualities of the inner man, or woman. Anne, and Jane Austen, find them in the rougher but sincere manners of the navy.

As I have tried to indicate, the usual sources, strongholds and tokens of social values have, in *Persuasion*, dried up, collapsed, or been eroded or travestied into meaninglessness. Even the family—which did seem to offer the possibility of a last stronghold in *Emma*—is at best a good-humoured confusion barely containing generational differences and at worst a hollow mockery or a claustrophobic prison of cohabiting egotists or a dreary vacancy. It may indeed have already 'broken up'—specifically in Anne's case, but that might be taken as a paradigm for a more general dissolution of the institution of the family. Mrs Smith seems to recognise this when she gives her opinion that 'even the smooth surface of family-union seems worth preserving, though there may be nothing durable beneath'. It would be idle to speculate whether or not this was Jane Austen's own opinion. It does indicate a felt apprehension that the 'family' was in danger of becoming an empty form, a mere name—or collective noun—when it should be the cornerstone and microcosm of society. The fate and future of 'the family' is an ongoing debate and problem in our own times. Jane Austen could already see that it was at a crisis point. We have very little to add to her diagnosis. What Jane Austen does offer as a potential source of new values, new bondings is the navy. About which now a few comments.

The specific dating of this novel—1814 and after—and its obvious significance has been mentioned. Britain has won the wars against Napoleon and primarily through her navy. Many specific references to the war—including Trafalgar—are made in the book, and indeed the whole novel is not properly comprehensible without appreciating the importance of this background. As Warren Roberts rightly states, '*Persuasion* could only have been written by someone whose life was deeply affected by the Revolutionary and Napoleonic wars' (see *Jane Austen and the French Revolution* for detailed evidence of the relationship between the novel and the wars). The 'peace' brings Captain Wentworth back to England; more generally, 'This peace will be turning all our rich Navy Officers ashore.' That many of them *were* rich—through capturing enemy ships and the like—is important, since, for example, it enables the Crofts to rent Kellynch Hall and makes Wentworth completely independent of any snobbish social disapproval (such as had separated him from Anne). Indeed, it makes him a 'somebody', since money was becoming a more powerful means of gaining social acceptance and esteem than land or even rank. But what is more important is that they bring back with them a wholly different scheme of values, and a potentially new model of an alternative society or community, alive and functioning where the traditional land society seemed to be moribund and largely 'stagnant'; a new community which, among other things, accepted wives as equals. Thus Anne delights in seeing the Crofts walk about Bath, meeting and warmly greeting their friends, and observing 'their eagerness of conversation when occasionally forming into a little knot of the navy, Mrs Croft looking as intelligent and keen as any of the officers around her'. That admiration and respect for 'a little knot of the navy' brings Jane Austen curiously close to Conrad and his sense of the hypocrisies of society on land and the values of fidelity within the ranks in the navy. (As it happens he also uses the word 'knot': 'the dark knot of seamen drifted in sunshine'—*The Nigger of the*

'*Narcissus*'.) This, if you like, is Jane Austen's ultimate displacement or shift of values in the novel: to redefine and relocate her vision of a 'possible' society in relation to that most potentially precarious of occupations engaged with the most unstable element—an unlanded and unrooted community of people committed to the sea. Hardly a stable and fixed community, since that 'knot' could be disassembled and reassembled, depleted and augmented, indeed 'tied' or 'untied', at any time and in any place. In truth, the extreme of a dispersed community, a floating, drifting, changing, population which would have seemed the antithesis of the kind of society Jane Austen was writing to secure or maintain. But by 1815 much had changed. For one thing it was the navy which—to Jane Austen's eyes—had saved England, while the ruling aristocratic class had done almost nothing. Seen in this light, the fact that at Uppercross 'there was a very general ignorance of all naval matters' is deplorable, while Sir Walter Elliot's unbelievably patronising and condescending attitude to naval officers is beneath contempt. Without the navy there quite possibly would no longer have been any society left in England. (Jane Austen must have been aware of the invasion panics.) Her transfer of allegiance and emotional investment from the English ruling classes (about whom she had clearly been growing more and more pessimistic) to the navy (which not only appealed to her patriotism but also embodied new and welcome alternative values) is doubly understandable at this point in English history. Among other things, *Persuasion* is notable for some uncharacteristically lyrical passages about the sea, which also help to give the novel its markedly different atmosphere. (Emma, we may recall, had never seen the sea, and one of her father's more significant fatuities is, 'I have been long perfectly convinced ... that the sea is very rarely of use to any body.' By this time the sea was 'of use'—of inestimable use—simply to the whole of England!) In the first description of the coast and sea at Lyme, so enchanting and beautiful in contrast to the 'melancholy looking rooms' and undistinguished buildings of the town, there is a curious sentence referring to the group 'lingering' on the seashore 'as all must linger and gaze on a first return to the sea, who ever deserve to look on it at all'. *Deserve* to look on the sea? Is this Jane Austen—or Melville? Here is a shift indeed. Not the awed and humble approach to Pemberley or Mansfield Park; but the privilege, for those who deserve it, of gazing at—the sea. Jane Austen seems to be turning her back on more than just the local inanities of a Sir Walter Elliot.

Of course the navy is on shore throughout the novel, and it is the effect they have there and the part they play in Jane Austen's redefinition and relocation of values that we must consider. At one point the enthusiastic Louisa

burst forth into raptures of admiration and delight on the
character of the navy—their friendliness, their brotherliness,
their openness, their uprightness; protesting that she was
convinced of sailors having more warmth than any other set of
men in England; that they only knew how to live, and they only
deserved to be respected and loved.

Allowing a little for her youthful hyperbole, this is in many ways—and with
moderation—the verdict of the book. Anne finds Captain Harville 'a perfect
gentleman, unaffected, warm and obliging'—it would seem that, by another
shift, only sailors can be true 'gentlemen': Mrs Harville is 'a degree less
polished' but has the 'same good feelings'. Above all, this naval group (or
knot) are sincere, hospitable, open, warm and genuinely friendly. What they
might lack in 'polish' they more than made up for in 'heart'. In any case, Jane
Austen never set great store by *mere* 'polish' and by now she clearly distrusts
it. The older values seem to have lost much of their force and degenerated
into snobbish reflexes. Where the older civilities are somewhat peremptorily
adhered to, it is often in 'an improper style'. Anne of course holds on to what
was best in the older practices and codes. She believes in 'duties', in
'prudence' in 'propriety'. If she is somewhat shy and reserved, she
appreciates the decent lack of these potentially inhibiting traits in others.
Quiet herself, she responds to 'heartiness'. She suspects Mr Elliot precisely
because he seems too controlled and good-mannered:

> Mr Elliot was rational, discreet, polished—but he was not open.
> There was never any burst of feeling, and warmth of indignation
> or delight, at the evil or good of others. This, to Anne was a
> decided imperfection. Her early impressions were incurable. She
> prized the frank, the open-hearted, the eager character beyond all
> others. Warmth and enthusiasm did captivate her still. She felt
> she could so much more depend upon the sincerity of those who
> sometimes looked or said a careless or hasty thing, than of those
> whose presence of mind never varied, whose tongue never
> slipped.

The passage speaks for itself; we remember that Emma's most significant
transgression occurs precisely because her tongue slips and she says 'a
careless and hasty thing' to Miss Bates, and to get some idea of the kind of
change in Jane Austen's values it represents just think how a Darcy or a
Knightley would appear if tested by these criteria. These are primarily the
manners of feeling, which may dispense with manners: spontaneity is always

likely to annihilate etiquette. If we want to see a 'Romantic' side to Jane Austen, it would be in such passages. In a sense Jane Austen was fortunate to have the navy to turn to. Otherwise it is something of a question whether she would not have had to have gone further afield—perhaps into socially 'dangerous' areas—to find suitable embodiments of these preferred values and characteristics.

Anne is also always 'useful', and willingly so, in anybody's home. (When Mary leaves her sick child in the care of Anne so that she can go to a dinner party, her excuse is 'I am of no use at home—am I?' It is the literal truth. In fact she is 'no use' anywhere. In this, she is not alone in the book.) When Anne speaks up for the navy—'The navy, I think, who have done so much for us, have at least an equal claim with any other set of men, for all the comforts and all the privileges which any home can give. Sailors work hard enough for their comforts, we must all allow'—Sir Walter speaks disparagingly of them as a class and merely allows that 'the profession has its utility'. But 'utility' is becoming a very positive word in this book. When someone is sick, Anne is glad to know herself 'to be of the first utility'. Whether or not there is some influence of Bentham here it is impossible to say. But it is clear that for Jane Austen 'utility' was becoming a word of approval. We must allow, for instance, that Sir Walter and his ilk have no 'utility' whatsoever. 'Utility' is something which Anne has in common with the navy. All the more appropriate that she should find her true home here at last. Of course, there is already an example of a 'useful' woman happily integrated into the 'little knot of the navy'—Mrs Croft. From the start we gather that she is no 'lady' of idleness leaving the 'real' world to men. She is in fact better at business than her husband. 'A very well-spoken, genteel, shrewd lady, she seemed to be ... [she] asked more questions about the house, the terms, and taxes than the admiral himself, and seemed more conversant with business.' Thus Mr Shepherd. When Anne meets Mrs Croft we are given the description of effectively a new kind of woman in Jane Austen's world. Quite outside any structure of dominance and deference, she seems to belong to no class at all. She is both inseparable from her husband—does all that may become a man—sharing all his travels; and also strongly independent—and still very much a woman. If she seems 'rougher' than many Jane Austen heroines, she is also in many not unadmirable ways tougher. Anne is not (yet!) like Mrs Croft. But she admires her.

> Mrs Croft, though neither tall nor fat, had a squareness, uprightness and vigour of form, which gave importance to her person. She had bright dark eyes, good teeth, and altogether an agreeable face; though her reddened and weather-beaten

complexion, the consequence of her having been almost as much
at sea as her husband, made her seem to have lived some years
longer in the world than her eight and thirty. Her manners were
open, easy, and decided, like one who had no distrust of herself,
and no doubts of what to do; without any approach to coarseness,
however, or any want of good humour.

Anne is 'pleased' with her, and so are we. So, obviously, was Jane Austen—
and in that depiction of Mrs Croft she is offering a new model of a new kind
of woman, scarcely imaginable in any of her previous novels. (One odd note:
she is childless. But then Jane Austen never does actually *show* us a good
mother. I think we must infer from this what we choose.)

A key area of the debate concerning old and new values concerns
resolution and wilfulness. A central problem here hinges on Anne's early
'yielding' to the negative persuasion of Lady Russell, which effectively
involved her suppressing the love she felt for Wentworth and preventing a
marriage both of them desired. Was she wrong? Did she show insufficient
resolution and belief in her own instinct and desires? We shall leave a final
adjudication until later, but her behaviour in fact poses a problem which
reverberates through the book. For instance, in talking to Louisa (who boasts
that she is not so 'easily persuaded' and derides 'nonsensical complaisance')
Wentworth praises her for her 'character of decision and firmness' and
speaks with understandable bitterness against the opposite: 'It is the worst
evil of too yielding and indecisive a character, that no influence, over it can
be depended on.... Everybody may sway it; let those who would be happy be
firm.' And to emphasise his point he picks up a hazel nut—one of the rare
emblematic aids to discourse in Jane Austen!—praising its exemplary
enduring strength and hardness, and asserting, rather foolishly, that its
'happiness' is a function of its unpunctured 'firmness'. A 'nutty' happiness
indeed, but not perhaps a very helpful model for a young—and virgin—
woman! Is this fair to Anne? Was she too easily 'swayed'—too indecisive and
lacking in firmness? It is at least something of a question. But Louisa's
'decision and firmness' reveal themselves most graphically on the Cobb. We
have been told that Louisa has the habit of 'doing as she liked' and believed
in 'the merit in maintaining her own way' (against 'parental wishes or
advice') and is quick to advance 'heedless schemes'. On the Cobb she also
wants her own way: this times it involves jumping from the steps into the
arms of Wentworth. Enjoying the sensation, she expresses a wish and an
intention to do it again. Wentworth 'reasoned' against it, but 'in vain': she
smiled and said, 'I am determined I will.' And 'maintaining her own way' she
jumps—too precipitously ('heedlessly'?)—and as everyone knows she falls

and suffers a dangerous concussion. There lies the 'nut' of 'decision and firmness'! She indeed would not 'yield' to any 'persuasion', however 'rational'—and she will not be 'swayed'. But how 'meritorious' or 'admirable' is that now? Is such a character trait of determined wilfulness a virtue or a rashness? Is it a real strength or an egotistical rashness (she not only causes damage to herself but great anguish and a lot of trouble to other people)? Is that jumping girl a finer character than the sedate and self-effacing—and apparently 'persuadable'—Anne? We might remember that another of the Musgrove children sustains a 'bad fall': young Charles falls and dislocates his collarbone in chapter 7. On that occasion 'Anne had every thing to do at once', since Mary retires into useless hysterics, and all the duties and responsibilities devolve on Anne. As, of course, they do after Louisa's accident on the Cobb. There even Wentworth reveals an uncharacteristic sense of helplessness: 'Is there no one to help me?' These are unusual words from a Jane Austen hero. He is not omnicompetent and once again all eyes turn to Anne for advice and direction. She effectively has to help and advise them all. These modern youngsters are attractive and lively, and perhaps engagingly adventurous and independent in their wilful heedlessness of external constraints—or advice. The Musgrove girls are 'wild for dancing', 'wild to see Lyme'—'wild' is one of their favourite words and, as a word, harmless enough as a youthful hyperbole (as for a more recent young generation everything was 'fabulous', 'fantastic', and so on). But are they perhaps in fact too wild? After all, Elizabeth Elliot is also accustomed to 'go her own way' and there is nothing at all attractive about her ice-cold selfishness. After the Cobb incident Anne might well wonder whether

> it ever occurred to him [Wentworth] now, to question the justness of his own previous opinion as to the universal felicity and advantage of firmness of character; and whether it might not strike him that, like all other qualities of the mind, it should have its proportions and limits. She thought it could scarcely escape him to feel, that a persuadable temper might sometimes be as much in favour of happiness, as a very resolute character.

Of course she is right. Louisa, in 'jumping' at will, shows herself to have a very 'yielding' character, but she yields to her own whims and caprices. At least Anne thought that she was 'rationally' persuaded to yield to Lady Russell. It comes back to the problem of authority in a period of change when all traditional sources of authority are in doubt, if not disqualified or defunct. Whose persuasion or advice should one—anyone—listen to? When Wentworth cries for help he is articulating a larger need. In the event, in this novel it is the apparently yielding but actually steadfast Anne who becomes the authority to whom others turn. Wentworth's 'nut' lies sufficiently crushed to make us (and him) realise that she would be in no way an appropriate wife for him. He says he wants 'A strong mind, with sweetness of manner' in any wife he chooses. There is of course only one candidate. Anne is not a 'nut'—that visual image for the ideal wife was curiously infelicitous. For nuts are either totally hard or totally smashed (I suppose they can also go rotten). Anne's strength of character is peculiarly human. Which means that it must combine flexibility and firmness, the concessionary and the adamant, the rights of self with the obligations of selflessness, in a complex, ever-demanding way. Wentworth is right in seeking for an alliance of strength and sweetness (the lion and the honeycomb). He is only wrong temporarily—and perhaps understandably— in not seeing that that ideal admixture is only to be found in one woman (in this novel). Anne. Only Anne.

How Anne will discover Wentworth's true state of feelings, how she will be able to convey her still 'unyielding' love for him, raises a problem familiar in Jane Austen's work: namely, that of private communication in a predominantly public world in which various taboos on certain forms of direct address between the sexes are still operative. It is again a problem of hermeneutics. 'Now, how were his sentiments to be read?' After his return they are 'repeatedly in the same circle', but that offers as many chances for misreadings (on both sides) as it does opportunities for reliable interpretation. People talk too little or too much. (As when Anne finds herself the unwilling repository of the 'secrets of the complaints of each house'. Regarded as nothing herself, a permanently available pair of hands or ears, she is 'treated with too much confidence by all parties'. On the other hand, the one man she wants to hear most from says least. She cannot control these asymmetries and excesses or shortfallings of communication.) Mary, inevitably, provides a constant example of lack of all communicative tact—as when she asks Anne to tell their father they have seen Mr Elliot. To Anne 'it was just the circumstance which she considered as not merely unnecessary to be communicated, but as what ought to be suppressed'. For Jane Austen the imperatives of verbal repression were as important as the obligations of communication: social harmony depends on getting the balance right. Needless to say, in the world of *Persuasion* most people have lost that tact. Anne often has to 'smother' her own feelings and preoccupations, realising that they are of little or no interest to her interlocutors. She knows what it is to have to 'converse' without 'communicating'. She also knows what it is like to talk without being heard. 'They could not listen to her description of him. They were describing him themselves.' But of course her main concern is somehow to communicate with Wentworth and this in fact provides the climax of the book. At the concert near the end she is sure of his feelings and desperate to communicate hers. But she cannot contrive the necessary propinquity. As other Jane Austen women do, she has recourse to the eye—trying to catch Wentworth's when she is prevented from speaking to him: 'she was so surrounded and shut in: but she would rather have caught his eye'. But she is trapped by the unwelcome attentions of Mr Elliot and the general 'nothing-saying amongst the party'. How to find or create a place or position which would make 'something-saying' possible is again a recurrent problem for Jane Austen's heroines. Interestingly, she manages to choose a seat on the bench with a 'vacant space' next to her. Wentworth nearly takes it, but Mr Elliot breaks in. Here is a small parabolic tableau of the problem for a woman. She can create a space for the man but cannot invite him to take it. Man has to initiate, and if there is any hesitation the wrong (and more assertive) male may take advantage of that space. Mr Elliot does this—and a jealous Wentworth takes his departure. Anne still has her problem: 'How was the truth to reach him? How, in all the peculiar disadvantages of their respective situations, would he ever learn her real sentiments?'

So crucial is this problem that Jane Austen revised her first—excessively simple—resolution of it into two longer chapters which dramatise in detail the strategies of indirection to which the lovers have recourse. This revision (chapters 22 and 23) is of great subtlety and importance and is worth some particular examination and comment. In the first version Admiral Croft crudely contrives to leave them alone in his house and very quickly everything is cleared up. There is 'a hand taken and pressed; and "Anne, my own dear Anne!" bursting forth in the fulness of exquisite feeling,—and all suspense and indecision were over. They were reunited.' This is summary to a degree and a very lame solution to a problem which has been growing in importance until it becomes *the* main problem in the book. The revised and substituted chapters do not merely prolong the suspense and defer narrative gratification through gratuitous complication of plot: they comprise an infinitely richer and more searching examination of the whole problem of communication between man and woman.

The revised chapters add much. We learn more of the 'odious insincerity' of Mr Elliot and his dubious connection with that other plotting 'hypocrite', Mrs Clay, whose name is suggestive enough of a weak vessel and whose 'freckles' not only indicate a flawed and 'spotted' moral interior but may indeed suggest the remnants or traces of syphilis. (In a very interesting letter to *The Times Literary Supplement* on 7 October 1983, Nora Crook points out that 'Gowland's Lotion', which Sir Walter recommends to Anne 'on the strength of its supposed benefits to Mrs Clay's freckles', contained 'corrosive sublimate of mercury', which 'had a particular connection with the old-fashioned treatment of syphilis'. Mrs Crook produces evidence from contemporary journals such as *Reece's Gazette of Health* and, while admirably tentative in drawing any conclusions, rightly points out that 'so few are references to actual trade-names in Austen that one feels that this one must have had some sort of function other than "realism"'. I agree completely and feel surer than she does—though on no more evidence—that a hint of syphilis must be intended. After all, Mrs Clay ends up in London as Mr Elliot's mistress and thus with a status little better than that of a prostitute. The fact that she was a welcome intimate of Sir Walter's and Elizabeth's, in preference to Anne, not only confirms the worst we feel about their utterly corrupted judgement: it also suggests the presence of the most ruinous sexual disease among the upper classes. She is a fitting 'partner' for the totally corrupt Mr Elliot—who is also the heir of Kellynch Hall. A fine end to be inscribed in that volume chronicling the 'history and rise of the ancient and respectable family'!) We learn that Louisa is 'recovered' but 'altered' (perhaps improved?). There is no 'running or jumping about, no laughing or dancing'. Her newly acquired 'stillness' is not the result of achieved moral poise and undistractability—the stillness which Jane Austen admired—but the timorous cowering of a nervous wreck.

But centrally there is the extended problem of how Anne can communicate with Wentworth. It is he now who is acting under an 'unfortunate persuasion': namely, that she loves Mr Elliot. In the crowded hotel scene 'he did not seem to want to be near enough for conversation' and the 'circumstances' only expose them to 'inadvertencies and misconstructions of the most mischievous kind'. Eyes and glances—surreptitious, anxious, inquiring—are again active. More venturesomely (or desperately) Anne speaks words to others which are meant obliquely for Wentworth—as when she loudly proclaims her complete lack of interest in a party being organised for the theatre which would include Mr Elliot. She trembles as she speaks, 'conscious that her words were listened to, and daring not even to try to observe their effect'. When they do have to exchange social conversation, Anne has recourse to another strategy. Referring to trivia—whether she still enjoys card games—Anne uses the occasion to transmit a second meta-message by emphasising that 'I am not yet so much changed', hoping that the generalising response will not be lost on Wentworth—though she still fears 'she hardly knew what misconstructions'. It is indeed a tricky and dangerous game when a lifetime's happiness depends on the outcome. We may wonder at the need for all these tormenting ploys of indirection. Why cannot Anne be open and, direct—qualities she admires in other people? The contrast is indeed made in the next chapter when Mrs

Musgrove is talking. Her talk is marked by 'open-hearted communication', but it is all concerned with personal 'minutiae' and Anne feels that 'she did not belong to the conversation'. The obstacle—effectively a double-bind—seems to be that you cannot speak 'openly' and 'directly' about such important matters as your feelings of love, *to* the person you love, until you have achieved a certain intimacy (tantamount to engagement) which *then* permits such open talk. But how do you ever manage to get intimate enough to be intimate, as it were? I don't think this is just a matter of tiresome, overdelicate etiquette or the repressive interdictions of propriety. It certainly has something to do with true modesty. More generally I think it dramatises the delicacy and difficulty of identifying and establishing the right sexual partner. That social conditions and codes made this particularly difficult in Jane Austen's period we can hardly doubt. But one feels that there is some deeper correlation between the delicacy of the approach and the value and quality of the ensuing union. We have gained much by our less inhibited and less formalised ways of achieving sexual and marital *rapprochements*. Arguably our loss has been no less great.

Be that as it may, we now approach the actual moment of full communication. How it is achieved—the context, the method—could hardly be more interesting. The general talk has become meaningless to Anne—'only a buzz of words in her ear'. She must look for (and send) the right signal in the noise. Then Captain Harville approaches Anne with a 'small miniature painting'. It is a portrait of Captain Benwick which was commissioned for Captain Harville's dead sister, Fanny. Benwick now wants it reset to give to Louisa, whom he is to marry. Harville finds the commission too painful and Wentworth has gallantly agreed to take care of it. He is seated nearby—'writing about it now', as Harville explains. Harville almost tearfully muses that 'Fanny ... would not have forgotten him so soon' and there ensues that debate about the relative constancy of men and women in their love. Anne argues that women do not forget so soon. 'We cannot help ourselves. We live at home, quiet, confined, and our feelings prey upon us. You are forced upon exertion ... continual occupation and change soon weaken impressions.' Then follows a famous exchange in which Harville has recourse to the evidence and authority of literature—writing:

> But let me observe that all histories are against you, all stories, prose and verse. If I had such a memory as Benwick, I could bring you fifty quotations in a moment on my side the argument, and I do not think I ever opened a book in my life which had not something to say upon women's inconstancy.... But perhaps you will say, these are all written by men.

Anne replies,

> 'Perhaps I shall.—Yes, yes, if you please, no reference to examples in books. Men have had every advantage of us in telling their own story. Education has been theirs in so much higher a degree; the pen has been in their hands. I will not allow books to prove any thing.'
>
> 'But how shall we prove any thing?'
>
> 'We never shall.'

Painting, writing, speech. The portrait is a fixed representation or 'quotation' of the man which he can dispatch to different women. The man changes in his affections; the portrait remains 'constant'. In this it is precisely a misrepresentation—an ideal image of the man which leaves all his emotional changeableness out. However accurate as to physiognomy, it is untrue to life. It is a detached token which can be sent through intermediaries—Harville, Wentworth—to now this woman, now that. And potentially any other. It is in all respects the opposite of an unmediated confrontation of, and communication between, a living man and a living woman. In this the portrait comes dangerously close to being like a piece of money, a coin of fixed, arbitrary 'value' which can circulate through different hands and purchase any object to be obtained at the price on the coin. There need be no relationship between the purchaser and the object. Indeed, the whole mode of transaction is marked by separation and impersonality. The model for this kind of 'relationship' is ultimately the open market. This is not to impugn the feelings of reciprocity which may have gone into the 'relationship' of Benwick, but only to point out that it is *excessively* mediated. Benwick is a man who lives in and by books. He woos and wins Louisa by quotations and a portrait (as he did Fanny and, we feel, would have tried to do with Anne). They are signs which are precisely *not* his own, not himself. They are substitutions for an essential absence—emotional if not ontological. Anne has no access to totally unmediated communication, but she must avoid the kind of mediation briefly but tellingly here alluded to. And so must Wentworth. Benwick's books and Harville's allusion to his 'quotations' might remind us that at the start of *this* book Anne was effectively written *out* of meaningful life because she was not written *in* to Sir Walter's 'book of books'. She has suffered from male 'writing' since indeed 'the pen has been in their hands'— starting with the originating male authority, the father. Her argument has of course a general and very important validity, relevant to the condition of all women in her—and our—society. But one crucial little incident gives it a vividly local and specific point.

As she is arguing with Harville—and of course her words have a double target and dual purpose, as she hopes that the nearby Wentworth, seated and writing, will hear them and detect the personal message contained in the general statements—a 'slight noise' draws their attention to Wentworth. 'It was nothing more than that his pen had fallen down.' Nothing more—in many ways it is the most quietly dramatic and loaded incident on the book. The pen may, generally speaking, be in 'their hands'; but at this crucial moment the pen—a specific one—had dropped from *his*—specific—hand. However unintentionally, however momentarily, he is disproving the generalisation which Anne is enunciating. He is, perhaps by a 'slip', excepting himself from—revealing himself as an exception to—the rule. We tend to read a lot of significance into 'slips' now, but, at no matter what level of conscious or unconscious intention, Wentworth's 'slip' in dropping the pen at that moment is perhaps the most important signal—or unvoiced communication—in his entire relationship with Anne. I am not concerned with possible phallic interpretations of 'the pen': literalness is quite powerful enough here. No single definitive reading of the incident is either possible or desirable. But we can say at least this: Wentworth at this critical moment has, however inadvertently, dropped (let go of, lost his grip on) that instrument which is at once a tool and a symbol of men's dominance over women; the means by which they rule women's destinies, literally *write* (through inscription, prescription, proscription) their lives. It is as if he is open to a more equal (unscripted) relationship in which the old patterns of dominance and deference are abandoned, deleted—dropped. Benwick quotes from already written books; Sir Walter wrote in his book according to an ancient and now non-functional scriptural tradition (his 'book of books' is only a bible for himself—a mere mirror instead of the authorising and authoritative sacred text). Wentworth was writing a commission for another person—he drops the pen and, after that crucial lacuna or interruption, when he picks it up again it is to 'speak' to Anne. Under the 'public' letter he writes for Harville and Benwick he now writes a 'private' letter—like a subtext—to Anne, which he hides under scattered paper. He goes out—formally—with Harville, and returning under false pretences (left gloves), furtively delivers the hidden—but 'true'—letter to Anne. Significantly the writing is 'hardly legible': we may guess that the impersonal 'public' letter was in a perfect hand. The hidden letter was indeed not really written, but rather 'spoken'. As he writes in it, 'I must speak to you by such means as are within my reach.' It is the desperate calligraphy of the heart—written under pressure and social constraints. No wonder it is 'hardly legible'. For this speech-writing is not done according to prescribed formulae or convention: it is an 'exceptional' writing which seeks to find a way through all the restraining and silencing rules and codes to communicate directly to the chosen woman. It attempts the apparently impossible—mediated im-mediacy. Like love. There is no need here to reproduce the contents of that letter-under-the-letter. With its delivery and reading the 'union' is assured. But two final points about it. Anne realises that, 'while supposed to be writing only to Captain Benwick, he had been also addressing her'. No doubt some of this final drama (or game) can be traced to the specific difficulties of intersexual communication in Jane Austen's society. But the episode points up and dramatises a larger truth. All 'writing' or communication is potentially double (at least esoteric and esoteric, to go no further: there may always be another message in—under—the ostensible message); we can 'address' more than one person at the same time, and likewise be 'addressed' by messages not apparently meant for us. Indeed, one might say that the addresser and the addressee of the letter—all 'letters'—are potentially indeterminate and plural. There is ultimately no single, definitively correct 'address'. The problems and difficulties which Anne and Wentworth have to negotiate are not a function of early nineteenth-century English society. They are inherent in language and communication itself. How important is this rather singular little parlour 'game'? Well—'On the contents of that letter depended all which this world could do for her!' Life, and all that it might offer, can indeed depend on 'the letter'. It is a final joke that informs us that, as Wentworth is now rich enough to be 'accepted' as a husband for Anne by her father, it 'enabled Sir Walter at last to prepare his pen with a very good grace for the insertion of the marriage in the volume of honour.' It is of course a dead volume by now and the paternal penis as irrelevant as it is powerless. Anne and Wentworth will 'write' their own marriage elsewhere, in a new book, in their own hands. Of course they will never 'prove' anything by the book, any book. When it comes to matters of love we can never *prove* anything—by writing, or speaking, or painting. And we never shall. When Othello asks Iago for 'ocular proof' of Desdemona's infidelity, he is lost. Her honour is 'an essence that's not seen'. You may fake 'proof' of infidelity (nothing easier for an Iago) and misread signs (and books) as evidence of inconstancy. But you cannot *prove* love—any more than you can 'see' honour or constancy. You must finally trust beyond the available evidence. The proof of the loving can only be in the living.

Before leaving the matter of language and communication in this novel, I want to draw attention to a rather surprising notion which Jane Austen inserts into Anne's thoughts while she is listening to another social conversation which combines the vacuous and the hyperbolic. 'Allowances, large allowances, she knew, must be made for the ideas of those who spoke. She heard it all under embellishment. All that sounded extravagant or irrational in the progress of the reconciliation might have *no origin but in the language of the relators*' (emphasis added). Of course social conversation can lie and fabricate—nothing unusual in such an observation. But Anne's thought is potentially more radical. Allow that language 'embellishes'; but what if *all* that people talk about has 'no origin but in the language of the relators'? Put it another way: language may be the origin of all that people relate. It is perhaps not such a new idea for us, but, coming out of the context in which Jane Austen was writing, the hint (it is perhaps no more) that language itself might be the origin of what we talk about—i.e. that language is the origin of what we think of as reality—is here startling. Language thus becomes capable of creating its own referents *and* referends—an awesomely autonomous, generative, and 'originating' power. If in fact we live primarily in the world we speak, then we should be careful indeed about the words we use. Jane Austen herself exemplifies that indispensable vigilance and scrupulousness.

What follows the final achieving of clarification and communication between Anne and Wentworth is characteristically summary. They stroll along a 'retired gravel-walk' and there can indulge their 'private rapture' in 'public view'. As usual Jane Austen does not pursue them into their private passional discourse. Whether we ascribe this to ignorance, repression or delicacy hardly matters. Jane Austen has shown us all that is essential to her novel; now she maintains a tactful distance.

> There they exchanged again those feelings and those promises which had once before seemed to secure every thing, but which had been followed by so many, many years of division and estrangement. There they returned again into the past more exquisitely happy, perhaps, in their re-union, than when it had been first projected....

And so on. There they are oblivious of the passing groups—'sauntering politicians, bustling house-keepers, flirting girls, nursery-maids and children'. The 'world' is temporarily lost, and well lost. They have made 'a separate peace'. But we should add a few words about Anne and her marriage. In some respects she is like Fanny Price, with her 'still' virtues, her essential loneliness, her general desire 'not to be in the way of any body'; her pleasure is only to be 'unobserved', her plight to be generally overlooked. She is glad just to do her duty and to be 'useful', however unappreciated. In her apparent weakness she is the real source of strength. But there is a crucial difference, related to the larger difference between the two worlds of the novels. At one point in the confusion of Uppercross, we are told of an

insuperable problem: 'How was Anne to set all these matters to rights?'
Fanny Price does effectively 'set to rights' all the wrongs, neglects, and
partial deteriorations of Mansfield Park—which becomes something of a
microcosm of society as it should be and might be. Anne's healing efforts are
necessarily more local and limited in the scattered and diffused world of
Persuasion. She would have put her father's house 'to rights' but is not allowed
to. She can nurse a sick child here, tend a wounded girl there, sympathise
with a grieving bereft lover, provide concrete help when Wentworth cries out
for it (a hint of a possible new equality there). But society is too far gone in
disarray to be 'put to rights' by an exemplary heroine. Fanny Price's marriage
to Edmund symbolises and seals the restoration and renewal of a whole social
order and structure. Anne's marriage to Wentworth signifies nothing larger
than their own refound and reconstituted happiness in love. Their 're-union'
is not a sign of any larger re-established harmony. To borrow that enigmatic
and resonant phrase of Jay Gatsby's, it is 'just personal'.

Their marriage is not grounded in property—as all the previous
concluding marriages in Jane Austen are. Mary—of course—gloats that Anne
'had no Uppercross-hall before her, no landed estate, no headship of a
family'. And indeed it is one of Anne's regrets that she has 'no relations to
bestow' on Wentworth, 'no family to receive and estimate him properly'. In
fact it is he who offers a family—the new 'family' of the navy. She brings to
him only her 'undistracted heart', in Henry James's memorable phrase. The
marriage itself does not portend an endless stability: there will always be 'the
dread of a future war'. She has to 'pay' for her marital happiness in a way
unknown to any previous Jane Austen heroine. Thus the conclusion: 'She
gloried in being a sailor's wife, but she must pay the tax of quick alarm for
belonging to that profession, which is, if possible, more distinguished in its
domestic virtues than in its national importance.' (Contrast the conclusion of
Mansfield Park and Fanny's return to the 'paternal abode' of Mansfield, which
formerly 'Fanny had been unable to approach but with some painful
sensation of restraint and alarm' but which 'soon grew as dear to her heart,
and as thoroughly perfect in her eyes as every thing else within the view and
patronage of Mansfield Park, had long been'. Her 'alarm' was definite but is
in the past, replaced by an extended future of assured happiness and
'perfection'. Anne's 'alarm' is indefinite and in the future—an integral part of
her happy marriage, out of an old society and into a new one, far away from
the abandoned 'paternal abode', with nothing assured except her joy in her
reciprocated love.) The final words of *Persuasion* effectively point to that
radical redefinition and relocation of values which marks the whole novel.
Established society and domesticity are now, as we say, 'all at sea'—

metaphorically (they are in a state of chronic confusion, chaotic flux) but also literally. For the new social and domestic virtues are now to be found, indeed, 'at sea'—for those 'who ever deserve to look on it at all'.

(To base a marriage almost exclusively on feelings, no matter how tested and proved those feelings may be, inevitably entails a *new* kind of 'risk'. It is more than apt that this new kind of model for a more personal society, in which actions come 'from the heart', is situated both metaphorically and actually on the sea—traditionally regarded as 'the unstable element'. Even though Anne and Wentworth are models of emotional stability and constancy, the emotions are by nature inherently potentially unstable, and, without the reinforcement of some forms— formalities—and conventions, any society based on feelings must be precarious and in danger of ensuring its own impermanence. In founding a possible new society on the sea, even metaphorically, Jane Austen was engaging deliberately in what is almost a contradiction of terms. It is some measure of her disenchantment with 'landed' society that she felt prepared, or compelled, to take that risk.)

Was Anne right to give in to the 'persuasion' of Lady Russell? There is rich ambiguity or hesitation here, and phrases such as 'the fair interference of friendship' in their poised ambivalence indicate that Jane Austen knew all about the multiple motivations which are at work in the impulse to exert some apparently beneficent control over a person in a weaker position. There is, perhaps, no point at which you can clearly distinguish persuasion from constraint or constraint from coercion. It is something of a blur, a confusion if you will—and it is out of just that confusion that Anne the nobody has somehow to come to clarification and remake her life. In discussing the point with Wentworth at the end of the book, when they are privately conversing while 'apparently occupied in admiring a fine display of greenhouse plants' (a somewhat more auspicious adjunct to a discussion of love than 'nuts'!), Anne defends her decision without wholly exculpating Lady Russell:

> I must believe that I was right, much as I suffered from it, that I was perfectly right in being guided by the friend whom you will love better than you do now. To me, she was in the place of a parent. Do not mistake me, however. I am not saying that she did not err in her advice. It was, perhaps, one of those cases in which advice is good or bad only as the event decided; and for myself, I certainly never should, in any circumstance of tolerable similarity, give such advice.

Lady Russell is by no means one of Jane Austen's malign characters. On the contrary she is a 'benevolent, charitable, good woman, and capable of strong attachments'. She is genuinely fond of Anne and truly appreciates all her qualities and virtues. Anne loves her to the end. She is indeed regarded by all who know her as a person of 'the greatest influence with every body', and that 'influence' is often wisely employed and invariably with disinterested concern for what is right or best. If she has a fault, it is not a kind of masked will-to-power masquerading as good advice. But 'she had prejudices on the side of ancestry ... a value for rank and consequence, which blinded her a little to the faults of those who possessed them'. In a word, she favours the old order of society and cannot always see its derelictions and delinquencies. She is not—as she insists—a 'match-maker', though we can see her as a 'match-marrer' when it comes to not appreciating the reality and value of Anne's and Wentworth's love for each other. But her real importance and significance is that, for Anne, 'she was in the place of a parent'—a surrogate mother. This brings me back to the central problem of the lack of any reliable properly constituted authority in the book. Effectively Lady Russell fills—and is allowed to fill—an authority vacuum. As far as my memory and my notes go, I think I am right in saying that that key word is only once applied to any character in the book, and that is Lady Russell. When Wentworth is explaining to Anne that he could only think of her as 'one who had yielded', who had been 'influenced by any one rather than by me', he is referring to his apprehensions about the persuasive power which Lady Russell might still be exerting over Anne: 'I had no reason to believe her of less *authority* now' (emphasis added). As Anne explains, she thought she was yielding to 'duty', and, while she now admits she was wrong, she makes the point that she was yielding to 'persuasion exerted on the side of safety, not of risk'. Perhaps she was too cautious, but she learnt her lesson and she is justified, in the event, when Wentworth comes to see where 'risk' can lead to—as in Louisa's foolish jump. (Emma, in her capricious wilfulness, often abuses her powers of 'persuasion': for example, in relation to Harriet's 'rejection' of the perfectly suitable Robert Martin—as Knightley angrily accuses her, 'You persuaded her to refuse him'; and in relation to herself, as when she excuses herself for her 'deficiency' in not visiting the Bateses by 'the persuasion of its being very disagreeable—a waste of time—tiresome women'—a perverse act of self-persuasion which, at 'heart', she herself knows to be a culpable rationalisation for a more selfishly and snobbishly motivated disinclination and neglect.)

Wentworth had to learn his own lesson, 'to distinguish between the steadiness of principle and the obstinacy of self-will, between the darings of heedlessness and the resolution of a collected mind'. The old order was wrong; but Louisa's reaction is not the right one—self-destructive rather than reconstructive. Lady Russell's 'authority' was capable of error, but with no other reliable authority available in this society-without-a-centre (as in Anne's family-without-parental-guidance), it seemed to Anne—as to others—the only reliable substitute. But it was a substitute. Lady Russell is *not* Anne's mother and she is not a true central authority in society. And it is the lesson that *she* has to learn that is as important as any in the book. It is a lesson which centres on her radically incorrect appraisals of the respective worth of Mr Elliot and Wentworth:

> She must learn to *feel* that she had been mistaken with regard to both; that she had been unfairly influenced by appearances in each; that because Captain Wentworth's *manners* had not suited her own ideas, she had been too quick in suspecting them to indicate a character of dangerous impetuosity; and that because Mr Elliot's manners had precisely pleased her in their *propriety* and *correctness*, their general *politeness* and suavity, she had been too quick in receiving them as the certain result of the most correct opinions and well regulated mind. There was nothing less for Lady Russell to do, than to admit that she had been pretty completely wrong and to take up a new set of opinions and of hopes. (Emphasis added)

There is no more important passage in the novel. We remember that Anne had been 'prudent' (an old and basic Jane Austen value) but had had to learn 'romance'. Similarly Lady Russell will have to learn to reeducate her 'feelings' when judging people and not rely on the once-reliable signs of 'propriety' and 'correctness', 'manners' and 'politeness'. In a changing society a more emotional, 'romantic' personal code is emerging as both desirable and necessary—with a proper appreciation of the difference between 'spontaneity' and 'impetuousness', between the mere rashness of 'risk' and the securely grounded independence of individual feelings, whether or not these seem to be approved and ratified by the old standards and codes of society. The lesson that Lady Russell has to learn is not in itself revolutionary or subversive, but it does represent a radical assessment—and turning away from—many of the old values. I have said that Anne was initially 'in between', an uncertain status both socially and ontologically. The novel shows that English society is similarly 'in between': in between an old social order in a state of decline and desuetude, and some new 'modern' society of as yet uncertain values, hierarchies and principles. It may precipitately 'jump' to its own destruction and wreckage (like Louisa). It may, though it is a slim hope, reconstitute itself and its values as Anne—and 'only Anne'—has learnt to do with Wentworth. Meanwhile the message within the message of the book, the not-so-hidden 'letter' under the text of the story, reads like this: 'There was nothing less for English society to do, than to admit that it had been pretty completely wrong, and to take up a new set of opinions and hopes.'

CLAUDIA L. JOHNSON

Persuasion: *The "Unfeudal Tone of the Present Day"*

*P*ersuasion has always signified more than what it singly comprises: its two slender volumes have been made to bear the imprint of Austen's entire career. Whereas *Pride and Prejudice* and *Emma* can be and most often are discussed without reference to Austen's other works, *Persuasion* is above all else the last novel, the apparent conclusion that determines the shape of everything that has come before. The critical tradition has designated *Persuasion* the "autumnal" novel, and this adjective brings with it a parcel of value-laden and often quite pedestrian assumptions about both the course of Austen's career and the course of literary history in general. Wistful and romantically unfulfilled in the twilight of her life, so the argument goes, the author grows tenderer on romantic subjects she had disparaged in the confidence and severity of her youth; with her own opening out onto a new world of emotion, eighteenth-century "objectivity" yields to nineteenth-century "subjectivity"; the assured, not to say simple-minded, gives way to the ambiguous and complex.[1] The underlying assumption that Anne's autumn and Austen's are complementary—in other words, that *Persuasion*, like the other novels, indeed like all novels by women, is the author's own love story, composed with little or no aesthetic distance—is of course teeming with fallacies, not the least glaring of which in this particular case are those which result from the imposition of specious teleology. *Persuasion*

From *Jane Austen: Women, Politics and the Novel.* © 1988 by The University of Chicago.

will not look so unequivocally like Austen's last and most mature word about love and the changing world before death stopped her lips if we recollect that *Sanditon*, which recapitulates the raucous energy and renews the literary debates characteristic of Austen's earliest work, followed so closely on its heels. Austen, unlike her latter-day readers, did not have the benefit of knowing that her impending death would be imparting a gently resigned, autumnal melancholy to all her observations. Many prominent, yet seldom-discussed, elements of *Persuasion* call the youthful *Sense and Sensibility* to mind—the apparently unfeeling allusion to Mrs. Musgrove's "fat sighings," the conventionalized villainy of William Elliot and the conspicuously artificial means of disclosing it, the overtness of its sarcasms at the expense of silly and uninformed people. To judge them in terms of the autumnal paradigm, with which they are at odds, these features can only be dismissed as unfortunate lapses in morbid foresight.

This of course is not to say that *Persuasion* gives us nothing new, but only that it should be considered without using the benefit of hindsight to beg so many important questions. Most readers note, for example, that *Persuasion* ridicules the ruling class. This fact appears distinctive, however, only when we assume that it is a departure from the practice of the earlier novels. But surely nothing said in *Persuasion* about the Musgroves or Elliots surpasses the satire to which the Middletons, Palmers, and John Dashwoods are treated in *Sense and Sensibility*. What is different about *Persuasion* is not that it shows how the improvident landowners, proving themselves unworthy of their station, have left England poised on the brink of a new world dominated by the best and the brightest, the Royal Navy. As one historian has observed, foolish and financially embarrassed landowners are nothing new to English social history or to Austen's fiction. Eventually, Sir Walter will reassume Kellynch, and yield it in the time-honored way to his heir William Elliot, a man who, knowing how to serve "his own interest and his own enjoyment" (P 250), will doubtless not, as Sir Thomas had, lose his hold on "the situation in which Providence has placed him" (P 248).[2]

But if in *Persuasion* the landed classes have not lost their power, they have lost their prestige and their moral authority for the heroine. Whereas *Pride and Prejudice* could, with elaborately wrought qualifications and finely modulated discriminations, finally vindicate the highly controversial practice of "prejudice," Lady Russell's "prejudices on the side of ancestry" and "value for rank and consequence" (P 11) are never allowed to be anything more than amiable but groundless articulations of self-interest. Like her idea of what constitutes a "little quiet cheerfulness" (P 134, 135) or, for that matter, Admiral Croft's idea of proper decor, Lady Russell's "prejudices on the side of ancestry" are not favored with any corroborative footing in "objective" reality. As Admiral Croft puts it, "Ay, so it always is, I believe. One man's ways may be as good as another's, but we all like our own best. And so you must judge for yourself ..." (P 127). *Sense and Sensibility* makes it hard to believe that Austen ever shared Lady Russell's prejudices, yet even there she evinces a heartier tolerance for booby squires than what she somewhat wearily musters here. For all his absurdity, Sir John Middleton's bluff generosity commands some respect. But whether darting eagerly after weasels, defending the claims of eldest sons, or extolling the virtues of "good, freehold property" (P 76), Charles Musgrove has little to recommend himself. His ideas, like his activities, are tediously predictable, and his "old country family of respectability and large fortune" (P 6) has no charm: Anne never regrets her refusal to attach herself to this inoffensive, but unredeemably mediocre gentleman and the long-established kind of domestic life he represents.

Persuasion,, then, distinctively minimizes problems which had before been so momentous to the heroines. By centering her novel on a maturer heroine, of course, Austen is free to explore female independence without being obliged to explore the concomitant impertinence which always seems to accompany the self-assurance of younger heroines. The duty of filial piety, for example—Fanny Price's "great rule to apply to" (MP 436)—is nowhere dignified with the status of being at issue here. Even though her "word" has "no weight" within her family circle (P 5), Anne, like Emma, is an autonomous heroine. For this reason, to conceptualize *Persuasion*, as readers so often do, as a debate between individualism and propriety is not only to employ an opposition already curiously loaded in favor of conservative arguments, but it is also to underestimate the degree of Anne's independence from traditional, paternal authority and to misplace the emphasis of the plot.[3] Starting as early as the second chapter, for example, when we learn that she regards paying one's debts as an "indispensable duty" (P 12), Anne distances herself from an impropriety that is specifically paternal. General Tilney's wrath with Catherine is the catastrophe of *Northanger Abbey*. But the crisis in *Persuasion*—Anne's decision to break off her engagement—has little to do with Sir Walter's paternal displeasure. On the contrary, it has everything to do with the advice, not the authority, of a trusted friend, Lady Russell, to whom Anne does not owe the comparable duty of obedience. Such is Anne's filial disposition at nineteen. At twenty-eight she pays Sir Walter even less mind. While Sir Walter pursues Lady Dalrymple, Anne visits a "nobody"—Mrs. Smith—without as much as informing him, let alone seeking his permission, and once his disapproval is expressed, it is ignored without fuss. For Anne, no hard conflict between duty and inclination is implied by defying or simply ignoring her father. Indeed, it is all too easy: "Anne kept her appointment; the others kept theirs" (P 158).

Although Anne's indifference to filial propriety can show us the distance Austen has come since *Northanger Abbey*, Austen's earlier novel is nevertheless tied up with *Persuasion*.[4] Published together posthumously in 1817, they seem unlikely companions, but in Austen's mind their partnership was deeper than the accident of their copublication. *Persuasion* itself speaks to problems that to all appearances pressed on Austen while she was reviewing, perhaps even revising, *Northanger Abbey* for publication. The "hand of time" may have been "lenient" (NA 201) to Catherine Morland's feelings, but Austen considered it harsh to her novel. In the "Advertisement" to *Northanger Abbey* she dwells on the "thirteen years" during which "places, manners, books, and opinions have undergone considerable changes," changes which render parts of her novel "comparatively obsolete." The "thirteen years" marked here, of course, are the same thirteen years that cause such dislocation in *Persuasion*. This novel is constantly calling attention to a temporal gap, to the time unwritten, but everywhere felt, to the missing third volume, as it were. Austen's handling of time in her plots is famously exact, carefully coordinated with reference to almanacs. But for all her exactitude, once Austen forges the temporal schemata of her narratives, she generally proceeds to submerge them, and only the most determined of students would wish to note down references to years and dates and then arrange them sequentially. But *Persuasion* is a calculated tangle of years and dates, and the passage of time itself is foregrounded. Here, as in no other novel, we are constantly being pointed backwards—to the knell-like repetition of "thirteen years" (P 6–7) that have left Elizabeth husbandless, to the heavy "eight years" (P 60) that have changed everything but Anne's feelings for Wentworth, to the tolled "twelve years" that have transformed the smart young Miss Hamilton into the poor and crippled Mrs. Smith (P 153); in short, to the inconjurable difference time makes.

The years alluded to in the "Advertisement" to *Northanger Abbey* and throughout *Persuasion* as the occasion of so much change are not just any years which would work changes at any time. With the benefit of hindsight, we look back upon those thirteen years as having sealed the reaction, but as they appear in *Persuasion* they do not present a repressive and politically monolithic aspect. Sir Walter himself seems firmly enough entrenched, to be sure, but he is not all there is. In his related capacities as general, pamphleteer, and stern paterfamilias, General Tilney is the obstacle in *Northanger Abbey* whose authority must be confronted and in some ways, however limited, overcome. But now, some two decades later, defenders of the nation appear under a different guise and are envisioned as alternatives to, rather than representatives of, the establishment. Admiral and Mrs. Croft are not gentry. Far from presiding over a neighborhood, they live most contentedly at sea, unconcerned with the production of heirs or the reproduction of ideologically correct values through the cultivation of local attachments. From some points of view, the differences between Admiral Croft and General Tilney may be minimal. The former, to be sure, nowhere expresses or implies progressive opinion. But to Anne, the difference is great. The years which bring the Admiral into prominence are those which mark off the disparity between the "old English style" of the senior Musgroves, and the "new" English style of their "accomplished" daughters (P 40), and which have brought changes with them accounting for what William Elliot calls the "unfeudal tone of the *present* day" (P 139, emphasis added). But the causes and the processes of such transformation are not themselves the subject of *Persuasion*. Instead they are the pervasive backdrop Austen establishes throughout *Persuasion* in order to consider the psychological impact that social arrangements have on women and the apparent possibilities which the "unfeudal tone of the present day" may hold out for them.

Of all Austen's novels, *Persuasion* is, in point of mere years, the farthest removed from the pressures of political controversy that animate the fiction of her time. And yet, though it is often viewed as a forward-looking novel, it makes a concerted effort to embrace a prerevolutionary context as well. Many of the most basic terms in the novel have a decidedly Johnsonian ring to them, and this should not surprise us, not only because Johnson is so sympathetic a figure to Austen generally, but also because he is probably foremost among the "best moralists" (P 101) Anne recommends to the stylishly melancholy Benwick. *Persuasion* continually contrasts the merits of fortitude, which can be "headstrong" (P 27) or daringly heedless (P 242), with the merits of prudence, which can be "over-anxious caution which seems to insult exertion and distrust Providence" (P 30). The opposition itself, of course, is Johnson's trademark. He frequently juxtaposes "heartless pusillanimity" to "heady confidence" (*Rambler* 25) and opposes the "presumption and arrogance" of expecting sure success to the "weakness and cowardice" of anticipating sure defeat (*Rambler* 43). Although neither Johnson nor Austen definitively resolve this opposition, both writers are self-consciously unconventional in refusing the moral authority of prudential maxims.

Writing when she does, however, Austen cannot treat temerity and timidity as neutral poles in a disinterested debate, nor can she omit scrutinizing their tacit reference to sexual difference. For Lady Russell, they are political attitudes. Lady Russell does not share the mindlessness typical of the squires, ladies, and baronets in this novel. Much to Elizabeth's irritation, in fact, she is always reading "the new poems and states of the

nation that come out" (P 215), and as we might expect, her opinions about
Anne's suitors bespeak her absorption in and sympathies for conservative
apologetics. She aims her approval of William Elliot at Anne in such a way
as to show Wentworth's boldness in what she considers to be the worst
possible light:

> He [William Elliot] was steady observant, moderate, candid;
> never run away with by spirits or by selfishness, which fancied
> itself strong feeling; and yet with a sensibility to what was amiable
> and lovely, and a value for all the felicities of domestic life, which
> characters of fancied enthusiasm, and violent agitation seldom
> really possess. (P 146-47)

Lady Russell's argument is a manifestly sentimental one whose object is to
establish the priority of that most basic unit of the social structure, the
patriarchal family. She awards the prize for true, as opposed to "fancied,"
feeling to the man whose sensibility evinces the most responsiveness to
women—the "amiable and lovely" being of course their province—and
dismisses Wentworthian impetuosity as only fitful in its loyalties and
subversive in its effects.

Of course Lady Russell is drastically wrong about Sir Walter's heir.
Like all the villainous gentlemen and peers of progressive fiction who
manipulate other people's domestic lives in order to secure their own power,
he is out for himself, and if a semblance of sensibility to the fair sex is needed
to acquire prestige, then so be it. Lady Russell is wrong about Wentworth as
well, although in this case her error is plausible, since Wentworth is a
complex figure whose own sensibility bears the deep marks of ideological
contradiction. The action of *Persuasion* begins eight years before the opening
of the novel, when Wentworth angrily spurns young Anne Elliot because he
believes she showed "feebleness of character" in relinquishing their
engagement. Wentworth's anger deserves particular attention, because it is
anything but customary to fault women for diffidence. In another kind of
novel by another kind of novelist, Anne's initial hesitation would strike
Wentworth and us alike as exemplary and he, like the enthusiastic Henry
Crawford glorying in his chains, would, rather than take umbrage at her
maidenly doubt, manfully seize an occasion to prove his worth. But
Wentworth does not appear to believe that the inconvenient modesty of the
maiden will be redeemed by the submission of the wife, or to value the
"feebleness" so often held to be part of woman's duty as well as her charm.
Conservative fiction and conduct literature tirelessly preach to women about
the duty of submission. In her avowedly counterrevolutionary *Letters*

Addressed to a Young Man, Jane West assures young men of the kingdom that they have every right to expect their wives to give way, whatever the "pestiferous doctrines" of revolutionaries urge to the contrary. The "wise and beautiful subordination which Providence has instituted to avoid domestic contention" dictates precisely the kind of persuadableness in women that Wentworth scorns: "submission is the *prescribed* duty of the female; peace must be preserved, and she must yield."[5]

Maria Edgeworth was, as we shall see, a careful reader of the very passages of *Persuasion* which specifically address how the different social conditioning of men and women creates differences in their psychological makeup. The political agenda of her *Practical Education,* co-authored with her progressive father, is not so unashamedly clear as West's. Here Edgeworth disclaims—though she does not outright dismiss—any progressive concern for the condition of women, illuminating their problems, but disavowing any intention to solve them: "Their happiness is of more consequence than their speculative rights." Accordingly, she recommends that female children should be taught restraint, sweetness, and submission, because these, like it or not, are to be expected from them throughout their lives as adults. Women, she continues, "must trust to the experience of others; they cannot always have recourse to what ought to be, they must adapt themselves to what is.... Timidity, a certain tardiness of decision, and reluctance to act in public situations, are not considered as defects in a woman's character." Edgeworth's statement, of course, is already a stunning piece of intertextuality, imbedded as it is with a number of conservative truisms: it is wiser to trust to the accumulated experience of others than to advance and pursue one's own ideals, to submit to what "is" rather than quixotically striving for what "ought to be," and to habituate male, but especially female, children to what Edgeworth a little later terms dutiful "forebearance" rather than self-willed "precipitation."[6]

Wentworth's contempt for what he perceives as Anne's failure to be decided, forward, and strong thus implicates and dissents from an already firmly established and widely available tradition of debate about women's manners. To Wentworth, a woman is guilty of "weakness and timidity" when she evinces a readiness "to oblige others" (P 61), and when, deferring to the judgment of family or friends, she credits fearful rather than hopeful predictions about her betrothed. A strong man himself, Wentworth knows, or at least thinks he knows, that he wants the same qualities in a woman. He "seriously described the woman he should wish to meet with. 'A strong mind, with sweetness of manner,' made the first and the last of the description" (P 62). Wentworth's description appears straightforward enough. But as his subsequent remarks attest, he is in fact caught within highly charged tensions

about women's manners, and his description of the ideal woman is
oxymoronic, because however much he may desire "strength" in women, he
considers it essentially inconsistent with the sweetness he also exacts. The
narrator's remarks on the "large fat sighings" of Mrs. Musgrove "over the
destiny of a son, whom alive nobody had cared for" (P 68) are relevant here.
They will appear less like the gratuitous and tasteless cruelties which the
subversive school has so relished when we consider them in light of
Wentworth's contradictory assumptions about women. The narrator in fact
brings up the grotesqueness of Mrs. Musgrove's grief only to ponder the
irrationality of our response to it: "Personal size and mental sorrow have
certainly no necessary proportions. A large bulky figure has as good a *right*
to be in deep affliction, as the most graceful set of limbs in the world. But,
fair or not fair, there are unbecoming conjunctions, which reason will
patronize in vain,—which taste cannot tolerate,—which ridicule will seize"
(P 68, emphasis added).

The tendency of *Persuasion* as a whole is to consider conjunctions
which perhaps have even less basis in reason, but which are so much more
pervasive that their arbitrariness is not even noticed. This discredited
association of physical size with emotional delicacy prefaces a debate
between Wentworth and Mrs. Croft about female manners, in which
Wentworth takes a position very different from what Lady Russell would
expect. If a large, bulky figure has a "right" to affliction, then conversely
perhaps a "graceful set of limbs" has a "right" to venturesomeness as well. To
Wentworth, however, the very idea seems as ludicrously incongruous, if not
indeed as repellent, as fat grief may be to us, and this despite his declared
wish to find "a strong mind, with sweetness of manner" in a woman. With
the haughtiness typical of him, Captain Wentworth announces his principled
opposition to carrying women on board ships precisely on account of their
delicacy. His objections, he explains, arise not from mean-spirited misogyny,
but rather from high-minded chivalry: "There can be no want of gallantry,
admiral, in rating the claims of women to every personal comfort *high*—and
this is what I do. I hate to hear of women on board, or to see them on board;
and no ship, under my command, shall ever convey a family of ladies any
where, if I can help it" (P 69). Having spent the best years of her life on a
man-of-war, Mrs. Croft regards her brother's opinions as "idle refinement!"
(P 69). But Mrs. Croft's claim that "any reasonable woman" can be "perfectly
comfortable" (P 70) on board actually loses points with her brother. To a
man fixed in his ideas about female delicacy, women so "reasonable" are
simply not ladies. He is willing to transport women on his ships insofar as
they are a dear friend's property—"I would bring any thing of Harville's from
the world's end, if he wanted it" (P 69)—but the possibility that women

themselves may not consider such journeys a violation of their lovely and amiable natures is obnoxious to him: "I might not like them the better for that, perhaps. Such a number of women and children have no *right* to be comfortable on board" (P 69, emphasis Wentworth's).

The objections not only to female sturdiness, but also to a female *"right"* to it, that Wentworth expresses here explain why it was and still is impossible for him to recognize "strength of mind" and "sweetness of manner" in Anne Elliot, until Anne's sturdiness and her forwardness to take control after the catastrophe at Lyme oblige him to surrender his notions about delicacy. Like female modesty, which is suspected to the same degree as it is commanded, female strength is disapproved to the same degree as it is desired. Although the introduction of the tearful Benwick and the domestic Harville upsets conventional conjunctions of ideas about gender, for Wentworth delicacy and strength are sex-typed oppositions reinforced by class, and where he finds them conjoined in women of his own class— officer's wives—he is by his own admission displeased. Mrs. Croft's extraordinary rebuttal seizes on what she regards as absurd in her brother's ideas about manners and class: "I hate to hear you talking so, like a fine gentleman, and as if women were all fine ladies, instead of rational creatures" (P 70). As we recall, Mr. Knightley can convincingly oppose the modish primitivism of Mrs. Elton's projected "gipsy party" to the "nature and simplicity of gentlemen and ladies, with their servants and furniture" (E 355), because *Emma* as a whole is predicated upon the worthiness of the gentry ideal and the gentlemen and ladies who comprise it. But in *Persuasion*, gentlemen and ladies are excluded from the category of "rational creatures." Not that rational creatures of either sex here abandon the amenities of life, like Mrs. Elton's impossibly idealized gypsies. Indeed, the conditions Wentworth imagines to be too grueling for a lady to bear turn out to be quite accommodating after all. It is Wentworth himself who ridicules land-loving civilians for supposing that sailors rough it, "living on board without any thing to eat, or any cook to dress it if there were, or any servant to wait, or any knife or fork to use" (P 64).

But though Mrs. Croft may not repudiate some of the comforts of gentility, she does repudiate the system of sexually differentiated manners ladies and gentlemen depend upon. Her views on the subject are actually quite remarkable, given the renewed importance ascribed to female manners during the period in question. Conservatives and radicals alike agreed that amiable weakness and loveliness in women guarantee the continuance of patriarchy itself. "The age of chivalry is gone," as Burke famously wailed in a passage of the *Reflections* which Lady Russell seems to remember, and along with the chivalric sensibility, he predicts, will die the conditions which make the old regime possible: the gallant disposition in men to feel fondly disposed to the amiable softness of women restrains the otherwise indecent and uncivilized rapacity of their appetites, and the retiring docility and dutiful chastity of women insures the identity and survival of the blood lines of good families. Of course not all of Burke's allies believed that the civilized world was held together by chivalrous opinion. Jane West, for one, opined that Burke's notions of chivalry bordered on idolatry, and granted women far more than they intrinsically deserved, filling their weak heads with silly ideas about their own importance, when it is they instead who should study to please, and to be sensible helpmates and useful companions rather than lovely and ever-distressed females.[7]

While conservative and progressive discourse sometimes intersects on the phrase "rational creatures," the insistence that men and women's shared status as rational creatures takes precedence over sexual difference in questions relating to their manners and their morals was generally perceived to be the progressive position. Wollstonecraft's critique of the cultivation of speciously differentiating delicacy in women was often treated as though it were a wholesale recommendation of grossly viraginous strength. Thus Robert Bisset, for example, scoffs that Wollstonecraft included among the *"rights of women"* the right to serve as "soldiers, sailors, senators, politicians, scholars, philosophers, and rakes.... She trusted the time would soon arrive when the sex would require high renown in boxing matches, sword and pistol."[8] Seen in this light, Mrs. Croft is a tour de force of characterization. Though her comportment has not the slightest hint of mannish impropriety about it—Lady Russell, for one finds her a pleasing and sensible neighbor— her manners are conspicuous by their lack of features usually construed as feminine, such as bashfulness, roundness, sweetness, and daintiness. She "had a squareness, uprightness, and vigour of form, which gave importance to her person" and "a weatherbeaten complexion, the consequence of her having been almost as much at sea as her husband" (P 48). She omits that self-doubt and reluctance that Edgeworth, for one, exacted from women, particularly in public situations. She looks "as intelligent and keen as any of the officers around her" (P 168), and her manners are "open, easy, and decided, like one who had no distrust of herself, and no doubts of what to do; without any approach to coarseness, however, or any want of good humour" (P 48). And finally, without ever really appearing to be the eccentric she is, Mrs. Croft prefers warships to the most comfortable manors in the kingdom, throwing overboard as needless weight the excellencies of the proper lady, and she "shares with him [Admiral Croft] in everything" (P 168).

Mrs. Croft appears never to consider robustness and self-confidence an oxymoronic violation of her feminine nature, and she could bid farewell to the age of chivalry without worrying much about the future of the civilized world. To her chivalry and the way of life it guarantees are superfluous: Wentworth's solicitude for women's comfort is a "superfine, extraordinary sort of gallantry" (P 69), which appears even more unnecessary in his case, since he in particular, as his sister implies, has the good fortune not to be a "fine gentleman" to begin with. Sir Walter, for his part, does not regard Wentworth as a "gentleman" at all, and his usage, however unpleasant, is far from idiosyncratic. Wielding a fortune in war prizes of mythically immense proportions, Wentworth is nouveau riche with a vengeance. Sir Walter restricts the term "*gentlemen*" to "some man of property;' and thus does not recognize the claim even of Wentworth's clerical brother to the title: "Mr. Wentworth was nobody, I remember; quite unconnected; nothing to do with the Strafford family" (P 23). He objects besides to the tendency of Wentworth's profession itself to contend with and confound the established networks of social prestige, for the military is "the means of bringing persons of obscure birth into undue distinction, and raising men to honours which their fathers and grandfathers never dreamt of" (P 19). In all fairness, the contempt is entirely mutual. To a man who prides himself on "the gratification of believing myself to earn every blessing that I enjoyed" (P 247) the famous "Elliot pride" (P 88) in membership within their own family—as well as the precedence-, title-, and pedigree-mongering that goes along with it—is offensive. Mary Musgrove's eagerness to assure him that she regards the Hayters as unworthy connections only arouses in him "a contemptuous glance, as he turned away, which Anne perfectly knew the meaning of" (P 86). Furthermore, the record of filial piety which makes up an important part of Darcy's characterization, for example, has no place in Wentworth's history, and his impatience with Anne's hesitation at nineteen to defy paternal displeasure surely suggests how little store he sets by paternal authority in general. Since Wentworth has no place in, and indeed is actually hostile to, the patriarchal world of family and neighborhood which Sir Walter represents, though none too well, his "superfine" gallantry has no rationale and operates at political cross-purposes with his own designs and energies.

Wentworth's argument with Admiral and Mrs. Croft does not settle any issues, for no sooner does the subject reach an impasse than Wentworth breaks off and withdraws altogether. To their assurance that he will change his mind when he marries, he rather angrily returns: "'I can only say, "No, I shall not;" and then they say again, "Yes, you will," and there is an end of it.' He got up and moved away" (P 70). Wentworth's words here both recapitulate his quarrel with Anne Elliot eight years ago and prefigure the same dilemma he will face in a matter of days when Louisa wants to jump down from the stiles at the new Cobb: "He [Wentworth] advised her against it, thought the jar too great; but no, he reasoned and talked in vain; she smiled and said, 'I am determined I will'" (P 109). Recurring to the imagery of hardness and to such related concepts as complaisance and determination, elasticity and fixation, impressionability and obstinacy, *Persuasion* continues to explore the antinomies of autonomy and authority that figure prominently in Austen's other novels as well. The subject of one of Elizabeth's and Darcy's first debates, after all, is the worth of ductility and resoluteness: "To yield readily-easily-to the *persuasion* of a friend," Elizabeth taunts, "is no merit with you" (PP 50, emphasis Elizabeth's). But while both novels attempt to delimit the legitimate boundaries of authoritative interference, the later novel deals with conflicts which, as with the conceit of fat sighings, "reason will patronize in vain" (P 68), and where persuasion accordingly is more problematic.

In *Persuasion* neither giving in on the one hand, nor holding out to get one's way on the other, are very attractive options. Conservative apologists, of course, cut the Gordian knot by submitting such conflicts to the arbitration of persons wisely vested by tradition with the authority to decide. But if *Persuasion* does not specifically indict this method, it also stops far short of adopting it, since the "authorities" so vested are inadequate. In Anne's case, an older woman friend, and no venerable father, carried the day. Lady Russell stands not in place of a mother, but rather "in the place of a parent" (P 246), and the very need to replace a living but morally dysfunctional father itself points to a problem with the conservative model. Moreover, although Anne is steadfast in refusing to apologize for having once been persuaded by a woman who takes the place of a parent, she soon eschews Lady Russell's prudential reasonings on the grounds that they "insult exertion and distrust Providence" (P 30), and she never allows herself to be persuaded again. When Anne receives a proposal from Charles Musgrove, she solicits neither her father's opinions nor Lady Russell's, but "left nothing for advice to do" (P 29). Anne's gentle imperviousness to interference is fortunate, for Lady Russell's approval of Charles Musgrove's suit and her championship of William Elliot's do not testify to her powers of discrimination. Like *Northanger Abbey*, *Persuasion* reflects on its own refusal to ratify received notions: the narrator validates the perseverance of young people in carrying their points even though doing so is, as she says, "bad morality to conclude with" (P 248). In erased notes of the cancelled chapter covering the same material, Austen dwells at greater length on her departures from conventional wisdom in fashioning a story where the older and unassailably "proper" woman is wrong, not once, but twice: "Bad Morality again. A young Woman proved to have ... more discrimination of Character than her elder—to have seen in two Instances more clearly what a

Man was ... But on the point of Morality, I confess myself almost in despair ... and shall leave it ... to the mercy of Mothers & Chaperons & Middle-aged Ladies in general" (P 282, n. 23). Even though Anne finally avers in defense of her own infelicitous, but not culpable, deference to Lady Russell, "if I mistake not, a strong sense of duty is no bad part of a woman's portion" (P 246), the efficacy of "submission" is, if not utterly undone, then at least called into question by authorially emphasized criticism of the principles which underpin and valorize such duty.

The unyielding firmness and independence Wentworth advocates is likewise tested and found wanting. After persuading Henrietta to visit Charles Hayter despite the interference of Mary Musgrove, Louisa proclaims:

> "And so I made her go.... What!—would I be turned back from doing a thing that I had determined to do, and that I knew to be right, by the airs and interference of such a person?—or, of any person I may say. No,—I have no idea of being so easily persuaded. When I have made up my mind, I have made it." (P 87)

This speech, and Wentworth's enthusiastic response to it, are not the simple assertions of principled self-determination they appear to be. Louisa, after all, did not disinterestedly supplement her sister's faltering powers of mind with the strength of her own. Instead, she took advantage of her sister's persuadability in order to clear the field for Wentworth and herself.[9] Further, Louisa recommends independence even as she congratulates herself for her own interference: "I made her go" (P 87). Finally, Wentworth disdains the feeble malleability of "too yielding and indecisive a character" (P 88) when it defies him as Anne's did, but he does not seem to mind or even to notice the same qualities when they malleably conform to his own influence. Louisa has really done no more than give Wentworth what he wants to hear, and unaware that Louisa's strength of mind is really only persuadability to him in disguise, he rewards her with his praise: "Happy for her [Henrietta], to have such a mind as yours at hand" (P 287).

Clearly, Wentworth's preference for singlemindedness is as indiscriminating and self-serving in its own way as Lady Russell's prejudice in favor of wealth and family is in its. If "complaisance" can be, as Louisa terms it, "nonsensical" (P 87), inflexibility can be so as well. Wentworth takes little notice of this possibility. "[L]et those who would be happy be firm," he intones, anticipating the moral of his parable about the hazelnut: "To exemplify,—a beautiful glossy nut, which, blessed with original strength, has outlived all the storms of autumn. Not a puncture, not a weak spot anywhere.—This nut ... while so many of its brethren have fallen and been trodden under foot, is still in possession of all the happiness that a hazel-nut can be supposed capable of" (P 88).[10] The most salient feature of the glossy hazel-nut, however, is not that it holds impressions well, but that it is not susceptible to them at all. The efficacy of determination is undermined when Louisa, "armed with the idea of merit in maintaining her own way" (P 94), withholds herself from advice and falls headlong onto the pavement at the Cobb. Even Wentworth eventually surrenders resolution so fixed and intransigent. After the accident, he turns desperately to Anne for help, to be ordered and told what to do. And throughout the novel, his immovable resentment of her loosens under the influence of other peoples' admiration of her. He arrives at Uppercross swearing that Anne has aged beyond recognition, but he changes his tune when he observes William Elliot to be struck by her, and later when connoisseurs of beauty sing Anne's praises in his hearing (P 177–78).

Wentworth's determination is generally considered to mark him as a "new man," temperamentally as well as ideologically opposed to the way of life Sir Walter represents. But like his gallantry towards women, his steadfastness to the point of inflexibility actually aligns him with Sir Walter, and he must mitigate his self-will before reconciliation is possible. When Anne defies him by suspending their engagement, she encounters "all the additional pain of opinions, on his side, totally unconvinced and unbending, and of his feeling himself ill-used by so forced a relinquishment" (P 28). Wentworth's tenacity in holding "unbending" opinions, his tendency to remain "unconvinced" by and inaccessible to opposition, and most alarmingly of all, his readiness to feel "ill-used" place him in the unflattering fellowship of none other than the Elliots themselves. Like spoiled children, Elizabeth and Sir Walter bitterly blame the world for the necessities their own debts place them under. They feel "ill-used and unfortunate" (P 10), and steadfast in their foolishness, they refuse to forego expensive "decencies"— "Journeys, London, servants, horses, table" (P 13)—that alone make life supportable even to "private" ladies and gentlemen. Having inherited "a considerable share of the Elliot self-importance" (P 37) without commanding any comparable hauteur, Mary Musgrove manifests their tyrannical self-pity in a particularly degraded form. She always fancies herself "neglected or ill-used" (P 37), always thinks with bullheaded obstinacy "a great deal of her own complaints" (P 33), and feels everything as a wound. Wentworth has his own version of the "Elliot self-importance" which prompts him in like fashion to be headstrong and absolute. True, he may not have behaved like "an ill-used man" (P 172) when Louisa falls for Benwick, but this is not, as the Admiral thinks, because he has "too much spirit" to kick against the goad, but rather because he came to regret their flirtation to begin with. As the Admiral could not have known, eight years ago, when it counted, Wentworth did feel like "an ill-used man," and he does "murmur" and "whine and complain" (P 172)—not with Mary's sorts of whimpers, but rather with icy vindictiveness nursed over a period of eight years.

In the Elliots' case, of course, self-importance is a birthright, a benefit conferred upon them by their social position. Sir Walter believes he is somebody to the "nobody" of virtually everyone else. But though Sir Walter is convinced that, as a public figure, he carries his importance around with him irrespective of place, people only three miles away at Uppercross are contentedly oblivious to "the affairs which at Kellynch-hall were treated as of such general publicity and pervading interest" (P 42) by Sir Walter himself. Anne's mortification to discover that Sir Walter and Elizabeth "see nothing to regret" in relinquishing "the duties and dignity of the resident land-holder" (P 138) bespeaks her lingering sympathy with the life of the manor, but landholders less distinguished than her father are not spared either. As presented in *Persuasion*, at least, landed existence itself fosters an immobility that fixes delusions of self-consequence which cause so much conflict. Anne is an adept in "the art of knowing our own nothingness beyond our own circle" (P 42), and this is what makes her wise. But the otherwise unobjectionable Musgroves, whose views are bounded by the narrowness of their neighborhood, cannot share such wisdom. Except in *Pride rind Prejudice*, where a countrified Mrs. Bennet takes umbrage at Darcy's cosmopolitan pretentions, only in *Persuasion* does Austen portray the provinciality of her characters as a disadvantage. Taken by himself, Charles Hayter, for example, could appear as an earnest and respectable gentleman. But placed alongside Frederick Wentworth and ineffectually pleading with a troublesome child, he fades into nonentity. And just as the Admiral's tendency to confuse Henrietta and Louisa suggests their indistinguishability, so the redundancy of Hayter's Christian name, doubling with that of Charles Musgrove, calls attention to what is undistinctive about eldest sons in general. And in no other novel is a gentry matron exposed to such painful comparisons with a woman with wider horizons. When Mrs. Croft summarizes her travels, adding "We do not call Bermuda or Bahama, you know, the West Indies," poor Mrs. Musgrove finds herself baffled: "Mrs. Musgrove had not a word to say in dissent; she could not accuse herself of having ever called them any thing in the whole course of her life" (P 70).

Landed life is not taken to task simply because it promotes mediocrity or ignorance, but rather because its insularity is psychologically damaging, especially for women. Conservatives laud membership within a neighborhood precisely on account of the strong and stabilizing attachments, the changeless pace, and the unceasing familiarity that it carries with it. But for women it also carries with it a particularly narrow and unwholesome confinement, and discussion of this problem in *Persuasion* is specific, prolonged, and dramatically charged. Whatever baronetcy does for Sir Walter, it has not helped a daughter who has reached the age of twenty-nine without marrying. For Elizabeth the *Baronetage* cannot be the never-ending fund of solace unalloyed it is for her father. Every reading mercilessly reiterates an ever-receding birthdate and an unchanging status as spinster. Mr Bennet's sarcasm—"a girl likes to be crossed in love a little now and then.... It is something to think of" (PP 137–38)—has a disturbing relevance to *Persuasion*, where such crosses are all that women have to think of. Being the mistress of Kellynch-hall—"doing the honours, and laying down the domestic law at home" (P 6–7)—is not as engaging, as satisfying, and as adequate to Elizabeth's imagination as running Hartfield and its environs is to Emma's. Elizabeth is haunted by her disappointment in love, and the cares and duties of "her scene of life" are not enough to keep her from revisiting and fixing her pain. Bitterness, mortification, regret, and worry are all she has "to give interest to a long, uneventful residence in one country circle, to fill the vacancies which there were no habits of utility abroad, no talents or accomplishments for home, to occupy" (P 9). Nor is Elizabeth's condition unique. Anne has more "resources," as they are termed in Emma, than her sister Elizabeth, yet she understands that her regret over Wentworth lingers because "no aid had been given in change of place ... or in any novelty or enlargement of society" (P 28) that could dislodge and eventually efface her painful impressions.

Whether it is because we typically exclude Austen in general from access to, capability for, or interest in arcana of any sort, or whether it is because we have a habit of regarding *Persuasion* in particular as a tender love story that is not conducive to such considerations, rather scant attention has been accorded to Austen's affiliation with the eighteenth-century tradition of liberal psychology.[11] But readers of Johnson's essays, who recall his fears about the corrosiveness of hopes and disappointments, his recommendation of "change of place" (*Rambler* 5, 47), and his anxieties about the "vacuities of recluse and domestick leisure" (*Rambler* 85), will recognize the provenance of her concerns and the character of her diction, and will appreciate how, by linking women's confinement within their changeless neighborhoods to the strength and longevity of their feelings, she develops this tradition with particular emphasis on women's problems. Anne herself tells Harville that women do "not forget you [men], so soon as you forget us" (P 232). But far from presenting the constancy of woman's love in the light of a virtue, for example, loyalty, she presents it as a burden—"our fate rather than our merit" (P 232). Men will love faithfully "so long as [they] have an object," but woman's love can subsist indefinitely as fantasy alone: "All the privilege I claim for my own sex ... is that of loving longest, when existence or when hope is gone" (P 235). A dubious privilege indeed, this liability to hopeless fixation. Anne's rather technical explanation for the stubborn durability of women's love combines social criticism with psychological acuity:

> "We live at home, quiet, confined, and our feelings prey upon us. You are forced on exertion. You have always a profession, pursuits, business of some sort or other, to take you back into the world immediately, and continual occupation and change soon weaken impressions." (P 232)

To Maria Edgeworth, whose access to moral psychology, unlike Austen's, is undisputed, Anne's analysis held special interest. The marginalia in her personal copy of *Persuasion* are very sparse until this episode, which prompts a flurry of scratches, underlinings, and comments. She, for example, reiterates Anne's socio-psychological argument here with "our mind is continually fixt on one object"; to the claims that occupation and change weaken impressions, she writes a heartily concurring "That it does"; and she brushes aside Harville's analogy between the strength of men's "bodily frames" and the constancy of their feelings (P 233) with an emphatic "No".[12] But whereas Edgeworth in conservative fashion upholds the traditional social arrangements that expose women to the problems she herself laments, on the grounds that defying such arrangements will not promote their happiness, *Persuasion* asks us to consider whether women's happiness may not be better served by cutting loose from those arrangements. Mrs. Croft disapproves of long and uncertain engagements because they expose women to perilous anxieties and fantasies—and her brother, eavesdropping, appears to acknowledge that the application to his own case with Anne has a compelling legitimacy which he had never before considered. Mrs. Croft's example as a wife suggests that life on the high seas, for all its dangers, is to be preferred to the "safety" of helpless immobility she experienced when she lived conventionally, as most wives such as Mrs. Musgrove do: "The only time I ever really suffered in body or mind, the only time I ever fancied myself unwell, or had any ideas of danger, was the winter that I passed by myself at Deal, when the Admiral (*Captain* Croft then) was in the North Seas. I lived in perpetual fright at that time, and had all manner of imaginary complaints from not knowing what to do with myself" (P 71).

The phenomena of change and relativity in *Persuasion* have long been considered symptoms of the dizzying modernity to come, a modernity usually described as either brave or degenerate, according to the axis of the critic. But to those characters who take notice at all, the deracination and relativity presented in *Persuasion* are not felt to be disturbing or disorienting. Except when she has pangs in tender remembrance of her dear mother, Anne cannot regret the Croft's tenancy at Kellynch-hall. She cannot say of her family seat what she knows social orthodoxy would have her say: "These rooms ought to belong only to us.... How unworthily unoccupied! An ancient family to be so driven away!" (P 126). Rather than feel that their removal to the diminished accommodations at Camden-place constitutes a fall, Sir Walter and Elizabeth themselves find more than enough "extent to be proud of between two walls, perhaps thirty feet asunder" (P 138). Anne is not bewildered to learn that our somethingness is tenuous and relative, or sad to confront her nothingness beyond her family circle—she, after all, is rather less than something in her family circle as well. Only from within a mentality which organizes people hierarchically from somebodies down to nobodies, and often according to whether or not they yield or are yielded to, does that status of nothingness feel so degrading. Anne does not possess such a mentality, and detached from a single neighborhood and a fixed world of traditional institutions that make that mentality possible, she allows the alienation she experiences upon first coming to Uppercross to be a benefit. Anne finds it "very fitting, that every little social commonwealth should dictate its own matters of discourse" (P 43), and by learning different social discourses she is able to be a citizen of many commonwealths. Accordingly, she considers it "highly incumbent on her to clothe her imagination, her memory, and all her ideas" (P 43) in Uppercross. Though first undertaken as a duty, this reinvestiture is later experienced as a boon. After leaving, Anne discovers that subjects which she had felt obliged to "smother among the Musgroves" assume only "secondary interest" (P 124). She is "sensible of some mental change": her sorrow about Kellynch and even her tenacious loyalty to Wentworth loosens, and she now entertains thoughts of Benwick, and even of Walter Elliot.

If processes of inuring can be therapeutic—Anne, for example, "was become hardened to such affronts" (P 34) as she receives at home—some kinds of malleability can bring relief as well, even if it makes possible a certain erasure. Anne finally refuses to take sides in the debate about hardness and softness, and determination and submission, setting her sights instead on "elasticity of mind, that disposition to be comforted, that power of turning readily from evil to good, and of finding employment" (P 154). When Wentworth wittily explains how in marrying Anne he is not getting what he deserves, he elaborates on this quality: "'Like other great men under reverses', he added with a smile, 'I must endeavour to subdue my mind to my fortune'" (P 247). The ironic mode of his statement is oddly fitting, for the "reverse" in question of course is the happiness of reconciliation, possible only after relinquishing the obduracy of his resentment and becoming susceptible to opposition. But the people in *Persuasion* who are preeminent for elasticity of mind are significantly far more remote than Wentworth, who after all by the end of the novel is acceptable even to Sir Walter. By the standards set in Austen's fiction, in fact, they are unusual, and by those set in conservative fiction, far too marginal to be the models they are here. They are mostly without the kinds of affiliations, idealized in such writing, that exact a high cost-confinement, unventuresomeness, fixity, boredom—for the stability they guarantee. Some Sir Walter regards as scarcely human: "A Mrs. Smith. A widow Mrs. Smith.... And what is her attraction? That she is old and sickly.—Upon my word, Miss Anne Elliot, you have the most extraordinary taste! Every thing that revolts other people, low company, paltry rooms, foul air, disgusting associations are inviting to you" (P 157). Yet Mrs. Smith above all others typifies the "elasticity of mind" Anne values, and this is not only despite the reverses that have marginalized her, but also in some ways because she has undergone them.

Insofar as salvos like these would console the unfortunate by contending that it is better to suffer after all, they condone the processes and conditions which cause such suffering to begin with, and so may be considered implicitly conservative. *Persuasion* is sometimes deeply tinged with such quietism. And yet Anne's preference of "low company, paltry rooms, foul air" to the companionship of her father and those he would choose for her is nevertheless a pretty piece of social criticism. Fortune, Providence, luck, chance—these are extremely prominent entities in the novel, and are emblemized here by the sea itself. And the person with "elasticity of mind"—the "choicest gift of Heaven" (P 154)—takes and resigns what they give with equal cheer, and makes her- or himself malleable to their impressions, much as the Crofts have let the sea air write itself onto their complexions without bothering with applications of Gowland's Lotion. On Mrs. Smith, who lives beyond the margins of "good" society, their marks have been the deepest: "She had been very fond of her husband,—she had buried him. She had been used to affluence,—it was gone. She had no child to connect her with life and happiness again, no relations to assist in the arrangement of perplexed affairs, no health to make all the rest supportable" (P 154). But though she is the least sheltered from fortune's blows—and as Mrs. Croft says, "We none of us expect to be in smooth water all our days" (P 70)—she is also the most resilient for having "weathered it" (P 154), the least inclined to feel "ill-used." Her bodily immobility—roughly similar in

kind, if not in degree, to the confinement undergone by proper ladies in their
provincial homes—serves only to highlight her resources more brilliantly. In
a similar way Harville lives just beyond society, bordering out onto the sea
itself, which has not served him a fraction so generously as it has Wentworth.
If his case is not so dire as Mrs. Smith's—he is less crippled, less cramped,
less destitute, and with a loving family, less disattached—by Sir Walter's
standards he still ranks as a "disgusting association." But though even Anne
herself suffers a "moment's astonishment" at the meanness of his lodgings,
she later regards them as the seat of "great happiness" (P 99).

       While the people Anne casts her lot with are well-traveled citizens of
many different commonwealths, to recall Anne's metaphor, they are
proprietors of none. Always ready to determine orders of precedence and to
feel "ill-used" if opposed or neglected, Mary Musgrove decides after only a
little consideration that even though Anne's accession to marriage restores
her "to the rights of seniority," her own situation is still superior: "Anne had
no Uppercross-hall before her, no landed estate, no headship of a family; and
if they could but keep Captain Wentworth from being made a baronet, she
would not change situations with Anne" (P 250). To Anne, however, these
lacks are a virtue. Religious intimations are more frequent in *Persuasion* than
in any of Austen's other novels and more enmeshed into its outlook. But
whereas in other novels the world of wealthy gentry in which Mary takes
such pride is either genuinely or at the very least nominally in the service of
such intimations, in *Persuasion* it is not. Characters here who are most like
the glossy but impermeable and therefore irredeemable hazelnut in
Wentworth's parable are not Wentworth himself, who finally yields after all,
but members of the privileged class, such as Sir Walter, who is devoted to
avoiding crow's-feet, and the "polished" William Elliot, who is suspect
precisely because he "endured too well" (P 161) and gives no evidence of
friction or wear.

       From the very beginning of the novel, Anne has valued "cheerful
confidence in futurity" and scorned to "distrust Providence!" (P 30). Peopled
more with friends than family, and accepting the "dread of war" that
sometimes dims the "sunshine" (P 252) of domestic felicity, the society Anne
finally selects—the "best" company (P 150)—removes itself from the
institutions of the country manor to front more directly and hospitably onto
Providence. But while the break Anne accomplishes with those institutions is
more complete than what we find in any other novel, and while her efforts at
accommodation are the most perfunctory, she and the alternative society she
joins are also the least prone to overt indictment, and this constitutes a
departure from Austen's early fiction especially. Whereas *Sense and Sensibility*
and *Northanger Abbey* derive much of their dramatic tension from the

defiance of tyrannical parents, *Persuasion* eludes, even frowns upon, overt rebellion. Social forms may be neglected—Anne dislikes "give-and-take invitations, and dinners of formality and display" (P 98)—but not outright opposed. Accordingly, Anne herself is capable of betraying some shame about her association with Lady Dalrymple and Miss Carteret, but she politely keeps it under wraps: "'Yes,' sighed Anne, 'we shall, indeed, be known to be related to them!'—then recollecting herself ... not wishing to be answered" (P 150–51). But William Elliot's history of expressed disrespect for rank itself is not acceptable. The narrator makes no bones about averring that "Sir Walter was not very wise" (P 24), but Anne shudders "with shock and mortification" to learn that his heir applies words as irreverent as "fool" (P 204) to him. But before we conclude that Austen's willingness to cover for Sir Walter betrays deplorable bad faith, or perhaps less damningly, loyalties too deep and residual to permit penetrating social criticism, we would do well to ponder the typically confounding twist in her characterization of William Elliot. Surely to identify the person who mouths social disrespect with the person who then panders to the very people of "credit and dignity" (P 151) whom he admits are "nothing in themselves" (P 150) is to underscore the particularly sterile conventionality of the entire system of "blood and connexion" (P 206) and the cynicism on which it subsists.

Of none of Austen's works, but of *Persuasion* perhaps least of all, can it be said, as Trilling has, "Nothing in the novels questions the ideal of the archaic 'noble' life which is appropriate to the great beautiful houses with the ever-remembered names—Northanger Abbey, Donwell Abbey, Pemberly, Hartfield, Kellynch Hall, Norland Park, Mansfield Park. In them 'existence is sweet and dear', at least if one is rightly disposed.... With what the great houses represent the heroines of the novels are, or become, completely in accord."[13] Northanger Abbey is far from a haven to Catherine Morland, and this is not because *she* fails to be "rightly disposed"; Norland Park provides no values with which the Dashwood sisters can accord; and Kellynch Hall, not even "ever-remembered" by its own proprietors, is bidden a rather wistful good riddance by a daughter far superior to what it now "represents." Works of fiction written on the conservative model tirelessly exhort us to accept infelicity as the condition of life and urge us instead to seek our modest satisfactions in the consciousness of prescribed attachments well honored, and duties well done. But Austen's novels are pervasively concerned, not with according ourselves to an existence "sweet and dear," but with achieving a more active, expansive, and personally fulfilling happiness, and they persistently suggest that this is well worth the striving. Sometimes, as in *Pride and Prejudice,* Austen contrives to locate such happiness within conservative institutions themselves, but as we have seen, it takes some work before Pemberly will accommodate Elizabeth. And once Pemberly does make a place for her, one suspects that it is the "great beautiful house" itself, rather than Elizabeth, that will be essentially improved for her presence there, because whatever its previous dignity, it never seemed a place of pleasure. The word "happy" rings as frequently across the pages of *Persuasion* as it does those of *Pride and Prejudice*, and it should tell us something that in *Persuasion* it is the nefarious Walter Elliot who wishes to dissuade Anne from pursuing the highest happiness she can conceive of. When he discovers that she prefers the "best" company to merely "good" company, he warns, "You have a better right to be fastidious than almost any other woman I know; but will it answer? Will it make you happy? Will it not be wiser to accept the society of these good ladies in Laura-place, and enjoy all the advantages of the connexion as far as possible?" (P 150). Fortunately, Anne's fastidiousness, like Elizabeth's, finally does "answer." But unlike Elizabeth's, it is achieved not at a great beautiful house with an ever-remembered name, but rather in a disposition only discernible in people who do not belong to such houses, people such as the Crofts, who walk "along in happy independence" (P 168), or like Harville, whose weather-beaten lodgings are a "picture of repose and domestic happiness" (P 98).

The interests of happiness, piety, and well-being demand removal from Kellynch Hall, its proprieties and priorities. But whether moving beyond Kellynch or any equivalent bespeaks a victory of autonomy from what a great house represents, or a despair of its ever improving enough to be desirable, is hard to say. Not surprisingly, since they belong exclusively to the years which assured the reaction, Austen's last three novels reflect a strong sense of the increasing immovability of established authority. While *Sense and Sensibility* concludes with an opposition and a withdrawal that are angry, permanent, and committed, in *Northanger Abbey* General Tilney finally does yield, if minimally, and in *Pride and Prejudice* Darcy is improved by confrontation, and eventually even Lady Catherine comes around. But even though Sir Thomas's judgment in *Mansfield Park* is thoroughly impeached, his authority is fixed. In *Emma*, when his kind of authority is transformed and feminized, and joined with Knightley's, it assumes a benign aspect. But in *Persuasion*, stately houses and their proprietors are no longer formidable, and their intransigence is matched only by their vapidity. Good characters depart from them without a breach, differ from them without defiance. Thus the overarching structure of *Persuasion* as a whole reproduces and asks us to accept the same sorts of unresolved tensions found in so many of its shorter, characteristically oxymoronic formulations—such as "fat sighings," or "she was deep in the happiness of such misery, or the misery of such happiness"

(P 229). *Persuasion* settles little: it resumes a debate interrupted eight years in the past without reaching an agreement, and without requiring one. Wentworth does not concede that Lady Russell had been right, Anne refuses to concede that yielding was wrong: "cheerful confidence in futurity" precludes such regret, and Providence has been equally served by delay. The "elasticity of mind" celebrated in *Persuasion* accepts and surpasses both of these, as well as the broader social conflicts the book details. It is tempting to see in this effort to define and endorse extensive difference from established institutions, without effecting an overt or impassible breach from them, as the perfection of the strategies and the positions that have marked Austen's fiction from the start. Austen, no less than Blake, wrote for an audience with what one critic has called "war-manacled minds," and her works, no less than Blake's, attempt—inevitably with only limited success— to shed those manacles which she perforce wore too.[14] Among the least doctrinaire of all her contemporaries, Austen from the outset took on the materials which political controversy endowed with such importance, without inviting or aggravating partisan impulses. During a time when all social criticism, particularly that which aimed at the institution of the family in general and the place of women in particular, came to be associated with the radical cause, Austen defended and enlarged a progressive middle ground that had been eaten away by the polarizing polemics born of the 1790s. If she very early opted definitely not to ratify the anarchism of the radical opposition, despite an allegiance to the liberal tradition which underlay much of it, she also avoided its irritability, its confusion, and its very early defeat. Conservative fiction was Austen's medium because it very quickly became the only fiction there was, other voices being quelled, and Austen persistently subjected its most cherished mythologies to interrogations from which it could not recover. The highly parodic style developed in the juvenilia, when applied to the stuff of conservative fiction, constituted a kind of piracy which commandeered conservative novelistic discourse and forced it to hoist flags of different colors, so to speak, to say things it was not fashioned to say—as when Catherine Morland, for example, assures herself with perfect trust that the good General Tilney "could not propose any thing improper for her" (NA 156); or when Marianne's "sensibility" and Elinor's "sense" turn out not to be antithetically opposed; or most optimistically, when Darcy himself absorbs the values of his antagonist in order to make her as well as himself happy. In none of the novels can conservative ideology be entirely overcome, but in all, as most forcibly in *Mansfield Park*, its basic imperatives—benevolence, gratitude, family attachment, female modesty, paternal authority—are wrested from their privileged claims and made, like Edmund Bertram, to relinquish their "moral elevation" (MP 158).

NOTES

1. For some of the many formulations of this view, see Virginia Woolf, *The Common Reader*, First Series, pp. 147–48; Nina Auerbach, *Romantic Imprisonment*, pp. 38–54, the chapter devoted to *Persuasion* in David M. Monaghan, *Jane Austen: Structure and Social Vision* (Totowa: Barnes & Noble, 1980).

2. For a historian's sceptical outlook on the way literary scholars have misused historical arguments about social change as reflected in *Persuasion*, see David Spring, "Interpreters of Jane Austen's Social World," in Todd, Jane Austen: *New Perspectives*, p. 65.

3. See, for example, Butler, *War of Ideas*, pp. 274–86; and Poovey, *Proper Lady*, pp. 224–40.

4. See B. C. Southam, "*Sanditon*: the Seventh Novel," in *Jane Austen's Achievement*, ed. Juliet McMaster (London: Macmillan, 1976), pp. 1–26. See also Joel J. Gold, "The Return to Bath: Catherine Morland and Anne Elliot," *Genre* 9 (1976): 215–29.

5. West, *Letters Addressed to a Young Man*, Letter 17, vol. 3, p. 371.

6. Maria Edgeworth, *Practical Education*, 2 vols. (London, 1798), pp. 167–68; 703–4.

7. West, *Letters to a Young Man*, Letter 14, Vol. 3, pp. 142–46; Cf. Hannah More, *Strictures on the Modern System of Female Education* (London, 1799), chap. 2.

8. Robert Bisset, *Modern Literature: A Novel*, 3 vols. (London, 1804), vol. 1, pp. 199–200; cf. the disgust with the idea of female vigor expressed in Benjamin Silliman, *Letters of Shahcoolen* (Boston, 1802). In an important discussion relevant to Mrs. Croft, David Monaghan argues that Austen differs from most contemporaries not only in granting "sex equality," but also in being willing to redefine gender roles in nontraditional ways; see "Jane Austen and the Position of Women," in *Jane Austen in a Social Context* (Totowa: Barnes & Noble, 1981), pp. 105–21.

9. I am indebted to the fine analysis in Tave, *Some Words*, p. 265.

10. For compelling discussions of the import of religious imagery throughout *Persuasion*, see Duckworth, *Improvement of the Estate*, pp. 195; and Jane Nardin, "Christianity and the Structure of *Persuasion*," *Renascence* 30 (1978): 43–55.

11. For some notable and welcome exceptions, see Frederick Keener, *The Chain of Becoming—The Philosophical Tale, the Novel, and a Neglected Realism of the Enlightenment* (New York: Columbia University Press, 1983), pp. 241–307; Lloyd W. Brown, *Bits of Ivory: Narrative Techniques in Jane Austen's Fiction* (Baton Rouge: Louisiana State University Press, 1971).

12. Edgeworth's copy of *Persuasion* is located in the Edgeworth Collection in the Special Collections Division of the University Research Library at The University of California, Los Angeles.

13. Trilling, *Sincerity and Authenticity*, pp. 71–74.

14. This phrase derives from David Erdman, *Blake, Prophet Against Empire* (Princeton: Princeton University Press, 1954).

JOHN WILTSHIRE

Persuasion: *The Pathology of Everyday Life*

That future of confinement to an unvarying, limited neighbourhood, supported with the spirits only of ruined happiness, sighted for a moment by Emma Woodhouse from the Hartfield windows on a miserable evening in July, becomes the actual condition of the gradually disclosed heroine of *Persuasion*, Austen's last completed novel. If *Emma* is a picture of health, the first volume of *Persuasion*, one can say with only a small exaggeration, is a portrait of suffering. Anne Elliot is a woman oppressed and insignificant, a 'nobody', discouraged by a burden of grief and regret that she has borne alone for the seven years prior to the novel's inception.

> Her attachment and regrets had, for a long time, clouded every enjoyment of youth; and an early loss of bloom and spirits had been their lasting effect ... No second attachment, the only thoroughly natural, happy, and sufficient cure, at her time of life, had been possible to the nice tone of her mind, the fastidiousness of her taste, in the small limits of the society around them. (28)

Having been persuaded to break of an engagement with a man whom she still loves, she wears her sadness and deprivation in her prematurely aging body and face. 'A few years before, Anne Elliot had been a very pretty girl, but her

---

From *Jane Austen and the Body: "The Picture of Health."* © 1992 by Cambridge University Press.

bloom had vanished early', now 'faded and thin', 'her spirits were not high', as her only friend Lady Russell admits, and this lack of resilience and of energy is evidenced in her first act in the novel, her intervention to persuade her sister Elizabeth about the ambitions of the hanger-on, Mrs Clay. Elizabeth arrogantly repudiates her advice, as she has foreseen. After a mild intercession from Anne, Elizabeth responds with renewed rudeness. 'Anne had done—glad that it was over, and not absolutely hopeless of doing good' (35). Anne's oppressed and marginal state—she has no energy to persist, and not being absolutely hopeless is her accustomed condition—is represented by her marginal position in the dialogue; her initiative is suppressed by the narrative, and Elizabeth's bullying instead allowed to dominate the page.

Anne's condition has been a prolonged, and private, mourning. Her loss and her grief are set by the novel within a continuum of other mourners who freely display their grief. Anne compares herself explicitly with Captain Benwick, the sailor who has suffered the unexpected loss of his fiancée, Fanny Harville, while at sea six months before. Everyone feels sympathy for him, '"And yet," said Anne to herself, as they now moved forward to meet the party, "He has not, perhaps, a more sorrowing heart than I have. I cannot believe his prospects so blighted for ever. He is younger than I am; younger in feeling, if not in fact; younger as a man. He will rally again, and be happy with another"' (97). This is Anne Elliot's lowest point in the novel, and it is characteristic of its mode of narration that she speaks only to herself, in a mood that marks her dissension, mild, but latently bitter, from the snood of those about her. Anne's authority in the narrative is promoted by the self-reflection that distinguishes the character's thoughts—by the perception that her own position as a woman is a determinant of her suffering—and here, additionally, by the accuracy of her prediction. Benwick, of course, does rally, and forgets Fanny Harville, but her brother, Captain Harville, though less the object of public attention, grieves for her longer and more poignantly. He cannot speak to Anne of his sister without 'a quivering lip' near the novel's close (232). The uncertain relationship of bereavement to its social signs is considered too in the extended presentation of Mrs Musgrove's demonstrative grief over the loss of her son, Dick, a grief that is 'real' as well as exaggerated and absurd, and by the mockery of woe carried about by William Walter Elliot, in his funereal livery and crape-banded hat, mourning for a wife he evidently does not grieve over.

These are not the only deaths which cast their shadows across the events of *Persuasion*. It is commonly agreed, in fact, that loss, and the human adjustment to loss, is a major theme of the novel.[1] There are losses of many kinds: of health, of hopes, of career, of one's home, of husbands and wives: perhaps, or so some critics argue, of a sense of stable value, even, some might claim, of the whole system of values that underpinned Jane Austen's other novels. 'By the time she wrote *Persuasion*,' argues David Monaghan, for example, 'Jane Austen seems to have lost faith in the gentry'.[2] Monaghan is one of many critics who read the Elliots' abdication of their country estate and their removal to Bath as symptomatic of a crucial transformation in English society, one indicative of a new hollowness in the code of polite manners, and the loss of the old order representing 'an ideal of civilised existence far beyond anything the Musgroves or the sailors could hope to achieve'.[3] 'In *Persuasion*', writes Mary Poovey, 'the fact that the social and ethical hierarchy superintended by the landed gentry is in a state of total collapse is clear not only from the fiscal and moral bankruptcy of Sir Walter Elliot but also from the epistemological relativity that is emphasised both thematically and formally'.[4] 'Just about all the previous stabilities of Jane Austen's world are called into question in this novel',[5] declares Tony Tanner, arguing that Austen in *Persuasion* demonstrates a 'crisis' or even 'chaos' in the gentry's values, and that this is in turn reflected in or signified by a shift in Austen's own priorities and narrative techniques. The novel is seen as Austen's farewell to a way of life. 'She is clearly undertaking a radical reassessment and revision of her system of values', claims Tanner.[6]

To read *Persuasion* as 'shaking the foundations of Austen's conservativism'[7] is to make Austen into a social historian of percipience indeed, discovering between the end of March 1815, when *Emma* was finished, and the beginning of August the same year, when *Persuasion* was begun, that the rural gentry were spiritually and financially bankrupt, foreseeing the modern condition, turning to newly discovered romantic values, and even more, it seems, anticipating the modern, or even postmodern, conviction of the relativity of all value and perception. David Spring has shown how unfounded are the historical assumptions upon which the view of *Persuasion* as depicting a social transformation rests: Sir Walter Elliot is not abandoning his estate in removing to Bath, and renting his property, he is simply repairing his fortunes in a time-honoured way. At the end of seven years he will return to Kellynch.[8] The navy men are not an alternative class, taking over power, their entrepreneurial initiative poised to take over the leading role in society vacated by the hollow gentry: they are gentry themselves, integrated and absorbed into the existing social order, as Benwick's eventual marriage to Louisa Musgrove exemplifies. The Musgrove family is ironised, but it is not a destructive irony: in all essential respects, they are a very good sort of people, uneducated and provincial perhaps, but the backbone of rural society. Mary Musgrove (née Elliot) has not come down in the world, and Charles Hayter, the educated young clergyman, is rising in it. There is no suggestion that such a society is either despicable, or in decline. Charles Musgrove is a representative and undistinguished country gentleman, but he does well for himself on the family's appearance in Bath, explicitly voicing opinions which the novelist's one cursorily contemptuous venture into Elizabeth's consciousness, when she decides not to invite the Musgroves to dinner, implicitly vindicates: 'It was a struggle between propriety and vanity; but vanity got the better, and then Elizabeth was happy again' (219). 'What's an evening party?' says Musgrove. 'Never worth remembering. Your father might have asked us to dinner, if he had wanted to see us' (223). When Mary protests that they have been invited to meet Mr Elliot—'the future representative of the family'—he replies roughly, 'Don't talk to me about heirs and representatives ... I am not one of those who neglect the reigning power to bow to the rising sun. If I would not go for the sake of your father, I should think it scandalous to go for the sake of his heir. What is Mr Elliot to me?' There is still vigour and conviction in the country gentry's code of values and in this speech they are seen to be congruent with the hospitality and independence celebrated in the naval figures. There are additional reasons of course why 'The careless expression was life to Anne, who saw that Captain Wentworth was all attention, looking and listening with his whole soul' (224) and certainly these things are seen from a point of view less implicated, less able to partake fully in the way of life they evoke than in earlier novels.

The view that *Persuasion* is a novel diagnosing radical shifts in social power, and that this vision corresponds to a radical recension in Austen's techniques and values seems to be motivated by the still-lingering embarrassment that a novel should be, to use the ironic phrase she used in defence of her art in *Northanger Abbey*, 'only a novel'. It is as if to vindicate or explain Jane Austen's status as a canonical or classic author it was necessary to make her into a social theorist, to make Austen prophesy the downfall of the class to which she belonged, or attribute to her, if not a radical politics, at least a 'radical' rethinking of her techniques. It is the easier, perhaps, to think of Sir Walter Elliot as a representative figure (rather than as a patent eccentric) because Bath, a real place, seems to function in this novel as the symbol—the structural embodiment and institutionalisation—of his own vanity and snobbery. One could easily suppose that Bath is presented in *Persuasion* as a specific microculture, a place in which traditional values have been replaced by commodity values, a built environment which seems to give concrete expression to a culture of narcissistic self-involvement. One could point, for instance, to the antithesis set up between Anne's thoughts of the autumn months in the country 'so sweet and so sad' and her dread of 'the possible heats of September in all the white glare of Bath' (33), and suggest that this is a hint at the false surface, the exclusion of the natural world and the inward turning that could be said to be characteristic of Bath's architecture. Eighteenth-century Bath is a city of enclosure, Squares and Circuses of geometric design explicitly sequestering the gentry who were to inhabit them from any natural wildness or irregularity. Describing John Wood's early eighteenth-century proposals for Queen's Square, the social historian R. S. Neale writes that 'Nature, except in the shape of a green turf and formal shrubs, was expressly excluded. There were to be no forest trees in the square, only low stone walls and espaliers of elm and lime'.[9] Later in the century, the lease of the Royal Crescent (1767–71) prevented the adjacent landowner from growing any tree more than eight feet high. The typical architecture of eighteenth-century Bath followed Wood's liking for 'enclosed spaces, designed to provide some isolation from the economic bustle of civil society and free from the intrusion of the labouring population who built and serviced the city'.[10] Separation of the gentry sections of the city both from the natural world and from the lower classes who were necessary to its existence was designed into its structure.

In Bath itself, in the novel, this social distribution of space is conveyed in the fact that addresses have a precisely calibrated economic and hence social value. Laura Place, for example, leased by the Elliots' cousin, Lady Dalrymple, a member of the (Irish, and therefore fringe) aristocracy, was an especially prestigious address, with one house built by John Eveleigh in 1702 advertised for letting at £120 per annum, with 'the special attraction of two water closets'.[11] The addresses are disposed in the novel as signifiers of social status—Camden-place, Gay Street, Lansdown Crescent, Marlborough Buildings—to be quickly, immediately, read as locating the addressee in a precise position on the social scale.[12] 'Westgate-buildings!' exclaims Sir Walter Elliot, 'and who is Miss Anne Elliot to be visiting in Westgate-buildings?—A Mrs. Smith ... And what is her attraction? That she is old and sickly' (157). Addresses are thus related to surnames and, as well, to fit and comely bodies, as markers of social rank.

Bath's *raison d'être* and subsequent prosperity was based upon its hot springs and medicinal waters. By Jane Austen's time it had become a resort which combined facilities for the renovation of health, and venues for the pursuit of social and sexual liaisons, a place in which the medicinal and the erotic were intertwined in an eighteenth-century Magic Fountain. 'Where the waters do agree, it is quite wonderful the relief they give', Mrs Elton tells Emma, and compounds the impertinence by adding 'And as to its recommendations to *you*, I fancy I need not take much pains to dwell on them. The advantages of Bath to the young are pretty generally understood' (E 275). Mrs Smith is one of those among its visitors who is lodging there for the purpose of health; she has come on the—arguably rational—grounds that the hot baths will relieve, if not cure, her rheumatism. But Bath had been for many years, as Defoe declared, 'the resort of the sound rather than the sick',[13] and its culture as an elegant watering place treats the body in another mode. The body is perceived as an object; it's to be prized or appraised, like handsome furniture, as a commodity. Thus when Elizabeth Elliot bestows a card upon Wentworth, her gesture is not a sign of forgiveness or reconciliation, a prompting of the inner moral life: 'The truth was, that Elizabeth had been long enough in Bath, to understand the importance of a man of such an air and appearance as his. The past was nothing. The present was that Captain Wentworth would move about well in her drawing-room' (226). The male body becomes an item of social circulation here as much as the female has always been, as for example at Netherfield. It is thus easy to elide Sir Walter Elliot's narcissism and vanity into representative status, as he stands 'in a shop in Bond-street' counting handsome faces as they go by (141–42). In its drawing rooms and evening parties the values he articulates can be seen to be reified, and he commodifies people on the streets as Lady Russell appraises handsome curtains.

Like all of Austen's novels, *Persuasion* is a study in the moral atmosphere of place. Obviously the novel contrasts, as does Anne Elliot herself, the warmth and hospitality of the Harvilles at Lyme, generous with their limited accommodation, with the cold formality of her father and sister in their two drawing rooms at Bath. The 'elegant stupidity' of their evening parties is evidently intended as typical of Bath society: on the other hand, as a resort, the city is atypical of the life of the gentry, and many aspects of the novel confirm this. *Persuasion* is certainly constructed in a more polarised mode than any other of Jane Austen's novels (even *Sense and Sensibility*): warmth, hospitality, enterprise, initiative, exertion and the future belonging—by and large—to the sailors, chill formality, snobbish self-regard, inertia and the past belonging—by and large—to the Elliots, their cronies and relations. But this simple polarity is actually greatly complicated by a number of features, not least of them the overlap, as I have already suggested, between the Musgroves and the Harvilles. The Musgroves are as hospitable as the Harvilles (one of the novel's subtle touches is the way the two families form all unobtrusive alliance as soon as events introduce them). Lady Russell is misguided and imperceptive, shares many of the dubious priorities of Sir Walter Elliot, but her value for rank does not prevent her from taking Anne to visit in Westgate Buildings, 'on the contrary, she approves it' (157). Bath is as hospital to the Crofts and their naval acquaintances as it is to the Elliots and their circle. Moreover it is a condition of the novel's plot that Anne Elliot's life be unusually confined and restricted so that opportunities for the depiction of representatives of the gentry other than the Elliots are necessarily curtailed.

Nevertheless, Bath and the Elliots are linked in a metonymic relationship, and the rest of the novel has a contrastive and interrogative function towards the corpus of values they represent. Bath excludes nature, excludes the labouring; and serving classes, and attempts to repress the knowledge of growth and change, of decay and death. Sir Walter lives out an infantile fantasy of narcissistic omnipotence.[14] Bath society represses that knowledge of the body as an unstable and imperfect subjective condition upon which its economy initially wholly, and still in part, depends, just as the labouring classes and wilderness are expunged from its spaces. But the novel discloses a 'real world' both inside and outside Bath in which the reader's intention is constantly being drawn to these necessary conditions of human life, to what Lady Russell calls 'the uncertainty of all human events and calculations' (159) and especially to thoughts about the human body very different from his simple equation of handsomeness and value.

Not being a great reader, Sir Walter Elliot is unlikely to have come across the quarto volumes of John Caspar Lavater's *Essays on Physiognomy*, widely as these circulated in the last decade of the eighteenth and the first of the nineteenth centuries, but if he had, he would have found there a notion of human nature not entirely at odds with his own. These heavy, profusely illustrated volumes outlined a theory of correspondence between features and moral character, between physical appearance and inner life. The many engravings of the faces of famous and unknown men and women with supplementary and elucidatory commentaries attempted to enforce the proposition that character can be read off from appearance, that, in Lavater's own words, 'virtue and vice, with all their shades, and in their most remote consequences, are beauty and deformity'.[15] Deviations from an ideal model of beauty were interpreted as 'symptomatic of analogous anomalies in the hidden psyche'.[16] 'Physiognomy', he wrote, 'is the science or knowledge of the correspondence between the external and the internal man, the visible superficial and the invisible contents'.[17]

But of course Sir Walter has no theory, and for him there is no correspondence: the 'invisible contents' might as well not exist: value exists only in appearance, and his moral world consists only of a hierarchy of assessments based exclusively on physical harmony and comeliness. Lavater is relevant to the novel he inhabits, none the less, because of the germ of truth, or of plausibility his new 'science' drew upon: the instinct, at its basis erotic or libidinal, to read health and vigour as virtue, to see handsomeness as integrity, an instinct in whose trap, for instance, Elizabeth Bennet is caught when she takes Wickham's presentation of himself as the injured but generous victim of Darcy's undeserved enmity on trust: 'Till I can forget his father, I never can defy or expose him', he asserts, piously enough. 'Elizabeth honoured him for such feelings', says the narrator, adding, 'and thought him handsomer than ever as he expressed them' (PP 80). It is an unconscious assumption often made in these novels, and *Persuasion*, which opens so decisively with a figure who equates value only with handsomeness, and who has, to all intents and purposes, no inner life or moral sense, carries the exploration of the problem of the relation between the face, the body, and the inner self further and into new, more disturbing areas. *Persuasion* is disturbed, too, by the collision between the enshrinement of that libidinal fantasy in the conventions of the romantic plot, and the promptings of a strenuous and critical realism.

Sir Walter thinks he and his like are immune from time: the narcissistic fantasy of his vanity expresses itself most powerfully in this delusion, which the novel subsequently underscores by emphasising the changes and vicissitudes wrought by time, and of the human body as an object besieged by its onslaughts. For time and vicissitude, the actions of nature, are more explicitly foregrounded in this novel than in any other of Jane Austen—with that touch of the traditional critical readings one can wholeheartedly agree— and it is their action upon the body which snakes the most salient contrast with the culture of Bath.

A. Walton Litz once claimed that *Persuasion* represents Jane Austen's most successful effort 'to build this sense of physical life into the language and structure of a novel'.[18] For Litz the 'deeply *physical* impact of *Persuasion*' is to be attributed to the novelist's 'poetic use of nature as a structure of feeling, which not only offers metaphors for our emotions but controls them with its unchanging rhythms and changing moods' and in the novel's development of 'a rapid and nervous syntax designed to imitate the bombardment of impressions upon the mind'.[19] Perceptive though these suggestions are, they fail to detect (perhaps because in one sense it is obvious) the series of occasions or events which refer explicitly to physical life and that are distributed through the novel as if to remind us (*pace* Sir Walter) that physical life is necessarily also physical vulnerability. After the opening Kellynch chapters in which he has been amply seen preening himself on his preservation from the ravages of time, Anne is claimed by Mary and goes to stay at Uppercross. Hardly has Wentworth been heard of in the neighbourhood, than her nephew falls and dislocates his collarbone, and Anne, faced with Mary's hysterics and the general confusion, takes charge of the household, eventually becoming the little boy's nurse, a situation which effectively delays her encounter with her former lover. Several of the scenes which follow depict her, specifically, in the role of nurse, attending to the child. The pretext for the shift of the novel's scene to Lyme is Wentworth's desire to see his old friend Harville, who 'had never been in good health since a severe wound which he received two years before' (94). Harville's lameness has curtailed his career and prospects in the navy, forced him into restricted accommodation, and makes it necessary for him to return home from their ramble in Lyme early, thus leaving only Anne and Wentworth to cope with subsequent events on the Cobb. Fatal injuries occur in civilian life too, and the scene of Louisa's jump, which climaxes events in the first volume of the novel, proves a turning point since it alters her personality and future and, in turn, the futures of Benwick, Wentworth and Anne Elliot. When, early in the second volume, Anne finally arrives in Bath, one of her first acts is to renew the friendship she had formed at school with a woman whom she had previously known 'in all the glow of health and confidence of superiority' and who is now poor and almost friendless, and, among her other misfortunes, is 'afflicted with a severe rheumatic fever, which finally settling in her legs, had made her for the present a cripple' (152). In each of the novel's main locales is found someone who is disabled as a result of injury or disease, or occurs an incident that serves to remind its of the vulnerability or fragility of the body. Pervading it all is Anne Elliot's unspoken sense of her own loss and deprivation, the result of the 'rupture' (28) with Wentworth. *Persuasion* is a novel of trauma: of broken bones, broken heads and broken hearts.

This reading of the novel then centres about the notion of injury, and for the most part, *Persuasion* depicts spiritual or mental pain and physical pain in the same terms, as when Wentworth speaks of Benwick's 'pierced, wounded, almost broken' heart. It's concerned with the ways people adjust to loss, or curtailment of life, and live through, or cope with, its deprivations. Mrs Smith appears now as an important figure, a significant commentary on the position of Anne. *Persuasion* is a short book, scarcely more than half the length of *Emma*. Even within this small compass, Mrs Smith is often considered a puzzlingly predominant flaw or intrusion, for conversations with her and discussions of her friend Nurse Rooke's ingenious ways of procuring advantages occupy two chapters in the second volume of the novel, the fullest just before its climax. The extended treatment the figure is given may be seen, in this light, as a crucial elaboration of the thought of the novel (though it cannot rescue the melodrama of her unmasking of Mr Elliot's 'hollow and black' heart) for the story of Mrs Smith, like the story of Anne Elliot, displays Jane Austen's intense interest in the resources of the human spirit in the face of affliction.[20] Austen's concern is not so much with accidents or misfortune as such, as with the positive human responses to suffering. In particular, she depicts (and critically examines) the isolated individual's attempt to gather the emotional resources to cope with chronic pain of a psychological nature, and the modes of support and nursing that enable others to endure and overcome their suffering and deprivation. And because pain and injury make so much of the material, it is inevitable that coping and nursing will also occupy the novel's attention.

Nurse Rooke's profession is a necessary element in the hidden economy of Bath: and, though essential to the plot of *Persuasion*, she is even more of an obscured figure in the novel she inhabits than Mr Perry is in his. Anne does not even notice her when she opens the door. Like Mr Perry in *Emma*, though, Nurse Rooke opens the door to one of *Persuasion*'s most important thematics. She is only one of a number of professional nursing figures who are momentarily noticed in the text, and who associate in the reader's mind nursing and femaleness, the nurse as the guardian of the small child with the nurse as attendant on the ailing adult. After Louisa Musgrove's fall, for example, Henrietta, her sister, wants to nurse her but 'Charles conveyed back a far more useful person in the old nursery-maid of the family, one who having brought up all the children, and seen the last, the very last, the lingering and long-petted master Harry, sent to school after his brothers, was now living in her deserted nursery to mend stockings, and dress all the blains and bruises she could get near her' (122). Nursing is thus linked not only with femaleness, but with social marginality. Sarah joins Mrs Harville, 'a very experienced nurse; and her nursery-maid, who had lived with her long and gone about with her every where, was just such another' (113). Mary has her favoured nursery maid too, Jemima. Nurse Rooke, besides her other professional duties, is a midwife. She attends the fashionable lady Mrs Wallis in her confinement, and as Mrs Smith with characteristic impudence says to Anne, 'She must be allowed to be a favourer of matrimony you know, and (since self will intrude) who can say that she may not have some flying visions of attending the next Lady Elliot, through Mrs Wallis's recommendation?' (208). Finally, as Anne and Wentworth take their reconciliatory stroll round Bath together they pass, unnoticed, 'nursery maids and children'. These glimpsed figures on the peripheries of the novel associate nursing with both mothering, and with social powerlessness: the nurse is a metaphor for both.[21] It is as if there were a necessary relationship between femaleness and nursing, as if true womanliness were expressed in devotion to the well-being of others, whether children or ailing adults.

Such was the view of moralists of this, as of later, periods. Thomas Gisborne's *Diaries of the Female Sex* of 1796 proposes that the 'unassuming and virtuous activity' of the female character is especially developed 'in contributing daily and hourly to the comfort of husbands, of parents, of brothers and sisters, and of other relations, connections and friends, in the intercourse of domestic life, under every vicissitude of sickness and health, of joy and affliction'.[22] Alistair Duckworth explains that the incident at

Uppercross in which Anne attends her nephew emphasises the 'utility' of her response: 'It suggests that the self, even when deprived of its social inheritance, may still respond affirmatively and in traditionally sanctioned ways, that deprivation need not lead to despair or to disaffection.'[23] This is certainly the view of Charles Musgrove, who announces that his son's dislocated collarbone is 'quite a female case' and need not prevent him dining out to meet Captain Wentworth, and underlined by Anne Elliot herself, who declares more mildly to Mary, put out that she is left at home, 'Nursing does not belong to a man, it is not his province. A sick child is always the mother's property, her own feelings generally make it so' (56). This conservative generalisation is immediately contradicted by Mary's alacrity at being released from the duty to her child by Anne's offer to stay at home. But the nobility of Anne's sacrifice is also qualified in this instance because of the ulterior motive behind her offer: her apparent dutifulness to the child is a means of protecting herself from the pain of an encounter with Wentworth. The social role, however 'traditionally sanctioned' here, as elsewhere, does not quite fit the emotions and motives of she who adopts it. Later, Anne's care of the child is to serve as a pretext for her not engaging in conversation with her former lover.

Femaleness and nursing are thus ideologically linked, but it is a curiously restricted femaleness. The nurse is a functional substitute for the nurturing and nurturant, supportive, mother in Alexander Pope's phrase, 'the tender Second to a Mother's care':[24] whilst being quintessentially female, her femaleness is thought of as Maternal, not sexual. A true woman will necessarily be a good nurse, but her womanliness will be one in which her own purposes and sexual desires will be subordinated to, and sublimated in, her ministrations to the child or to the patient. Her hands are intimate with the body, and she has therefore a quasi-sexual relation to the subjects whom she attends, but her own sexuality is necessarily screened or suspended. Anne Elliot is assigned, or assigns herself, to a range of ancillary roles in the households at Uppercross and Lyme—listener, confidante, 'umpire' between husband and wife, accompanist on the piano—but her role as nurse subsumes these others, and it is precisely as a nurse that she values herself most and is most valued by those around her. In positioning herself thus as mother-substitute, as she does, for instance, by taking over the care of the injured child from Mary, she expunges herself as a desiring subject. In effect, she is representing to herself, and allowing her circle to assume, that her romantic story is closed, is in the past, that she does not entertain ambitions or desires on her own behalf, but only on behalf of those to whose well-being she attends. The role of nurse is eminently female, not without initiative, and not without strength, but without desire. It is a role in which Anne comes to be valued, but her value is predicated upon the obliteration (or suspension) of her own bodily needs. Whilst she plays, her hands mechanically at work, 'equally without error and without consciousness' (72), others engage in the courtship dance; whilst she attends to Mrs Musgrove or her injured nephew, Wentworth narrates the history of how he was 'made', regales the admiring Musgroves with his exploits: he re-creates himself as an active, desiring principle, whilst she salvages what identity she can as listener and as confidante of others.

Anne's laborious and demanding attentions to the child (she has Mary to worry about, too, of course) are amusingly juxtaposed with the merely verbal solicitude of the Musgrove sisters for 'dear, good Dr Shirley's being relieved from the duty which he could no longer get through without most injurious fatigue', Dr Shirley being the elderly rector of Uppercross, whose curacy they have their eyes on for Charles Hayter. On the beach at Lyme, Anne listens and encourages once again, amused to detect the motivation of Henrietta's enthusiasm for Dr Shirley's settling by the sea; 'The sea air always does good', that artless young lady exclaims, 'There can be no doubt of its having been of the greatest service to Dr Shirley, after his illness, last spring twelvemonth' (102). Once again, like Mr Perry setting up his carriage, talk about health serves to disguise the economic and, in this case, sexual motives which are actually in operation. That caring for others may afford substitute gratifications is not, I think, a point the novel dwells on, but it is clear that nursing gives Anne a pretext for a semi-permanent adoption of that role of bystander to which she has consigned herself, and in which she takes both comfort and pride.

Yet because *Persuasion* depicts the body as fragile and vulnerable, nursing does emerge as an important value, despite its association with the sexually and socially subordinate. The companionate marriage of the Crofts is a good example. Mrs Croft herself remarks that the only time she has ever been ill was when she was left on shore, separated from her husband. 'I lived in perpetual fright at that time, and had all manner of imaginary complaints from not knowing what to do with myself ...' she tells Mrs Musgrove (71). When they come to Bath, the Admiral is 'ordered to walk, to keep off the gout, and Mrs Croft seemed to go shares with him in every thing, and to walk for her life, to do him good. Anne saw them wherever she went' (168). But this turns into genial parody as altruistic female attendance becomes self-injury. A week or so afterwards Anne sees Admiral Croft talking alone. Croft, asking her to take his arm, makes a remark that matches his wife's earlier ones. 'I do not feel comfortable if I have not a woman there', and explains why he is out without her. He may have kept down the gout, but she has become the invalid: 'She, poor soul, is tied by the leg. She has a blister on one of her heels, as large as a three shilling piece' (170).

More importantly, the novel puts nursing in a new light by assigning nursing functions, or something equivalent to them, to the heroic male, Wentworth. The scene where he is first displayed (and displays himself) for example, is intercepted by a passage in which he exchanges places with the listening, attendant, Anne. His bragging of his achievements and prizes, his careless boasts of nonchalance in the face of danger are rendered indirectly, through her listening consciousness. Then when Anne's attention is claimed by Mrs Musgrove, he recedes into silence. In the foreground is Mrs Musgrove and her thoughts about her lost, apparently 'worthless' son, Dick.

> 'Ah! Miss Anne, if it had pleased Heaven to spare my poor son,
> I dare say he would have been just such another by this time.'
>   Anne suppressed a smile, and listened kindly, while Mrs Musgrove relieved her heart a little more; and for a few minutes, therefore, could not keep pace with the conversation of the others. (64)

When Wentworth is in turn appealed to by the grieving mother, his attitude replicates Anne's, and is relayed by her. She detects 'an indulgence of self-amusement' in his face at first, but 'in another moment he was perfectly collected and serious; and almost instantly afterwards coming up to the sofa, on which she and Mrs Musgrove were sitting, took a place by the latter, and entered into conversation with her, in a low voice, about her son, doing it with so much sympathy and natural grace, as showed the kindest consideration for all that was real and unabsurd in the parent's feelings' (67–8) This is not that showy gallantry towards women which his sister shortly criticises him for, but a quick and intuitive solicitude that precisely matches Anne's. This passage is an example of the flexibility of the point of view in this novel: though the listening consciousness still remains Anne's, the narrative moves seamlessly away from her to inform us of the speech of Wentworth (which she could hardly hear) and even penetrates to the quality of Mrs Musgrove's feelings.

'No summons mocked by chill delay': Wentworth's responses to appeals for help and sympathy are always ready 'instantly'. The word is habitually tagged to his gestures, movements, and actions, an index of that bodily ease and confident physical efficiency which support his enterprise and daring. The most signal example of his humanity is recounted by Captain Harville just prior to the fall on the Cobb. Anne and Harville are talking of Benwick's recent bereavement. Fanny Harville died in June, but the news was not known to him until August, when he came home from the Cape. 'I was at Plymouth,' says Harville, but Benwick's ship was due to dock at Portsmouth. 'There the news must follow him, but who was to tell it?':

'Nobody could do it, but that good fellow, (pointing to Captain Wentworth.) The *Laconia* had come into Plymouth the week before; no danger of her being sent to sea again. He stood his chance for the rest—wrote up for leave of absence, but without waiting the return, travelled night and day till he got to Portsmouth, rowed off to the Grappler that instant, and never left the poor fellow for a week; that's what he did, and nobody else could have saved poor James. You may think, Miss Elliot, whether he is dear to us!'

Anne did think on the question with perfect decision, and said as much in reply as her own feelings could accomplish, or as his seemed able to bear. (108)

Wentworth, in effect, nurses Benwick through the worst of his grief. (On the other hand, Mr Elliot, we are told, refused to help the widow of his friend, and by refusing to act as his executor, greatly increased her distress (209).) Harville's tribute has the narrative function of displaying Wentworth as a courageous and enterprising as well as sympathetic man just before the incident which is to present him as very nearly inadequate or impotent, as he faces a crisis of a more complicated sort.

Wentworth's capacity for sympathetic attentiveness (what I have called nursing) is displayed, of course, most fully in his attentions to Anne Elliot herself. If we are to explain 'the deeply physical impact' of *Persuasion* we look first, I think, at the intensity of Anne Elliot's responses to her former fiancé's physical presence, and to the indirect, mediated evidence of his awareness of her. Anne and Wentworth are kept apart in the first scenes at Uppercross partly because (as David Monaghan suggests) Anne relegates herself to a peripheral position which the Musgroves do not have the perception or intelligence to see is less than she deserves. Wentworth's lingering resentment and Anne's modesty keep the two former lovers apart, since there is no one with any appreciation of Anne's value to give her the more prominent role that might have brought her to Wentworth's notice. Their intercourse is a minimal one of polite manners and careful avoidance. Wentworth arranges to avoid even the perfunctory physical contact of shaking hands that a formal introduction would require (59). In the subsequent scenes at Uppercross, good manners and politeness, 'the exchange of the common civilities', acts as a barrier to closer intercourse, as the two ex-lovers manoeuvre to keep out of each other's way, even when they are in the same room.

But a child of two has no manners, none of these polite inhibitions, and therefore can be the agency through which the two people whom politeness would have kept 'perpetually estranged' (64) can be brought together. Anne is forced to stay in the room with Wentworth because the sick boy demands her, and imprisoned by the younger child, who 'began to fasten himself upon her, as she knelt, in such a way that, busy as she was about Charles, she could not shake him off', she is rescued by Wentworth's resourceful action: 'In another moment, however, she found herself in the state of being released from him: some one was taking him from her, though he had bent down her head so much, that his little sturdy hands were unfastened from around her neck, and he was resolutely borne away, before she knew that Captain Wentworth had done it' (80). The child is a 'transitional object' to borrow Winnicott's term: Wentworth relieves Anne's body through the agency of his physical contact with the body of the child. The breach of strict decorum is admissible because it appears in the guise of solicitude, and the incident is kept below the level of socially embarrassed consciousness by the silence in which it is transacted. The rescue leaves Anne quite speechless, overwhelmed with confused emotions. They are not due merely to being the recipient of an act of courtesy.

A similar act of solicitude, but this time wholly volunteered by Wentworth and thus showing a fuller attention to Anne, comes in the next chapter where on the return from Winthrop the party meets the Crofts in their gig, who offer a ride to any lady who might be tired. Anne's tiredness has not been dwelt on, though Charles Musgrove's inattention to her has, so that when Wentworth 'cleared the hedge in a moment to say something to his sister' and then, the Crofts having offered a place to Anne, 'without saying a word' turns to her and 'quietly obliged her to be assisted into the carriage' (91) the reader perceives it as a strikingly solicitous action. These deeds may be read as Anne reads them, fully persuaded as she is from the conversation she has just overheard between Wentworth and Louisa, that Wentworth is now indifferent about her: but his detection of Anne's fatigue (the topic has not come up—she has made no complaint) suggests that for a man supposedly courting another woman, his mind is unusually occupied with her. In Highbury misplaced attention to bodily well-being reflects ignorance about or obliviousness to the subject's inner life. In these two instances, in a wonderful twist to the Highbury mode, nursing concern for the body becomes the permissible vehicle in which awakening (or latent) desire can find a plausible and socially sanctioned, because apparently sexually neutral, expression. Anne misreads Wentworth's behaviour in just this way, as chivalry or solicitude without sexual motivation: 'though becoming attached to another, still he could not see her suffer, without the desire of giving her relief'. The irony is far more muted than the irony that attaches to Emma Woodhouse's misconstruings, but Anne's supposition is not unqualified by the narrational circumstances.

In a parallel way, Wentworth's awakened or awakening love for Anne is expressed in his regard for her in that woman's exemplary role as a nurse. It is clear that everyone in the novel values Anne as a nurse, or rather that her value, unrecognised until then, is made visible when she emerges as a nurse, or needs to be used as one, but there is something more to that moment after the accident on the Cobb when Anne, coming downstairs, overhears Wentworth praising her competence:

> '.... If Anne will stay, no one so proper, so capable as Anne!'
>
> She paused a moment to recover from the emotion of hearing herself spoken of. The other two warmly agreed to what he said, and she then appeared.
>
> 'You will stay. I am sure; you will staff and nurse her;' cried he, turning to her and speaking with a glow, and yet a gentleness, which seemed almost restoring the past.—She coloured deeply; and he collected himself and moved away. (114)

To speak publicly in praise of Anne in the role of nurse is permissible, because of that separation of nursing from sexuality I have described. Whilst the relation is actually one of desire, it is conducted here, once more, according to the canons of solicitude. Wentworth's feeling for Anne can thus be masked by its ideological vehicle. In fact, though, as Anne intuits, he is expressing love for her, and the mutual embarrassment of this passing moment circles round this unspoken, almost unthought, disclosure.

It is through such moments of mutual caring and embarrassment that Anne and Wentworth progress towards their knowledge of each other's heart. Far more to the foreground in the first volume of the novel, though, is Anne's attempt to find solely within herself the resources by which to live through her neglect and isolation, an attempt predicated upon the hopelessness of ever fulfilling her desire. The first volume, after the introduction of the Elliots, comes to focus on the psychology of Anne, as she attempts to school herself into composure and 'reason' when faced with the agitation and distress, as well as awakened desire, brought about by Wentworth's reappearance in her circle. She has 'become hardened' (32) to the affronts of her family, but the wound that opened in her psyche with the rejection of Wentworth, and her recognition that the rejection was a mistake, has not been healed by a second attachment. 'She could not hear that Captain Wentworth's sister was likely to live at Kellynch, without a revival of former pain; and many a stroll and many a sigh were necessary to dispel the agitation of the idea. She often told herself it was folly, before she could harden her nerves sufficiently to feel the continual discussion of the Crofts and their business no evil' (30). To harden her nerves, to inure herself against suffering, is the emotional programme Anne Elliot adopts.

Jane Austen's favourite brother Henry, who published *Persuasion* and *Northanger Abbey* after her death in 1818, delivered during the same year a sermon at 'the chapel of the British Minister at Berlin' in which he spoke of 'the beautiful, the instructive part of Joseph's character' which was, he declared, 'deeply to feel, and strictly to command his feelings'.[25] It is evident from *Persuasion* that Jane Austen shared this ideal of the moral character, for the first volume of the novel consistently depicts Anne Elliot attempting to live the life of the Christian stoic. She feels deeply, but she seeks means, through the exertion of 'reason', to combat her feelings, and to generate, if possible, an independent, autonomous self. 'That man should never suffer, his happiness to depend upon external circumstances, is one of the chief precepts of the Stoical philosophy' as Johnson had stated in his sixth *Rambler* essay (1750). He goes on to outline how a Christian can make some use of the stoic ideal, adapting it into a more provisional, more contingent attempt to foster a state of mind which is secure against the destructive invasion of external influences. 'We may very properly enquire', he wrote,

> how near to this exalted state it is in our power to approach, how far we can exempt ourselves from outward influences, and secure to our minds a state of tranquillity: for, though the boast of absolute independence is ridiculous and vain, yet a mean flexibility to every impulse, and a patient submission to the tyranny of casual troubles, is below the dignity of that mind, which however depraved or weakened, boasts its derivation from a celestial original.

Like the stoic, Anne Elliot, in Foucault's phrase, 'is called upon to take [her]self as an object of knowledge and a field of action'.[26] The exclusively male ethics and practices developed during the first centuries of Christendom become, in the eighteenth and nineteenth, a means by which the socially disempowered woman converts her powerlessness into self-definition. Though not codified formally, enough features of the stoic regimen are displayed incidentally in the first volume of *Persuasion* to demonstrate that Anne Elliot has absorbed many of the characteristic exercises through which the stoics both guarded and constituted the self. Like them, she 'makes herself familiar with the minimum',[27] thinking, for instance, as Mary and Charles depart, that 'she was left with as many sensations of comfort, as were, perhaps, ever likely to be hers.' 'What was it to her', she asks, 'if Frederick Wentworth were only half a mile distant ...?'

(58). Like them, Anne takes for granted that life will afford her little more comfort than the comfort of a clear conscience. Her attempts to 'harden' herself are a version of the stoic's armour against calamity. Like the stoics, she attempts to argue herself into a state of emotional aloofness from outer hazards, and the most original feature of the novel's prose, as Litz and others have pointed out, is the freedom with which it imitates the nervous swings of Anne's feelings as she struggles to command them, aroused by the sight of Wentworth once again:

> 'It is over! it is over!' she repeated to herself again, and again, in nervous gratitude. 'The worst is over!'
>
> Mary talked, but she could not attend. She had seen him. They had met. They had been once more in the same room!
>
> Soon, however, she began to reason with herself, and try to feeling less. Eight years, almost eight years had passed, since all had been given up. How absurd to be resuming the agitation which such an interval had banished into distance and indistinctness! What might not eight years do? Events of every description, changes, alienations, removals,—all, all must be comprised in it; and oblivion of the past—how natural, how certain too! It included nearly a third part of her own life.
>
> Alas! with all her reasonings, she found, that to retentive feelings eight years may be little more than nothing.
>
> Now, how were his sentiments to be read? Was this like wishing to avoid her? And the next moment she was hating herself for the folly which asked the question. (60)

'Reasoning with herself', Anne Elliot takes herself as an object of knowledge, even though, as represented here, her 'reasonings' are a scrambling together of frail defences against the onslaught of unassuaged emotion. But the transparency with which Austen now can present the invasions of feeling—a technical achievement in the development of an open and un-Johnsonian prose—does not, of course, imply revised or fluctuating values: such a telling enactment of the failure of the rational faculty to control or contain the promptings of desire does not impugn 'reason' in itself as an ideal to be striven towards. It is within the ethic of stoicism, too, that Anne's response to hearing that Wentworth has said she is 'so altered that he should not have known her again!' is inscribed. 'These were words which could not but dwell with her. Yet she soon began to rejoice that she had heard them. They were of sobering tendency; they allayed agitation; they composed, and consequently must make her happier' (61). 'Always making sure that one does not become attached to that which does not come under our control'[28] Anne seeks a state of emotional equilibrium or 'composure', not far from the stoic ideal of 'apathia'.

Composure is both an ideal of inner disposition and of social demeanour, and each can foster or augment the other. Sometimes social manners may camouflage an agitated or turbulent mind, as they do most remarkably for Lady Russell who 'had only to listen composedly' on hearing of Wentworth's probable engagement to Louisa Musgrove, 'but internally her heart revelled in angry pleasure, in pleased contempt' at this apparent vindication of her opinion of Anne's former suitor. Usually, for Anne, inner agitation cannot but be expressed physiologically—in tears, in paleness or in blushing—and therefore social devices have to substitute for lack of inner composure. When Wentworth relieves her of the scrambling child, Anne bends over little Charles to hide her face, which otherwise would display her 'confusion of varying, but very painful agitation', before making off to her room to 'arrange' her feelings (80–1). Or a screen for her agitations may conveniently be provided by Mrs Musgrove. When Lady Russell tempts her to accept Elliot by suggesting that Anne would thereby take the place of her mother 'Anne was obliged to turn away, to rise, to walk to a distant table, and, leaning there in pretended employment, try to subdue the feelings this picture excited' (160). In an instance of the symmetry between the lovers that is so consistent in his novel, Anne perceives in, or projects onto, Wentworth, her own typical strategies, as he hides his face after the accident. 'He sat near a table, leaning over it with folded arms, [his] face concealed, as if overpowered by the various feelings of his soul, and trying by prayer and reflection to calm them' (112).

'In *Persuasion* the sense of community has disappeared and the heroine finds herself terribly alone', Litz had written in his earlier book on Austen of 1965.[29] This is another version of the novel as an epochal break with the earlier work, for in it Anne is said to experience the 'despair' of the 'modern "personality"'. The language perhaps belongs rather to the crisis of liberal humanism than to the mood, even the saddest mood, of Anne Elliot, for there is no terror in her comparative emotional isolation, and her self-reflection and self-consciousness are depicted as at least in part a strength, a resource. The attempt to reason herself out of her agitation demonstrates the presence within her of a culture of personal self-determination, but in many ways the most convincing achievement of the novel in this sphere is to show how Anne's 'cultivated mind' is manifested indirectly, not in the self-regulating exercises she performs, but as part of that mind's fabric, in the apparently involuntary and smilingly ironic self-reflection with which she sees the parts she herself plays within her culture.

The novel's dialogue with earlier texts about suffering is carried through two main set-piece scenes, one with Captain Benwick, the bereaved sailor, the other with the crippled and impoverished school-friend, Mrs Smith. Anne and Benwick discuss poetry together, but romantic poetry is presented as dangerously self-absorbing, like the 'sweets of poetical despondence' with which Anne had consoled, and indulged, herself on the walk to Winthrop. Finding that Benwick uses his reading only to amplify his grief, Anne makes 'some suggestions as to the duty and benefit of struggling against affliction':

> she was emboldened to go on; and feeling in herself the right of seniority of mind, she ventured to recommend a larger allowance of prose in his daily study; and on being requested to particularise, mentioned such works of our best moralists, such collections of the finest letters, such memoirs of characters of worth and suffering, as occurred to her at the moment as calculated to rouse and fortify the mind by the highest precepts, and the strongest examples of moral and religious enduranccs. (101)

Some issues of Johnson's periodical, *The Rambler*, especially perhaps number 32, 'on patience, even under extreme misery' would certainly be among those books Anne takes leave to recommend. It was this number of the *Rambler* that was singled out by Boswell in his famous commendation of the work in the *Life of Johnson*, which Austen had, of course, read. 'In no writings whatever can be found *more bark and steel for the mind*, if I may use the expression,' he wrote, 'more that can brace and invigorate every manly and noble sentiment'.[30] This idea of the book as fortifying the male is wonderfully parodied, and perhaps subverted, by the very first sentence of *Persuasion*, conspicuously Johnsonian in its cadence, where Sir Walter Elliot reads the Baronetage to find 'occupation for an idle hour and consolation in a distressed one' and where 'his faculties were roused into admiration and respect...' It is subverted once again by the detachment with which, her rather solemn ministrations completed, Anne Elliot views the episode:

> When the evening was over, Anne could not but be amused at the idea of her coming to Lyme, to preach patience and resignation to a young man whom she had never seen before; nor could she help fearing, on more serious reflection, that, like many other great moralists and preachers, she had been eloquent on a point in which her own conduct would ill bear examination. (101)

'That few men, celebrated for theoretic wisdom, live with conformity to their precepts, must be readily confessed', wrote Johnson in *Rambler* 77. 'Do not be too hasty ... to trust, or to admire the teachers of morality: they discourse like angels, but they live like men', Imlac the sage warns Rasselas. Anne's humorous self-inflation is neatly reflected by Wentworth's equally ironic boast later in the novel. 'Like other great men under reverses', he declares, 'I must endeavour to subdue my mind to my fortune. I must learn to brook being happier than I deserve' (247). The novel thus continues a predominantly masculine literary and moral tradition in its presentation of Anne Elliot's care of the self,[31] but it is a tradition which can include too the humorously self-subversive attitudes which frame the heroine's tendency towards earnest idealism. The questioning of stoicism is carried even further in the depiction of Mrs Smith, as well as Anne's propensity to see life just a little through the spectacles of books.

Mrs Smith is the first invalid in Jane Austen's novels whose distresses are indubitably real.

> She was a widow, and poor. Her husband had been extravagant; and at his death, about two years before, had left his affairs dreadfully involved. She had had difficulties of every sort to contend with, and in addition to these distresses, had been afflicted with a severe rheumatic liver, which finally settling in her legs, had made her for the present a cripple. She had come to Bath on that account, and was now in lodgings near the hot-baths, living in a very humble way, unable even to afford the comfort of a servant, and of course almost excluded from society. (152–53)

It is Mrs Smith who is to reveal the true nature of the impeccably well-mannered Mr Elliot, an exposure that is, strictly speaking, superfluous since Anne has already made up her own mind not to trust him. She also introduces an element that, given how close the story of Anne comes to romance, is necessary: her story insists on the harsher realities of life. Anne, for example, has elevated notions of the nurse's experience: 'What instances must pass before them', she declares, 'of ardent, disinterested, self-denying attachment, of heroism, fortitude, patience, resignation—of all the conflicts and all the sacrifices that enoble us most. A sick chamber may often furnish the worth of volumes'. The volumes Anne is no doubt thinking of would contain those examples of moral and religious endurances which she had preached about to Benwick not long before, and which in a more self-reflective or tough-minded moment she had seen as contradicted or at least qualified by her own behaviour. Mrs Smith's reply contains a note of astringent realism that serves to dampen the ardour of Anne's romantic and even sentimental claims: '"Yes" said Mrs Smith, more doubtingly, "sometimes it may, though I fear its lessons are not often in the elevated style you describe. Here and there, human nature may be great in times of trial, but generally speaking it is its weakness and not its strength that appears in a sick chamber; it is selfishness and impatience, rather than generosity and fortitude, that one hears of"' (156). One function of Mrs Smith is to anchor the romantic idealism of Anne (to be fully demonstrated in the speeches to Harville which precipitate Wentworth's proposal) to the grim conditions of survival. She restrains the novel's impulse to a day-dream-like wish-fulfilment (the past restored, the rift healed) by setting against it a view of life characterised by day-to-day tenaciousness and an integrity qualified by necessary expediency. The lesson of the sickroom Mrs Smith is to demonstrate is not quite of the elevated kind Anne imagines.

Mrs Smith's liveliness and adroitness are very closely linked to economic advantage and survival. She has had to develop new skills (even literally, like the knitting Nurse Rooke has taught her) in order to survive. She needs tact, address and diplomacy to maximise her possible advantage from Anne's prospective marriage with Mr Elliot. No matter that Elliot has wronged her, no matter that he has betrayed and neglected her, no matter that Anne may be about to marry a cold-hearted villain. To warn Anne is a luxury she cannot afford, to advise caution is the privilege of those whose own economic status is secure. Mrs Smith must adroitly calculate what possible advantages there might be to her in whatever opportunities present themselves. These are the pressing exigencies of the poor. Naturally some readers feel uncomfortable with Mrs Smith's 'cynicism' and with her apparent duplicity towards Anne in concealing what she knows of Mr Elliot, as well as her 'unqualified bitterness' towards him when she is free to speak; they feel that this violates the atmosphere of the novel and that the details of Mr Elliot's perfidy unnecessarily interrupt its progress towards gradual romantic affirmation. But what her presence does is remind us of the social security, as well as the luck, that afford Anne the privilege of her untarnished romantic idealism, and that makes the final fulfilment of her desires such a rare and exceptional apotheosis. 'Prettier musings of high-wrought love and eternal constancy, could never have passed along the streets of Bath, than Anne was sporting with from Camden-place to Westgate-buildings. It was almost enough to spread purification and perfume all the way' (192), is how Austen describes Anne's journey to the interview. In part this is a reflection on the decadence of Bath. 'Oh! who can ever he tired of Bath?' had exclaimed Catherine Morland, the seventeen year old heroine of *Northanger Abbey*.

'Not those who bring such fresh feelings of every sort to it, as you do', replies Henry Tilney. 'But papas and mammas, and brothers and intimate friends are a good deal gone by, to most of the frequenters of Bath and the honest relish of balls and plays and every-day sights, is past with them' (NA 79). The comment in *Persuasion* is similarly an amused and partly ironic glance at the still-intact and reality-defining ardour of his much older heroine. To spread purification is to imply that the stencil of decay might otherwise prevail. In other words, Mrs Smith makes plain that though Anne is a romantic (and it happens miraculously in this instance that her idealism is vindicated and her dreams are fulfilled) Jane Austen is not.

Mrs Smith is surviving, and can be charitable to those poorer even than herself, because she has developed an informal, female network of support, through her landlady and Nurse Hooke, more desperate, more tenuous, but analogous to the mutual support of the sailors. Considering her 'cheerless situation' (worse even than Fanny Price's at Portsmouth) Mrs Smith seems to be astonishingly resilient, and her cheerfulness prompts Anne to an implicit reflection upon her own coping strategies:

> Her accommodations were limited to a noisy parlour, and a dark bedroom behind, with no possibility of moving from one to the other without assistance, which there was only one servant in the house to afford, and she never quitted the house but to be conveyed into the warm bath.—Yet, in spite of all this, Anne had reason to believe that she had moments only of languor and depression, to hours of occupation and enjoyment. How could it be?—She watched—observed—reflected—and finally determined that this was not a case of fortitude or of resignation only.—A submissive spirit might be patient, a strong understanding would supply resolution, but here was something more; here was that elasticity of mind, that disposition to be comforted, that power of turning readily from evil to good, and of finding employment which carried her out of herself, which was from Nature alone. It was the choicest gift of Heaven... (154)

This initial impression is perhaps to be modified, as more is seen of what this adaptability means, and qualified too, by the resentment Mrs Smith is later shown to harbour towards Elliot, but it is clear that Mrs Smith is certainly not 'the Christian Stoic of *Persuasion*'.[32] She is a refutation of the notion that one can retain one's independence within patriarchal society only through the ethic of self-discipline, through patience and resolution and the cultivation of the self. Her 'elasticity', her power of interest in the world about her, and her delight in her imagination, remind us, I think, of another Jane Austen woman who delights to detect the signs of romance in the faces of others. Mrs Smith eagerly constructs from the gossip she has heard and from Anne's bright eyes the hypothesis that she is to marry Elliot:

> '... You need not tell me that you had a pleasant evening. I see it in your eye. I perfectly see how the hours passed—that you had always something agreeable to listen to. In the intervals of the concert, it was conversation.'
>
> Anne half smiled and said, 'Do you see that in my eye?'
>
> 'Yes, I do. Your countenance perfectly informs me that you were in company last night with the person, whom you think the most agreeable in the world, the person who interests you at this present time, more than all the rest of the world put together.'
>
> A blush overspread Anne's cheeks. She could say nothing. (194)

The presumption and eagerness of Emma Woodhouse are recaptured briefly in these characteristically emphatic speech rhythms ('perfectly ... perfectly ... all the rest of the world put together'). 'If you prefer Mr Martin to every other person: if you think him the most agreeable man you have ever been in company with, why should you hesitate? You blush, Harriet ...' (E 53). Mrs Smith's elasticity is related to Emma's spirit—a quality that is a moral anomaly, that offends almost as much as it alarms, but that ensures her survival, even in the most defeating conditions of personal deprivation.

Though she tells Anne in her bitterness at Elliot's betrayal, that her 'peace' has been 'shipwrecked' (196), she has earlier claimed to have 'weathered' the most acute of her distresses (154). It is obvious enough how—Austen links, through these metaphors, Mrs Smith's mode of survival in her cramped rooms with Mrs Croft's 'weathered face' and happiness in confined quarters, and links them also with the survival and resiliance of Captain Harville, another crippled victim of hazard and misfortune, and as I have suggested, her informal support system is an underclass reflection of the male bonding of the sailors. What is more, Nurse Rooke's enterprise in wringing from her convalescent patients both useful gossip and charitable donations reflects the commercial imperatives and initiatives that rule the lives of the men the novel asks us to admire. (It is amusing to see critics who unquestionably accept the sailors' right to plunder French frigates getting upset at this 'nurse-accomplice'[33] taking minor advantage of her wealthier clients.)

The accident which forms the climax of the first volume of the novel is its turning point, since Louisa Musgrove's jump and its aftermath supposedly lead Wentworth to rediscover his love for Anne, and at the same time release him from obligations to her. The incident, so he says later to Anne, teaches him a lesson: 'There he had learnt to distinguish between the darings of heedlessness and the resolution of a collected mind': a conduct-book moralism (young ladies should always be prudent) that is best regarded as his attempt to rationalise than as an exhaustive account of the incident's meaning. Certainly it convincingly illustrates Anne Elliot's competence in a medical emergency. Whilst Henrietta faints, Mary has hysterics and Wentworth, overcome with shock, staggers against the wall for support, she thinks quickly, resourcefully, and intelligently, making herself the effective temporary commander of this floundering human ship.

Anne keeps her wits when all about her are losing theirs—and to read some critics, it is this which revives Wentworth's love. The occasion is revelatory, though, not determinant. Wentworth is already, perhaps unknown to himself, in love with Anne Elliot, and the incident is only one of a series of moments which confirm his awakening feelings. Austen pairs this incident on the steps of the Cobb with the equally accidental moment at the same place when the Mysterious Stranger, later revealed as Mr Elliot, looks admiringly at her as she passes by.

> She was looking remarkably well; her very regular, very pretty features, having the bloom and freshness of youth restored by the fine wind which had been blowing on her complexion, and by the animation of eye which it had also produced. It was evident that the gentleman, (completely a gentleman in manner) admired her exceedingly. Captain Wentworth looked round at her instantly ... (104)

Wentworth says later that he was 'roused' by the other man's glance (242). Wentworth's preoccupation with Anne—made clear on the Winthrop walk—is here brought a stage closer to consciousness.

A Jane Austen young lady who leaps from a high step and knocks herself out embarrasses everyone, and the critics have accordingly given Louisa Musgrove, 'whose headstrong resolution of course leads to her fall',[34] a good dressing down. Outbidding Austen herself in callousness towards members of the Musgrove family, Mary Lascelles remarked that 'the catastrophe which the spectators think they are witnessing is an illusion. Louisa is not dead or even injured. True, she has fallen on her head, but it had never been a very good one, and the blow seems to have cleared it...'[35] Tony Tanner also plays with the idea that Louisa is 'improved' by her 'alteration', though he goes on to remark that Louisa's demeanour after the fall 'is not the result of achieved moral poise and indistractability ... but the timorous cowering of a nervous wreck'.[36] Even critics who normally read accurately like Stuart Tave and Claudia Johnson attribute a degree of deviousness and guile to Louisa at variance with the suggestions of the text.[37] One can see why they do so; to take the aftermath of the accident seriously, to see that the concussion has totally altered Louisa's personality and future role in life, is to face the problem that the punishment seems monstrously to outweigh any conceivable crime, and it therefore violates the sense, so strong in Jane Austen's novels, that the moral world is coherent and meaningful and ultimately rationally ordered. If sufficient fault can be attributed either to Louisa or to Wentworth, symmetry can he restored, and the vicissitudes of the physical can be seen literally to embody the trials of the spirit.

Of course the accident has been prepared for (one can always see these things with the benefit of hindsight). Louisa is high-spirited, enthusiastic, and has been flattered by the attentions of an unusually attractive and forceful man. Anne Elliot has overheard him, at Winthrop, encouraging her to be resolute. 'Your sister is an amiable creature; but *yours* is the character of decision and firmness, I see. If you value her conduct or happiness, infuse as much of your own spirit into her, as you can' (88). So she has been 'armed with the idea of merit in maintaining her own way' (94) and encouraged too, to believe herself of special interest to the man who thus flatters her. Reflecting back to Wentworth the dualities he says he values, she avails herself of the physiological latitude and promptitude assigned to him and having been jumped down the steps once, 'instantly' runs up them again.

> In all their walks, he had had to jump her from the stiles; the sensation was delightful to her. The hardness of the pavement for her feet, made him less willing on the present occasion; he did it, however; she was safely down, and instantly, to show her enjoyment, ran up the steps to be jumped down again. He advised her against it, thought the jar too great; but no, he reasoned and talked in vain; she smiled and said, 'I am determined I will:' he put out his hands; she was too precipitate in half a second, she fell on the pavement on the Lower Cobb, and was taken up lifeless! (109)

It is as if Julia or Maria Bertram, in squeezing beside the gate into the Ha-Ha, were to impale herself on a spike. Louisa's moral fault whether it is recklessness, or, more subtly, to offer herself as an emblem of what another values) immediately precipitates its own physiological punishment.

But it takes two to make the accident, and if the critics have hastened to blame Louisa, Wentworth blames himself. 'It was my fault entirely', he says, 'If I had not been weak, she would not have been headstrong.' 'Oh God!', he cries in the carriage on the way back to Uppercross, 'that I had not given way to her at the fatal moment! Had I done as I ought! But so eager and so resolute! Dear, sweet Louisa!' (116), and he is to reiterate these sentiments later in the novel (183). This is very natural, but the crucial phrase is 'the fatal moment'. To recover meaning out of arbitrary assaults of fortune, fatal or tragic illness and accident, human beings renarrate them so as to locate their origin in some fault of their own, however tenuous the connection of this moral fault may be with the final outcome. By taking to himself the blame for this incident Wentworth is enabled to remaster events, to gain some frail hold over contingency and 'fate', to position himself once more as the dominant and controlling male. Of course, Louisa's spiritedness and Wentworth's hesitation both contribute to the accident: but that does not exhaust its significance in the novel. It is the most crucial of the many fortuitous circumstances[38] which make up the narrative and prepare for the eventual reunion of Anne Elliot and Wentworth, a graphic reminder that human-beings are bodies as well as minds, and that the fortunes of the one are not necessarily congruent with the fortunes of the other.

There is another account of the fall's meaning that ought to be taken notice of. Perhaps it is best considered as an instance of the psychopathology of everyday life:

> Falling, stumbling and slipping need not always be interpreted as purely accidental miscarriages of motor actions. The double meanings that language attaches to these expressions are enough to indicate the kind of phantasies involved, which can be represented by such losses of bodily equilibrium. I can recall a number of fairly mild nervous illnesses in women and girls which set in after a fall not accompanied by any injure, and which were taken to be traumatic hysterias resulting from the shock of the fall. Even at that time I had an impression that these events were differently connected and that the fall was already a product of the neurosis and expressed the same unconscious phantasies with a sexual content, which could be assumed to be the forces operating behind the symptoms. Is not the same thing meant by a proverb which runs: 'When a girl fills she falls on her back?'[39]

Louisa's escapade can readily be seen as a partly unconscious aspect of her courtship of Wentworth since it invites him to confirm the self-image he has helped to create, and because she is inspirited by his presence (as by the weather, the occasion, and her own bodily vitality): and his failure to reciprocate can he read erotically too. He is not feeling and responding as she is feeling: their missing each other's hands at 'the fatal moment' is a sign that he cannot 'attach himself' to her which he already unconsciously knows. When Wentworth and Anne are reunited, and he looks back on his 'attempts to attach himself to Louisa', the word itself is used: 'He persisted in having loved none but her ... he had been constant unconsciously, nay unintentionally ...' As for loving Louisa, 'he protested that he had forever felt it tot be impossible' (242). At this moment Wentworth's promptitude in emergencies, that instantaneous movement that is his gift, deserts him. He does not reciprocate, either with firmness or with partnership. Louisa's fall then is not far from a parapraxis, since it does enact each of the participant's unconscious processes.

What seems to be inadmissible is the claim that the event is an adequate representative of deliberate considered behaviour, and therefore that it can function as an adequate sample of Louisa's moral character and offer a tenable parallel to Anne's. If this incident is meant as a contrast to Anne's persuadableness in breaking off the engagement (she interprets the incident, with understandable bias towards herself, this way) then one can only say that it is a bad parallel: delight, even heedlessness, in jumping from a step is hardly analogous to (say) wilfully persisting in carrying through a wrong-headed engagement despite advice. In this instance the meaning that Austen is so skilful in loading into nuances of manners and every-day behaviours has gone awry. The analogy between the mind and the body doesn't work so readily and the moral sense which discovers a narrative rationality in events is now in conflict with the novel's other pervasive reminders of mutability and accident in the course of life. Blame Louisa or blame Wentworth? As well blame the wind that made the high part of the new Cobb unpleasant, so that the party had to go down the steps, the wind that blows through Admiral Croft's cupboard, the wind that blew for four days and four nights and would have done for the poor old *Asp* and for Captain Wentworth, if he had not had the luck to bring her into Plymouth Sound six hours previously, the wind that, only minutes before the accident, miraculously blew new bloom into Anne Elliot's face at the precise moment her cousin was passing by on the Cobb.

It is sometimes remarked how careless Jane Austen has been in providing no motivation for William Walter Elliot to be in Lyme at the same time as the Uppercross party. And indeed a postmodern joke might be

Wentworth's remark that 'we must consider it to be the arrangement of Providence, that you should not be introduced to your cousin' when the mourning livery and the hanging of the great-coat over the arms prevents Mary from discovering that William Elliot is staying at the same inn (106). But Heaven and Providence are commonly, and usually seriously, invoked in *Persuasion*, as is often observed, most memorably perhaps in the first full statement of Anne Elliot's feelings and beliefs: 'How eloquent could Anne Elliot have been,—how eloquent, at least, were her wishes on the side of early warm attachment, and a cheerful confidence in futurity, against that over-anxious caution which seems to insult exertion and distrust Providence!' (30).[40] At the same time it is a novel that makes much of this very human capacity for work and for exertion—the capacity that turns Harville's small house into a place of happiness, that helps Anne Elliot live through her deprived life without resorting to Elizabeth's arrogance or Mary's sense of ill-usage. The structure of the second volume of *Persuasion* exactly parallels the first, with Wentworth's reappearance after six chapters replicating his original introduction after six: and his reappearance elicits a brief recapitulation of the stoic theme, as Anne says to herself after their first encounter 'She hoped to be wise and reasonable in time; but alas! alas! she must confess to herself that she was not wise yet' (178). They are still much at the mercy of chance, as their meetings and exchanges are criss-crossed, interrupted and thwarted by the intrigues and designs of others. Anne once again tries to believe in her autonomy:

> to dwell much on this argument of rational dependance—'Surely, if there be constant attachment on each side, our hearts must understand each other ere long. We are not boy and girl to be captiously irritable, misled by every moment's inadvertence, and wantonly playing with her own happiness.' And yet, a few minutes afterwards, she felt as if their being in company with each other, under their present circumstances, could only be exposing them to inadvertencies and misconstructions of the most mischievous kind. (221–22)

'*Persuasion*', as Judy van Sickle Johnson writes, 'is Jane Austen's most unreservedly physical novel'. Its power, as she describes it, 'resides in Austen's success in sustaining the credibility of a renewed emotional attachment through physical signs. Although they are seemingly distant, Anne and Wentworth become increasingly more intimate through seductive half-glances, conscious gazes and slight bodily contact'.[41] But the problem is, both for the figures and the narration, that these bodily signs are not enough in themselves to achieve the final rapprochement. Wentworth's 'manner and look … sentences begun which he could not finish—his half averted eyes and more than half expressive glance' (185) may give warrant to Anne Elliot's belief in his returned or returning affection, but by themselves they do not inevitably convey the meaning she divines, nor overcome the obstacles that their life in the social world, as well as the inhibitions generated by their past history, present to the articulation or fulfilment of the lovers' desires. In the original climactic chapter, the embarrassment and the self-consciousness that are the recurrent motif of their meetings, he 'looking not exactly forward', her emotion 'reddening [her] cheeks, and fixing her eyes on the ground' (182) become intensified, and the final reconciliation is achieved, in fact, by a scene in which body language is made to seem an effective substitute for the spoken word, and to communicate that full and precise meaning of which the previous manifestations of feeling were scarcely decipherable tokens:

> He was a moment silent. She turned her eyes towards him for the first time since his reentering the room. His colour was varying, and he was looking at her with all the power and keenness which she believed no other eyes than his possessed.
>
> 'No truth in any such report?' he repeated. 'No truth in any *part* of it?' 'None.'
>
> He had been standing by a chair, enjoying the relief of leaning on it, or of playing with it. He now sat down, drew it a little nearer to her, and looked with an expression which had something more than penetration in it—something softer. Her countenance did not discourage. It was a silent but a very powerful dialogue; on his side supplication, on hers acceptance. Still a little nearer, and a hand taken and pressed; and 'Anne, my own dear Anne!' bursting forth in the fulness of exquisite feeling,—and all suspense and indecision were over. (258)

The power of the 'dialogue', by its own admission, can only be rendered in language, in words, and therefore this moment, however appropriate a climax to the series of physical signs which have communicated the lovers' feelings to the reader, and however skilfully tumescent emotion is conveyed in the continuous tenses, is bound to seem perfunctory.

Added to this, the machinery creaks by which the two figures are brought together in a room without a third person. The two chapters which replace the original volume II, chapter X are, in their fulness and richness—representing the whole cast of characters in the novel—much superior. By having her speak, and speak eloquently and fully, if indirectly, of her own experience and love, the famous climactic scene at the White Hart Inn grants Anne Elliott a central position for the first time in the novel. At the same moment it keeps to the narrative logic whereby what finally brings the pair together is also an accident, or providential, since Anne speaks from her heart, without being sure whether Wentworth, who is seated in the same room writing a letter, can in fact, with the preternatural alertness of the lover, overhear her.

The length and eloquence of Captain Harville's and Anne Elliot's speeches form a consummate duet, almost operatic in its final affirmative intensity, on the theme of constancy. That their dialogue fulfils the desire, repressed or suppressed throughout the novel, for Anne to speak, to be eloquent, that Anne and Wentworth change their typical narrative positions—she speaking, he hanging on her words, she narrating (if indirectly) her deepest experience of life, actively speaking her passive experience, he the dependent listener, at that moment performing a service for a colleague, whose pen drops whilst she (and Austen through her) affirms the experience of women: these aspects of the scene have been in their turn eloquently commented upon. Anne holds the floor at this point, and finds, in terms of the narrative, her fulfillment. She speaks, he writes. In a reversal of the original intention, the role of bodily communication is minimised; only lips and fingers move, and it is through language, not nervous gesture or looks, that the truth is revealed. Anne's speeches combine the authorising procedures of rational debate with the authenticity of (indirect) confession. The presence of the body is in fact reduced to a metaphor, in this disputatious discourse, but one which brings apparently casually to the surface a theme, or a problematic that can be seen, in retrospect, to be deeply embedded in the novel.

Captain Harville believes in 'a true analogy between our bodily frames and our mental; and that as our bodies are the strongest, so are our feelings; capable of bearing most rough usage, and riding out the heaviest weather'. Anne takes up the analogy, to argue her own position: man is more robust than woman, but he is not longer lived, and if women live longer than men, they also love longer (233). And this relation between bodily frailty and strength of attachment is given a precise enactment in Anne's final contribution to the dialogue:

> 'All the privilege I claim for my own sex (it is not a very enviable one, you need not covet it) is that of loving longest, when existence or when hope is gone.'
>   She could not immediately have uttered another sentence; her heart was too full, her breath too much oppressed.
>   'You are a good soul,' cried Captain Harville, putting his hand

on her arm quite affectionately. 'There is no quarrelling with you.
And when I think of Benwick, my tongue is tied.' (235–6)

Is there an analogy, in fact, between the body and the spirit? How is the
body to be read, and just how does the body disclose or communicate the
secrets of the self? These are questions about which *Persuasion* has circled on
a series of occasions. To read from the face and the body to the soul, Lavater
claimed, was infallibly possible, but depended upon hermeneutic skills which
he did not trouble to impart. How the body feels, still less how the body
looks, may be far from a reliable guide to its own condition, and say still less
about the inner life. But it is common to assume a parallel or analogy
between the two, or to take one for the other,—to read, as Highbury reads,
body as access to total self. For Sir Walter and Elizabeth Elliot nothing could
be simpler: there is no question of an analogy between the body and the
mind or spirit, since questions of spirit or value are resolved merely into
questions of the comeliness or otherwise of the body and face. Mrs Smith's
name, her address, and her infirmity sit together on a continuum read
according to a primitive scale of 'objective' value. Of course, the novel
deconstructs this summarily as soon as Sir Walter's disposition to overlook
Mrs Clay's freckles and awkward wrist is demonstrated. But the desire to see
a correspondence between bodily condition and inner nature, to read one as
a sure transcription of the secrets of the other, is strong enough for critics, in
their turn, to suggest that Mrs Clay's freckles, for which Sir Walter has
recommended Gowland's lotion, are the outward sign of her inner
corruption—since Gowland's lotion can be linked to venereal disease.[42]
    Enough to say that this novel is sometimes troubled and sometimes
amused by the mismatchings that occur between inner being and outer
appearance. Simple contrastive irony about body and spirit abounds, for
wounded and disabled bodies are pictured as emblems of healthy living and
spiritual resource. Wentworth is reported as saying that Anne is 'so altered
he should not have known her again', speaking of her appearance after seven
years, but she is in fact, unaltered, unchanged in spirit, and this very
constancy is not unrelated to her decline in looks. In the first draft of the
conclusion, after the *rapprochement*, as the lovers retrace the past, and
Wentworth goes over his feelings, Anne is said to have 'the felicity of being
assured that in the first place (so far from being altered for the worse), she
had gained inexpressibly in personal loveliness'. In the revised version this is
amplified to form a little moment of muted comedy: Wentworth tells her
that he fled to his brother's after the accident at Lyme:

'He enquired after you very particularly; asked even if you were
personally altered, little suspecting that to my eye you could
never alter.'

> Anne smiled, and let it pass. It was too pleasing a blunder for a reproach. It is something for a woman to be assured in her eight-and-twentieth year, that she has not lost one charm of earlier youth: but the value of such homage was inexpressibly increased to Anne, by comparing it with former words, and feeling it to be the result, not the cause of a revival of his warm attachment. (243)

Anne smiles at the blundering offence against chivalry and it is her feelings rather than Wentworth's that now become 'inexpressible'. In smiling she demonstrates her own maturity and cultivation, her own self-irony, but also acknowledges the erosions of time and the inexact correspondence between human emotions or desire and the physical objects that are their focus and motivation. The first incident was a gratifying narrative of dream fulfilment: in its reworking and rephrasing Austen incorporates within the same moment two themes deeply relevant to her novel—acknowledging both time's depredations and the contingencies of human subjectivity—and thereby authenticates the romance she is simultaneously qualifying.

But the problematic is exposed most thoroughly in Austen's representation of Mrs Musgrove's grief in chapter VIII of the first volume. To quote only part of the notorious passage: 'while the agitations of Anne's slender form, and pensive face, may be considered as very completely screened, Captain Wentworth should be allowed some credit for the self-command with which he attended to her large fat sighings over the destiny of a son, whom alive nobody had cared for' (68). If there were a true harmony between body and spirit, then the dismissal of the body as grotesque could stand for dismissal of the feelings: the problem is that each demands a different, but concurrent, simultaneous, response. Austen cannot resolve the problem of her attitude here. Partly the writing insists there is an analogy, at the very least, between our bodily frames and our emotions, otherwise why describe Mrs Musgrove's sighings as 'fat'? But another part of the intention is to mark the disjunction, the separation between 'deep affliction' and 'a large bulky figure': the fact that appraisal of the body, whether approving or otherwise, can make no claim to knowledge or valuation, none whatsoever, of the inner life. Is Mrs Musgrove's sorrow, then, to be framed comically or tragically? The text is at this point riven between the tone adopted for its introspective, subjective narration of Anne's sufferings, a tone inflected towards the nuanced presentation of internal processes—'all that was real and unabsurd in the parent's feelings' and which it here extends towards this minor character and its wish to instantiate, once again, the irony that body and spirit may tell off in different directions. But here the narrative capitulates to that crude reading of the body as a decipherable text which the novel examines and repudiates almost everywhere else. The result is a paragraph of defensive floundering.[43]

The puzzle of relations between body and spirit is brought up once again in the little comic aftermath to the proposal scene. Even after reading Wentworth's passionately penned declaration—which shows him as agitated and nervous as ever Anne has been—her troubles are not finished. Overwhelmed, this time with happiness, her body takes over. What she is feeling is joy, what it displays is illness, and her chance to meet Wentworth on the way home is threatened, momentarily, when the Musgroves notice how she looks:

> She began not to understand a word they said, and was obliged to plead indisposition and excuse herself. They could then see that she looked very ill—were shocked and concerned—and would not stir without her for the world. This was dreadful! Would they only have gone away, and left her in the quiet possession of that room, it would have been her cure; but to have them all standing or waiting around her was distracting, and, in desperation, she said she would go home.
>
> 'By all means, my dear,' cried Mrs Musgrove, 'go home directly and take care of yourself, that you may be fit for the evening. I wish Sarah was here to doctor you, but I am no doctor myself. Charles, ring and order a chair. She must not walk.' (238)

In this coda to the emotional heights of the declaration scene, the kindly, uncomprehending Musgroves enact a brief farcical replay of Highbury's misplaced solicitude about Jane Fairfax. But for the most part in *Persuasion*, as I have been suggesting, nursing and solicitude, if not 'doctoring', are central and serious matters. Because *Persuasion* is so much more than *Emma* about the miscarriages of life, about suffering and vulnerability, it has also necessarily brought to a finer focus the role, as well as the profession, of the nurse, and advocated more urgently the need, the seriousness of care, coping and support. The novel is shot through with recognitions of the body's fragility and instability, and of the tenuousness of the emotions and valuations that are forever seeking an anchor in its immanent truths. This is a novel about 'the art of losing', to quote Elizabeth Bishop's very apposite poem, 'One Art': the art of existing without bitterness, despite multiple deprivations, of care of the self, the art of composure that is, for the writer, simultaneously the art of composition. If I have argued, too, that *Persuasion* was no radical revisioning of Jane Austen's social world, and that the historicist dimension of the novel may well he exaggerated, it is impossible to deny that the next work she undertook, to which the thematics of ill health are even more germane, was certainly to focus on contemporary social developments.

NOTES

1. See, for example: Laura G. Mooneyham, 'Loss and the Language of Restitution in *Persuasion*' in *Romance, Language and Education in Jane Austen's Novels*, 1988, pp. 146–75; Julia Prewitt Brown, *Jane Austen's Novels: Social Change and Literary Form*, Cambridge, Mass., and London, 1979, p. 148 (Brown notes (pp. 179–80) the number of widows and widowers); Alistair M. Duckworth, *The Improvement of the Estate*, Baltimore and London, 1971, p. 180.

2. David Monaghan, *Jane Austen: Structure and Social Vision*, 1980, p. 143.

3. Monaghan, *Austen*, p. 157.

4. Mary Poovey, *The Proper Lady and the Woman Writer*, Chicago, 1984, p. 224.

5. Tony Tanner, *Jane Austen*, 1988, p. 211.

6. Tanner, *Jane Austen*, p. 225.

7. Penny Gay, 'A changing view: Jane Austen's landscapes', *Sydney Studies in English*, 15, 1989–90, p. 62. See also John Wiltshire, 'A romantic *Persuasion*?', *The Critical Review*, 14, 1971, 3–16.

8. David Spring, 'Interpreters of Jane Austen's social world, literary critics and historians', in *Jane Austen, New Perspectives, Women and Literature*, (New Series). 3, ed. Janet Todd, New York and London, 1983, pp. 53–69. I have used examples of the same fallacies published later than the examples discussed in Spring's article. See also Daniel P. Gunn, 'In the vicinity of Winthrop: ideological rhetoric in *Persuasion*', *Nineteenth Century Literature*, 41, 1987, 403–18.

9. R. S. Neale, *Bath, 1680–1850, A Social History*, 1981, pp. 193–6.

10. Neale, *Bath*, pp. 207, 205.

11. Neale, *Bath*, p. 246.

12. Patricia Bruckman, 'Sir Walter Elliot's Bath address', *Modern Philology*, 80, 1, 1982, 56–60, notes the precision of the novel's assignment of lodgings to its various characters and especially the location of Sir Walter in Camden Place, a never completed, architecturally flawed Crescent. See also Sir Nikolaus Pevsner, 'The architectural setting of Jane Austen's novels', *Journal of the Warburg and Courtauld Institutes* 31, 1968, 404–22.

13. Quoted in Roy Porter, *English Society in the Eighteenth Century*, Harmondsworth, 1982, p. 215.

14. Freud described the primary narcissism parents project upon their infant child: 'Illness, death, renunciation of enjoyment, restrictions on his own will, shall not touch him; the laws of nature and society shall be abrogated in his favour'. Sigmund Freud, 'On Narcissism' (1912) in the *Standard Edition of the Works*, ed. J. Strachey et al, 1957, reprinted 1986, XIV, p. 91.

15. John Caspar Lavater, *Essays on Physiognomy for the knowledge and the love of mankind*, trans. Thomas Holcroft, second edition, 4 vols., 1804, I, p. 175. For Lavater's influence see Graeme Tytler, *Physiognomy in the European Novel: Faces and Fortunes*, Princeton, New Jersey, 1982.

16. Barbara M. Stafford, John La Puma and David L. Schiedermayer, 'One face of beauty, one picture of health: the hidden aesthetic of medical practice', *Journal of Medicine and Philosophy*, 1989, 213–30. The authors note that Lavater's contemporary, Georg Christoph Lichenberg, opposed his theories, and suggest that Lichenberg's most profound

insight was that, to be in relationship with anything, be it another person or the world, is by definition to be constantly deformed ... Life erodes geometrical perfection; it distorts edges and roughens contours ... a calibrated central form ... can be maintained only in narcissistic isolation (p. 224).

17. Lavater, *Essays on Physiognomy*, p. 19.

18. A. Walton Litz, '*Persuasion*: forms of estrangement' in J. Halperin, ed., *Jane Austen, Bicentenary Essays*, Cambridge, 1975. p. 225.

19. Litz, 'Forms of estrangement', pp. 223, 228.

20. I am indebted to my colleague Ann Blake for this phrase, as well as much else in this discussion of suffering in *Persuasion*.

21. Claire Fagin and Donna Diers, 'Nursing as metaphor', *American Journal of Nursing*, September 1983, 1362. I am indebted to Meg McGaskill for this reference.

22. Thomas Gisborne, *The Duties of the Female Sex*, second edition, 1797, pp. 11, 12.

23. Duckworth, *Improvement of the Estate*, p. 188.

24. Quoted from his translation of the *Odyssey* by Pope in a letter of 7 Nov. 1725. *The Oxford Book of Friendship*, edited by D. J. Enright and David Rawlinson, Oxford, 1991, p. 192.

25. Rev. Henry Thomas Austen, A.M., *Lectures upon Some Important Passages in the Book of Genesis delivered in the Chapel of the British Minister at Berlin in the year* 1818, 1820, p. 207.

26. Michel Foucault, *The Care of the Self*, (*The History of Sexuality*, Vol. 3), trans. Robert Hurley, Harmondsworth, 1990, p. 42.

27. Foucault, *The Care of the Self*, p. 60.

28. Foucault, *The Care of the Self*, h. 64.

29. A. Walton Litz, *Jane Austen*, A Study of her Artistic Development, 1965, pp. 153, 154.

30. *Boswell's Life of Johnson*, ed. G. B. Hill, revised by L. F. Powell, 6 vols, second edition, 1964, reprinted 1975, I, p. 215.

31. Foucault, *The Care of the Self*, pp. 36–68.

32. Mooneyham, *Romance, Language and Education*, p. 156.

33. Duckworth, *Improvement of the Estate*, p. 192.

34. John Davie, 'Introduction' to World's Classics edition of *Persuasion*, Oxford, 1980, p. x.

35. Mary Lascelles, *Jane Austen and her Art* (1939), Oxford, 1969, p. 78.

36. Tanner, *Jane Austen*, p. 238.

37. 'What [Wentworth] does not know is that Louisa's firm powers of mind have been used to eliminate her sister from the competition and leave Captain Wentworth all for herself' (Stuart M. Tave, *Some Words of Jane Austen*, Chicago, 1973, p. 265). Claudia Johnson writes similarly, acknowledging Tave, that 'Louisa, after all, did not disinterestedly supplement her sister's failing powers of mind with the strength of her own. Instead, she took advantage of her sister's persuadability in order to clear the field for Wentworth and herself' (*Jane Austen, Women, Politics and the Novel*, Chicago 1988, p. 156). Austen's stress is repeatedly on 'that seemingly perfect good understanding and agreement together, that good humoured mutual affection' of the sisters (41): Anne Elliot 'did not attribute guile to any' (82). Anne may of course be mistaken, but the textual basis for assigning guilt, of whatever kind, to Louisa is skimpy.

38. Paul Zeitlow, 'Luck and fortuitous circumstance in *Persuasion*: two interpretations', *English Literary History*, 32, June 1965, 179–95, remains the classic reference for this aspect of the novel.

39. Sigmund Freud, *The Psychopathology of Everyday Life* (1901), in *Standard Edition of the Works*, ed. J. Strachey et al, 1957 reprinted 1986, VI, pp. 174–5.

40. C. S. Lewis remarked on 'the Johnsonian cadence of a sentence which expresses a view that Johnson in one of his countless moods might have supported' ('A note on Jane Austen', *Essays in Criticism*, 4, 1954, 364). Compare, for example, 'that anxious inquietude which is justly chargeable with distrust of heaven' (*Rambler* 2).

41. Judy van Sickle Johnson, 'The bodily frame: learning romance in *Persuasion*', *Nineteenth Century Fiction*, 38, June 1983, 43–61.

42. Tanner, *Jane Austen*, quotes (p. 237) Nora Crook in *The Times Literary Supplement*, 7 Oct. 1983.

43. D. A. Miller. 'The late Jane Austen', *Raritan*, 10, 1990, 55–79, includes a witty analysis of this passage, pp. 60–2.

ADELA PINCH

Lost in a Book: Jane Austen's Persuasion

*P*ersuasion is a book that is interested in people's indebtedness to books, in the capacities of books to provide consolation, and in the adequacy of books to consciousness. The novel opens, for example, upon "Sir Walter Elliot, of Kellynch-Hall" reading the entry under "Elliot of Kellynch-Hall" in his favorite book, the Baronetage:

> Sir Walter Elliot, of Kellynch-Hall, in Somersetshire, was a man who, for his own amusement, never took up any book but the Baronetage; there he found occupation for an idle hour, and consolation in a distressed one; there his faculties were roused into admiration and respect, by contemplating the limited remnant of the earliest patents; there any unwelcome sensations, arising from domestic affairs, changed naturally into pity and contempt, as he turned over the almost endless creations of the last century—and there, if every other leaf were powerless, he could read his own history with an interest which never failed— this was the page at which the favorite volume always opened:
> ELLIOT OF KELLYNCH-HALL[1]

From *Studies in Romanticism* 12, no. 1 (Spring 1993). © 1993 by the Trustees of Boston University.

Austen suggests that Elliot reads this book, not only as an amusement, in idle occupation, but as "consolation." Reading the Baronetage can reroute "any unwelcome sensations arising from domestic affairs" into other feelings with other subjects. This paragraph asserts that a book can have such "powers"; but of course in this case those powers are the powers of vanity. Sir Walter is a particularly narcissistic reader, and the book confirms his own social superiority: reading arouses his feelings not into an Aristotelian "pity and terror," but rather into a snobbish "pity and contempt." The page that has the most power bears his own history. However, by presenting Sir Walter not simply with his family name, but with virtually the same first words that meet our eyes when we open her book—"Elliot of Kellynch-Hall"—Austen broaches the subject of what it is that attaches us to books in a way that embraces not only Sir Walter, but also the readers of her fiction. Even in this perfect marriage of man and book, moreover, the adequacy of books is in question. The "book of books," as it is later called, proves insufficient as a record of personal catastrophe: Sir Walter must supplement the printed text of his family history "by inserting most accurately the day of the month on which he had lost his wife" (3).

Persuasion's explorations of the powers of books might be situated within the context of debates that took place in England from the mid-eighteenth century on, debates about *women* and reading: about whether and in what ways women are particularly susceptible to the effects of reading, and the extent to which this susceptibility can be either dangerous or beneficial to women's minds. This is an issue that is taken up in one way by Charlotte Lennox's *Female Quixote*, appears frequently in conduct books and treatises on women, and it is an issue that Austen explores in *Northanger Abbey*. In that novel, the reading of gothic romances often laughably exaggerates Catherine Morland's perceptions of reality, but it also renders her highly sensitive to some rather real social threats. I would like to argue that Austen takes up this issue in *Persuasion* as well, though in more oblique and phenomenological ways. *Persuasion* explores what it feels like to be a reader. It does so by connecting this feeling to what the presence of other people feels like. It explores, that is, the influence reading can have on one's mind by comparing it to the influence of one person's mind over another's.

The question of the influence of other minds figures most centrally in Anne Elliot's great act of submission to duty and propriety, her refusal of Captain Wentworth. She refuses him, persuaded that her "engagement was a wrong thing—indiscreet, improper, hardly capable of success, and not deserving it" (27). The duties to which Anne submits herself belong to the scheme of things outlined in the Baronetage her father loves to read—the preservation and perpetuation of the landed gentry through marriage. Anne submits, however, under no terrors, no parental threats and prohibitions. She gives in under the gentler ministrations of a friend, Lady Russell, who substitutes for her family's indifference to her. Devoted to registering the repercussions of Anne's act of renunciation, *Persuasion* is about what it is like to be subject to the influences of others, and conceives of this as particularly a woman's predicament. (Indeed, one critic has argued that for contemporary readers the word "persuasion" would have resonated specifically with the question of parents' rights over the marriage of daughters.)[2] The novel's treatment of this issue, however, must be seen as fundamentally shaped by the aesthetic qualities that seem to set this Austen novel apart from the others, the qualities that make up what is frequently called the novel's lyricism. People seem drawn to discussing *Persuasion* in relation to romantic lyric poetry. Its emphasis on memory and subjectivity have been called Wordsworthian, its emotional tone has been likened to Shelley and Keats, and its epistemological strategies compared to Coleridge's conversation poems. Its modernity has been hinted at through allusions to the lyric fiction of Virginia Woolf.[3] What does it mean to call a novel lyric? What are the effects of this lyricism on the novel's politics? I think it is useful to use the category of the "lyric" to describe certain aspects of the novel—its emphasis on loss, its de-emphasis of plot and its emphasis instead on temporality and repetition, and its interest in voice and in noise. But I will, in addition, be defining the lyric in *Persuasion* as a particular way of rendering consciousness' apprehension of the social.

This essay will take as its starting point Austen's treatment of the pressures of other people. It will then consider how she represents first the presence of the beloved, and then the influence of books.

I

Persuasion is striking for the ways in which the presences of other people are apprehended as insistently sensory phenomena. Mary Musgrove, who has more of the "Elliot pride" than does Anne, and who is constantly fretting that her in-laws do not give her the "precedence" that is due to her, registers their claims as a physical pressure. She complains after a dinner party:

> It is so very uncomfortable, not having a carriage of one's own. Mr. and Mrs. Musgrove took me, and we were so crowded! They are both so very large, and take up so much room! And Mr. Musgrove always sits forward. So, there was I, crowded into the back seat with Henrietta and Louisa. And I think it very likely that my illness today may be owing to it. (39)

Mary feels the Musgroves' proximity to be a threat, their bodily presence capable of making her ill. Anne, however, also frequently finds herself crowded in by other people, in rooms, on furniture. She feels "astonishment" at finding herself, at the Harville house in Lyme, in "rooms so small as none but those who invite from the heart could think capable of accommodating so many" (98). She is crowded on a sofa by Wentworth and the "substantial" Mrs. Musgrove. Perhaps the best emblem for Anne's tendency to be swamped by family duties is the moment in Chapter Nine (to which I will return) in which, as she busily attends to one of her nephews, another one fixes himself upon her back. Her family is literally crawling all over her.

Families, and the Musgrove family in particular, are often represented in terms of the space they take up, the noise they make. Austen describes the Musgroves at Christmas as a collection of noises, a room full of "chattering girls," "riotous boys holding high revel."

> the whole completed by a roaring Christmas fire, which seemed determined to be heard, in spite of all the noise of the others. Charles and Mary also came in, of course, during their visit, and Mr. Musgrove made a point of paying his respects to Lady Russell, and, sat down close to her for ten minutes, talking in a very raised voice, but, from the clamour of the children on his knees, generally in vain. It was a fine family-piece. (134)

The emphasis on family noise may remind us of the representation of the Price family at Portsmouth in *Mansfield Park*. To the "delicate and nervous" Fanny, the noise at Portsmouth is "the greatest misery of all":

> Here, every body was noisy, every voice was loud.... Whatever was wanted, was halloo'd for, and the servants halloo'd out their excuses from the kitchen. The doors were in constant banging, the stairs were never at rest, nothing was done without a clatter, nobody sat still, and nobody could command attention when they spoke.[4]

But in *Mansfield Park*, noise is attached to one particular social sphere: it underlines the novel's need to separate the superior Fanny Price from her distinctly inferior family. In contrast to the heavily weighted description of the Price family noise, Austen's description of the Musgrove noise is rather detached. In *Persuasion*, noise is everywhere, vaguely menacing but at the same time strangely neutral, and even the best of families, such as the Harvilles, are perceived as crowds. Domestic spaces, much as they are the typical containers of dramas and conversations in domestic fiction, have a way of impressing themselves upon us in this novel as containers of bodies as well. Furniture often seems the register of the pressures that the characters tend to feel from other people. The furniture of the Musgrove drawing room has grown shabby "under the influence of four summers and two children" (37). Mrs. Croft is especially recommended to the Elliots as a tenant because "a lady, without a family, was the very best preserver of furniture in the world" (22). And Anne, using a word that makes several strange appearances in this novel, thinks of her house occupied by others in this way: "All the precious rooms and furniture, groves and prospects, beginning to own other eyes and other *limbs*" (47; my emphasis).

It is not simply other people's bodily presence that conditions mental life in this novel; mental life seems crowded in by bodily life in general. In Chapter Eight, we find the estranged lovers Anne and Wentworth, divided from each other by the physical form——"no insignificant barrier"——of Mrs. Musgrove, whose body, Austen declares, "was of a comfortable substantial size, infinitely more fitted by nature to express good cheer and good humour, than tenderness and sentiment" (68). Anne and Wentworth are listening to her "large fat sighings over the destiny of a son, whom alive nobody had cared for." Austen comments:

> Personal size and mental sorrow have certainly no necessary proportions. A large bulky figure has as good a right to be in deep affliction, as the most graceful set of limbs in the world. But, fair or not fair, there are unbecoming conjunctions, which reason will patronize in vain,—which taste cannot tolerate,—which ridicule will seize. (68)

This passage has baffled readers as a piece of gratuitous viciousness. It is vicious; Austen applies the language of neo-classical aesthetic judgement ("unbecoming conjunctions ... taste cannot tolerate") to Mrs. Musgrove's expressive body, as if she were a bad poem or book. The result is not far from the physical snobbery of Sir Walter Elliot: deeply offended and disgusted by the weather-beaten looks of Navy-men, Sir Walter deems them "not fit to be seen," and to spare the world the sight of them, opines, "It is a pity they are not knocked on the head at once, before they reach Admiral Baldwin's age" (20). But if extreme physical snobbery has already been represented and ridiculed within the novel in the characters of Sir Walter and Elizabeth Elliot, finding the narrator raising similar questions suggests that a serious inquiry of some kind about the relationship between personal form and mental life is taking place here. In spite of the rational disclaimers of the first two sentences, the last seems to be admitting that there are, in fact, "necessary proportions" between body and mind. The notion that there might be no connection between body and mind seems a foreclosed option— foreclosed even by Austen's use of metonymy. By the second sentence of this passage, there are no heads, no mental spaces for mental sorrow to take place in: "deep affliction" is located in either a "large bulky figure" or a "graceful set of limbs."[5]

The dislocation of head from limbs here recalls the one line, one paragraph verdict on Louisa Musgrove's accident at Lyme: "Louisa's limbs had escaped. There was no injury but to the head" (112). The phrasing of this assertion puts into question our sense of priorities. Again it sounds like something Sir Walter—always more concerned for people's appearances than for their inward states—might say. But, as is often the case in Austen, certain ideas are simultaneously repudiated and raised as serious suggestions; and heads, as in Austen's metonymy, Louisa's accident, and Sir Walter's quip about sailors, seem somewhat cavalierly treated, and perilously at risk in this novel. The humorous Admiral Croft, on surmising that there is some relationship between Wentworth's part in Louisa's fall, and his supposed romantic interest in her, exclaims:

> Ay, a very bad business indeed.—A new sort of way this, for a young fellow to be making love, by breaking his mistress's head!...—This is breaking a head and giving a plaster truly! (126)

And in a strange figure towards the end of the novel Austen comments on Anne's deferral of making public the crimes of Mr. William Elliot, "Mr. Elliot's character, like the Sultaness Scheherazade's head, must live another day" (229). Austen repeatedly warns that the rights of heads to bear thoughts and feelings of their own may be precarious.

The question of "persuasion," of the pressures that one mind can put on another, assumes, at the phenomenal level, less gentle, or at least more physical forms. The novel repeatedly figures an acute awareness of others, an exaggerated sense of the contingency of mind. This hypersensitivity to the presence of others allows Austen to register a certain resistance to women's place in this social environment. As the issue is phenomenalized, it seems to become absolutely pervasive, extending to reach all the ways in which mental life is crowded in by the presence of other people, even by the body. The text's emphasis on the phenomenal nature of the presence and pressures of others is naturally accompanied by an emphasis on sensation as the form of apprehension of these pressures. Readers have often pointed out that perceptions of the outside world seem to make their way into *Persuasion* more than in any of Austen's other novels. There are allusions to specific dates, military events, glimpses of people from all walks of life—farmers, boat-men, and nurses. What interests me, however, is the way in which the novel foregrounds the sensory nature of perception. In the disquisition on noises which Austen interjects right after her picture of the noisy family-piece at Uppercross, she highlights the sensory, and the pleasurable or unpleasurable aspects of noise:

> Every body has their taste in noises as well as in other matters; and sounds are quite innoxious, or most distressing, by their sort rather than their quantity. When Lady Russell, not long afterwards, was entering Bath on a wet afternoon, and driving through the long course of streets from the Old Bridge to Camden-place, amidst the dash of other carriages, the heavy rumble of carts and drays, the bawling of newsmen, muffin-men and milk-men, and the ceaseless clink of pattens, she made no complaint. No, these were noises which belonged to winter pleasures; her spirits rose under their influence. (135)

In this novel, in which scenes of overhearing are so important (the hedge-row scene, for example, and the climactic scene at the White Hart), noise and sound have special prominence. Spoken language is often apprehended as sheer sound. This passage is an urban pastoral in the tradition of Swift, where instead of pastoral sounds the car is met with the sounds of the town, which are ranged in a list, from "the dash of other carriages" to "the ceaseless clink of pattens." Both the listing and the conjunction of sound with the word "ceaseless" (a conjunction which will occur again) evoke an atmosphere of continuous, unhierarchized sound. I will return to the topic of noise later.

II

The courtship between Anne and Wentworth provides Austen with an especially vivid arena for exploring what the presence of other people feels like. Anne's experience of her gradual reunion or re-courtship with Wentworth takes particularly sensational forms. They are reunited through a series of encounters that Anne experiences as shocks to her consciousness. Their courtship takes its sensuous forms precisely *because* it is a re-courtship: the shocks are not the shocks of newness impressing themselves upon a "virgin" consciousness. Having already "done" this before, and with the same man, Anne substantially revises the *tabula rasa* quality of most eighteenth-century heroines, for whom love and courtship are new sensations. Fanny

Burney's youthful and innocent Camilla, for example, not only doesn't seem
to know what she is doing, but she seems not to remember very much from
one moment to the next. Her courtship consists of blind repetitions of
embarrassing moments. The nature of Anne's and Wentworth's courtship is
the result of its taking place within a context heavy with memory and
repetition. Anne is always "resuming an agitation" (60), experiencing a
"revival of former pain" (30).

The temporal structure of the plot, its concern with the reunion of
lovers whose actions and feelings are always in reference to an earlier
courtship, shapes the novel's understanding of the origins of feelings. It is the
existence of this past desire, and past submission to prohibition, that makes
Anne a "romantic" person today:

> How eloquent could Anne Elliot have been,—how eloquent, at
> least, were her wishes on the side of early warm attachment, and
> a cheerful confidence in futurity, against that over-anxious
> caution which seems to insult exertion and distrust Providence!—
> She had been forced into prudence in her youth, she learned
> romance as she grew older—the natural sequel to an unnatural
> beginning. (30)

"Romance" in this context would seem to mean, roughly speaking, "feelings
first," as well as all the other things we mean by "romance." But in this novel
romance does not mean spontaneous, innocent feeling: Anne and
Wentworth's early involvement is discussed rather perfunctorily: "He had
nothing to do, and she had hardly any body to love." Romance comes late, is
about belatedness: Austen stresses that it may have "unnatural" origins which
defy our conventional expectations of the effects of maturation and
chronological time.

In *Persuasion*, the realm of feelings is the realm of repetitions, of things
happening within a strong context of memory. The sensational quality of
Anne's and Wentworth's encounters arises not from the newness of stimuli
but rather from stimuli which take place on a consciousness already prepared
by memories of earlier sensations. Anne's conscious recollection seems to
function the way Walter Benjamin, following Freud, describes the function
of consciousness: formed for the protection against stimuli rather than the
reception of stimuli, consciousness serves as a protective shield that puts its
energies against energies from the outside world. In *Beyond the Pleasure
Principle*, Freud models the origins of consciousness on that of a primitive
organism whose exterior develops into a "crust" "baked through" by
stimulation. Consciousness, pursues Benjamin quoting Freud, is "located in

a part of the cortex which is 'so blown out by the effects of the stimulus' that it offers the most favorable situation for the reception of stimuli."6 The job of consciousness is to register energies from the outside world as shocks; the more readily it does so, the less likely they are to have a traumatic effect. This account of consciousness and sensation consists of paradoxes: what allows one to resist stimuli from the outside world is precisely the condition of having been traumatized by them before; at the same time, what allows one to go on registering outside stimuli is the condition that makes one resistant to them.

We can perhaps sharpen our sense of the ways in which the impressions Wentworth makes on Anne are conditioned by repetition and recollection by comparing them to Wentworth's effects on Mrs. Musgrove. For Wentworth is a blast from the past not only for Anne but for the Musgrove family as well. He activates a sense of loss for their deceased and always troublesome son, when Mrs. Musgrove remembers that Wentworth was the very name of the Captain her son had spoken of in the only letters he'd ever written:

> In each letter he had spoken well of his captain; but yet, so little were they in the habit of attending to such matters, so unobservant and incurious were they as to the names of men or ships, that it had made scarcely any impression at the time; and that Mrs. Musgrove should have been suddenly struck, this very day, with a recollection of the name of Wentworth, as connected with her son, seemed one of those extraordinary bursts of mind which sometimes do occur. (51)

This "burst of mind" spurred by the name "Wentworth" throws Mrs. Musgrove "into greater grief" for Richard "than she had known on first hearing of his death" (51). Anne, of course, has also to cope with sensations arising from hearing the name of Wentworth repeated so often (52). However, Mrs. Musgrove's burst of mind is a moment of *memoire involuntaire*, a random, unforeseeable moment when something which barely entered consciousness the first time around pops into consciousness, bringing with it an emotional force that belongs not to itself but to its associations. As for Mrs. Musgrove here, for Anne impressions typically take the form of repetitions. But Anne's memory is the opposite of Mrs. Musgrove's; she practices sustained and conscious recollection. Of the memory of pain she says, "when the pain is over, the remembrance of it often becomes a pleasure" (184). Of all of her experiences it might be said, as it is said of her stay at Uppercross, "she left it all behind her; all but the recollection that such things had been" (123). Anne leaves very little behind her.

Indeed, Anne is often so occupied with her own rumination and recollection that impressions from the outside seem to have a hard time finding their way in. This is not to say that Anne seems self-absorbed; rather, the way Austen frequently represents Anne's consciousness is as *absorption*. While many readers have stressed Anne's acute preceptions of the outside world, I'm interested in the way in which Austen's representation of Anne's innerness takes the form of an *inwardness* that oddly seems only penetrated from the outside with difficulty. A locution that Austen uses frequently when Anne is addressed by the outside world is "Anne found herself": in the carriage on the way home from Lyme, Anne "found herself" being addressed by Wentworth (117). At Uppercross she "found herself" having the child removed from her back (80). This phrase has a way of suggesting that what precedes these moments of contact is a state somewhat like unconsciousness: it is an absorption within. At the concert hall: "These were thoughts, with their attendant visions, which occupied her too much to leave her any power of observation; and she passed along the room without having a glimpse of him, without even trying to discern him" (186). In the climactic scene at the White Hart hotel, Anne, absorbed in her thoughts, becomes "gradually sensible" that Captain Harville is addressing her (231). Sensations from the outside are often surprises, like physical shocks, as when she is "electrified" by Mrs. Croft's suddenly saying something of interest (49).

It is above all, as many of these examples suggest, contacts with Wentworth that take these sensory, sensational forms. Their renewed courtship takes place through moments of physical contact—as when Anne finds herself handed into the carriage—which are both erotic and strangely intrusive, described as impingements from the outside world on her mind. It seems fitting that their whole re-courtship is framed by the fact that Wentworth's family—and Wentworth himself—have taken over Anne's house.

This combination of eroticism, claustrophobia and sensation can be found above all in the scene in Chapter Nine in which Wentworth removes the child from Anne's back. Maria Edgeworth singled out this passage in a letter, drawing attention to its surprising tactility:

> The love and lover are admirably well-drawn: don't you see Captain Wentworth, or rather *don't you in her place feel him* taking the boistrous child off her back as she kneels by the sick boy on the sofa? (my emphasis)[7]

This scene constitutes a pivotal moment. It seems on the one hand a moment where Wentworth asserts his potentially liberating role in Anne's life, by freeing her from the claustrophobia of family duties, actually removing a burden from her back. But the agitation it produces in the "nervous," "overcome" Anne ("such a varying, but very painful agitation, as she could not recover from") seems to come not only from Anne's confusion over Wentworth's motives—his coming to her aid, his attempts to avoid her thanks—but also from the sheer physicality of this moment of contact between them. Wentworth removes a physical pressure from her back, but also creates a physical sensation there, at a part of the body where we are most vulnerable. In our semiotics of knowledge, we associate knowledge of others conceptually with vision, with facing forward towards the object of apprehension: to have this moment of contact at the back stresses how removed Anne's experience of Wentworth is from normal knowledge of others' presence.

Organized around moments such as these, the structure of Anne and Wentworth's relationship produces many of the aspects of the text we evaluate as "lyric." Austen's depiction of their courtship stresses sensory experience, touch, sound; Anne's experience of the beloved is organized into heightened moments of "shock." Anne and Wentworth's courtship allows Austen to conduct a typically lyric investigation of the claims of and resistances to the outside world.[8] The text's organization of experience into heightened moments of shock might recall for us Benjamin's discussion of the experience of "shock" as the condition of possibility for the production of post-romantic lyric poetry in the essay on Baudelaire. For Benjamin, the modern world—and he is specifically writing in this essay about the experience of being surrounded by the urban crowd—is fundamentally unassimilable for "poetic experience" unless consciousness meets it as discrete shock-like encounters. We tend to think of the romantic and post-romantic lyric as a mode which involves the repression or exclusion of the social; for Benjamin, lyric is a mode of registering the social.

Because of the way in which Austen represents Anne's consciousness, the presence of her lover is apprehended as invasive, much as the presence of others is. This may seem surprising, since to some extent *Persuasion* conceives of Wentworth, and the realm of romantic love he represents, as an alternative to the pressures of other people. We could, perhaps, see this as a strategy that attempts to reconcile or resolve a conflict in the novel between Anne's submission to duty in refusing Wentworth in the past (which Anne, at least, maintains to the end of the novel was the right thing to do), and her fulfillment of her own desires in the present by marrying him.[9] Indeed, Austen seems to break down the distinction between persuasions from without, and internal states and desires, by, for example, frequently using the word "persuasion" to signify either external forces, or inner convictions.

Anne, for example, feels the "persuasion" of having pleased the despondent
Captain Benwick with her conversation about poetry (100). And later, Austen
reveals the "internal persuasions" which lead Elizabeth to decide not to
invite her relatives to dinner (219). And Austen renders Anne's experience of
Wentworth so as to suggest that love itself is a form of persuasion. At the end
of the novel, Wentworth acknowledges Anne's influence over him in terms
of "the perfect, unrivalled hold" her mind "possessed over his own" (242).

But if the novel's lyricism helps to resolve this conflict, it does so only
by simultaneously highlighting how thoroughly consciousness is conditioned
by the presence of others, *and* representing a kind of consciousness that is
constituted *as* resistance to outside influence, much like Freud's "baked
crust," or the glossy hazel-nut that Wentworth ironically holds out to Louisa
Musgrove as an illustration of "firmness of mind" (88). There are moments
in *Persuasion* which reveal the proximity of Benjamin's "shock" to another
aesthetics of trauma, the sublime. Anne's crucial encounters with Wentworth
are accompanied by overwhelming moments of access to the outside world.
These moments often seem claustrophobic, moments when she is crowded
in by or at least surrounded by her awareness of her environment. At Anne's
first meeting with Wentworth, as "a thousand feelings" rush in on her, she
has the following impression: "the room seemed full—full of persons and
voices" (59). Anne experiences Wentworth's sudden presence as something
that ushers in acute awareness not only of him but of the presence of all
around her. This "all" loses its normal perceptual form—individual persons
who speak particular utterances—and turns into bloated abstractions.
"Persons" are separated from "voices."

As the novel progresses, Anne's moments of shock and inundation
increasingly take a typically sublime turn: a trauma from without is parried
and inverted to become part of a power within. What before seemed to bring
an inundation by the outside world, now becomes part of her resistance to it.
In the Octagon Room at the concert hall in Bath, a wash of noise signals her
subjectivity's dominion over the outside world:

> In spite of the agitated voice in which [Wentworth's speech] had
> been uttered, and in spite of all the various noises of the room,
> the almost ceaseless slam of the door, and ceaseless buzz of
> persons walking through, [Anne] had distinguished every word.
> (183)

Here too, heightened awareness of Wentworth's presence ushers in as well a
heightened awareness of all that is not Wentworth, a room full of persons
and voices. As is often the case in *Persuasion*, sensory experience is rendered

primarily in terms of aural interference. But here, the narrator impresses these noises upon us in order to assert that Anne can subordinate them. The sounds of the room are reduced to ceaseless (the word is repeated), abstract, continuous sound, affirming the capacity of mind, even as it has been traumatized by the rushing in of sensations, to reduce the external world to a blur. But the outside world never goes entirely away. When, reunited at last, Anne and Wentworth retire to the gravel walk, it might seem that the outside world intrudes into the text only to affirm the characters' absorption in each other:

> And there, as they slowly paced the gradual ascent, heedless of every group around them, seeing neither sauntering politicians, bustling housekeepers, flirting girls, nor nursery maids and children, could they indulge in those retrospections and acknowledgements ... which were so poignant and so ceaseless in interest. (241)

Anne and Wentworth are no longer in a crowded concert room, but rather in a more expansive public space: the outside world gets bigger and more populous even as they become more enclosed in each other. The listing of urban characters here is reminiscent of Austen's earlier urban pastoral of the sounds of Bath (135). The listing serves to stress that a sense of the presence of other people does not go away. It maintains, as in the earlier "sounds of Bath" passage, its continuous, one-thing-after-another form. The progress that organizes the list—from politicians to housekeepers to flirting girls to infants—might seem to follow a descending scale of political importance— though from an early nineteenth-century woman's perspective, this list may not be descending in its claims to attention. The appearance, however, of the word "ceaseless" here, previously linked to the "white noise" of the world, signals the inversion which has occurred. Here, what is "ceaseless" are not the noises of the outside world, but the absorptions of love.

III

I'd like to return now to the question of the value of the literary in *Persuasion* that I raised at the beginning of this essay. If we read *Persuasion* in part for its lyric pleasures, what do the characters in the novel read for? Sir Walter is not the only reader in the Elliots' world. Even Mary Musgrove seems to read: she enjoys her stay at Lyme in part because she gets so many books at the library, "and changed them so often" (130). Elizabeth Elliot's rejection of the books Lady Russell lends her is surely a sign of her complete apostasy (215). But

Austen herself sometimes appears to reject the notion that a taste for reading accompanies a higher moral sense, a deeper emotional sensitivity. Captain Wentworth seems to think that because Captain Benwick is "a reading man" (182), he must be subject to deep mental sufferings and long-lived feelings:

> He considered his disposition as of the sort which must suffer heavily, uniting strong feelings with quiet retiring manners, and a decided taste for reading. (97)

Captain Wentworth is of course wrong about Benwick, who quickly overcomes the loss of Fanny Harville to fall in love with Louisa Musgrove. Books do not prepare or extend the psyche's receptivity to pain; they do not supplement or aid memory. Nor, as Anne Elliot discovers, does literature always provide consolation. On the walk to Winthrop in Chapter Ten, Anne mediates her enjoyment of the autumn day,

> repeating to herself some few of the thousand poetical descriptions extant of autumn, that season of peculiar and inexhaustible influence on the mind of taste and tenderness, that season which has drawn from every poet, worthy of being read, some attempt at description, or some lines of feeling. She occupied her mind as much as possible in such like musings and quotations. (84)

When she overhears a disturbing conversation between Wentworth and Louisa, however—"Anne could not immediately fall into a quotation again" (85). But Austen's most condemning and grotesque suggestions about the literary concern Louisa Musgrove, whose conversion to literature seems the effect of a fall, not into quotation, but onto her head:

> The idea of Louisa Musgrove turned into a person of literary taste ... was amusing, but she had no doubt of its being so. The day at Lyme, the fall from the Cobb, might influence her health, her nerves, her courage, her character, to the end of her life. (167)

Louisa, recovered, is later described as a kind of semi-vegetable, responsive only to violent sensory stimuli, and poetry:

> She is altered: there is no running or jumping about, no laughing or dancing; it is quite different. If one happens only to shut the door a little hard, she starts and wriggles like a dab chick in the

water; and Benwick sits at her elbow, reading verses, or whispering to her, all day long. (218)

Here, in the figure of Louisa Musgrove, the novel's meditations on consciousness, sensation, and literature begin to come together. Louisa is now the opposite of the hazel-nut that Wentworth held up to her as an image of firmness of mind. She has no "baked crust" of consciousness to parry sensations from the outside world. The "slam of the door" that Anne was able to subordinate in the Octagon Room works on Louisa as a physical trauma. Louisa falls into literature because it is all she can take.

The only people in *Persuasion* who have satisfying relations to books are men. Both Sir Walter Elliot and Captain Wentworth find pleasure and consolation in reading books which mark their own place in national history, Sir Walter in the Baronetage, and Wentworth in the Navy List, a "precious volume" he cradles in his hands (66). While men can find their past in books of public chronicle, women, like Anne Elliot, can turn only to personal memory, for which there is no book. Not only Baronetages and Navy Lists exclude women from finding consolation and adequate representation in books. In the climactic debate between Anne Elliot and Captain Harville about the comparative strengths and duration of the feelings of both sexes, Harville appeals to books as his witnesses:

> If I had such a memory as Benwick, I could bring you fifty quotations in a moment on my side of the argument, and I do not think I ever opened a book which had not something to say upon women's inconstancy. (234)

Harville's last phrase suggests that to read at all is to read about women's fickleness. But Anne Elliot, who has a memory full of quotations, claims that quotation is no good:

> If you please, no reference to examples in books. Men have had every advantage of us in telling their own story the pen has been in their hands. (234)

It seems, then, that the gap between mind and books that emerges in *Persuasion* is in part an indictment of a masculine literary tradition. But the issue is more complicated than this. As Daniel Cottom has pointed out, Anne and Harville's debate is in a way quotation itself—from one of the *Spectator* papers. In *Spectator* 11, "Ariella" is arguing with a gentleman about women's inconstancy: when he refers to "Quotations out of Plays and Songs," she, like

Anne Elliot, claims that male authors have maligned the whole sex.[10] And
one thing that had happened over the course of the eighteenth century,
between the date of the *Spectator* and Austen's "quotation," was that
literature, penned by both men and women, had become full not of
inconstant and unfeeling women, but of abandoned and perpetually feeling
women.

Austen also calls our attention to herself as a writer, and as a woman
writer, here. Shortly before Anne protests that literature is no good record of
women's feelings because "the pen has been in [men's] hands," Anne and
Harville hear a noise, coming from where Wentworth has been sitting and
writing:

> A slight noise called her attention to Captain Wentworth's
> hitherto perfectly silent division of the room. It was nothing
> more than that his pen had fallen down, but Anne was startled at
> finding him nearer than she had supposed, and half inclined to
> suspect that the pen had only fallen, because he had been
> occupied by them, striving to catch sounds, which yet she did not
> think he could have caught. (233–34)

In a novel in which noises frequently are the means by which the presence of
others is made felt, it seems appropriate that in this climactic scene Anne is
once again "startled" aurally into an awareness of Wentworth's presence. But
this noise is also an interruption of writing, a pen "which has been in their
hands" falling down. This noise, I would suggest, also calls our attention to
the fact the pen is now in Austen's hands. (I imagine this moment to be
somewhat like that at the end of *Alice in Wonderland* when Alice, frustrated
by the ineptitude of the jury animals at the trial, snatches the pencil out of
one of their hands, as if to signify that she is becoming gradually conscious
that she is the author of the dream.) Using a metaphor, that seems
appropriate to *Persuasion*'s poetics of noise and absorption, William Gass has
said about reading, "It seems incredible, the ease with which we sink through
books quite out of sight, pass clamorous pages into soundless dreams."[11]
This moment serves to startle us from our soundless absorption in the text,
into self-consciousness about the "noise" of its production.[12]

The notion that there may be some doubling at the end of *Persuasion*
between the characters' experiences in the text, and our experiences of the
text—that there is a foregrounding of authorial rustlings and of our
sensations as readers and that we, like Anne, are being startled out of a
certain kind of absorption—is confirmed as well through the device of the

letter that Wentworth has been writing.[13] When letters are set into a novel there is, of course, always a sense in which reader and character find themselves in the same place, as both are supposedly reading the same words at the same time. For a number of reasons this effect seems especially strong here. The effect of this letter upon Anne is overwhelming:

> Such a letter was not to be soon recovered from. Half an hour's solitude and reflection might have tranquilized her, but the ten minutes only, which now passed before she was interrupted, with all the restraints of her situation, could do nothing towards tranquility. Every moment rather brought fresh agitation. It was an overpowering happiness. (238)

And the reader? Certainly, if I may draw on my own adolescent experience, the crowning glory of rereading *Persuasion* (which I did often—reading, perhaps, like Sir Walter, to escape from "unwelcome sensations arising from domestic affairs" [3]) was getting to read Wentworth's letter: indeed, I remember on occasion opening the book just to read the letter alone. That Anne and the reader may be aligned here tempts me to point out the way in which the temporal structure of Anne's story—the repetition between the first courtship and the second courtship—produces an isomorphism between the doubling of first courtship and second courtship, *and* the doubling of Anne's experience and a reader's experience. Critics sometimes point out that *Persuasion* seems to begin where the "typical" Austen novel ends—that it seems not unlike a "second novel" that begins where a "first novel" has gone wrong.[14] The text itself suggested earlier that Anne's romance, or feelings, are the belated effect of "unnatural" origins—from being "forced" to follow a conventional story of first love and family prohibition; Anne's early experience is like a text that she is now repeating with renewed feeling. But if there is something literary in the temporal structure of the novel, there are also aspects of Anne's experience that seem like that of a reader. Frequently figured, as I've argued, as absorbed in a consciousness that registers other persons as sensations, Anne's state seems not unlike the kind of absorption Gass refers to. The novel presents us with several images of readerly absorption. Anne is so "engrossed" in Mary's letter from Uppercross that she cannot hear what her father is saying to her (162). Admiral Croft is the very image of absorption when Anne finds him in such "earnest contemplation" of a print in a shop window that she is "obliged to touch as well as address him before she could catch his notice" (169). And Mary exclaims of Captain Benwick (after Charles says "Give him a book, and he will read all day long"):

> Yes, that he will! ... He will sit poring over his book, and not know
> when a person speaks to him, or when one drops one's scissors, or
> any thing that happens. (132)

Readers—or people in reading-like states of absorbed contemplation—
appear to attain the kind of imperviousness to the outside world which is how
the novel often figures autonomy of mind.

But do books merely function as a kind of persuasion that simply
shields us from other influences and presences? I'd like to return to the walk
to Winthrop, where it appeared that Anne could not fall into quotation,
where literature failed to protect her from unwelcome sensations from the
outside world. It is here above all that Austen's critique of the limits of
literature as consolation is accompanied by a pervasive intimation of
literature's inevitability. This chapter is notable both for its seeming satire on
the idea of mediating one's relation to both nature and one's own feelings
with literature, and for its own heightened literariness. Somewhat like the
trip to Sotherton in *Mansfield Park*, the walk to Winthrop on a lovely
November day seems to take characters into a heightened literary
atmosphere. It is in part the scene's autumnal tones, in such evident harmony
with Anne's predicament, tones, which, as Austen points out, had become by
this point synonymous in English literature with the poetical itself.
Repeating poetry to herself, Anne clearly has done the kind of reading that
would furnish her with what late eighteenth-century conduct book writers
and anthologists advised for women, a "mind ... stored with a lasting treasure
of sentiments and ideas."[15] In her disquisition on female reading in Chapter
Five of *Northanger Abbey*, Austen satirized anthologies. But like Catherine
Morland in Austen's earlier novel, Anne has clearly "read all such works" that
women must read in order to "supply their memories with those quotations
which are so serviceable and so soothing in the vicissitudes of their eventful
lives."[16] Austen pokes fun at the conduct books' functionalist attitudes
towards women's reading, but she nevertheless supplies the memories of her
heroines with "such like musings and quotations." And while Anne may not
be able to "fall" into a quotation readily after this interference, the text insists
on supplying her with one in any case:

> Anne could not immediately fall into a quotation again. The
> sweet scenes of autumn were for a while put by—unless some
> tender sonnet, fraught with the apt analogy of the declining year,
> with declining happiness, and the images of youth and hope and
> spring, all gone together, blessed her memory. (85)

This autumn walk is most thoroughly literary even at the moments when real life is said to push literature aside. This is especially true in the passage where, pursuing their walk,

> After another half mile of gradual ascent through large enclosures, where the ploughs at work, the fresh-made path spoke the farmer, counteracting the sweets of poetical despondence, and meaning to have spring again, they gained the summit of the most considerable hill. (85)

The structure of this sentence seems itself to enclose more poetical images, rather than expelling them, while the diction here animates the scene with pathetic fallacy. This is poetical agriculture, the georgic, which extends the poetical rather than counteracting it.

Thus, while the walk to Winthrop stresses the limits of literature as consolation, it simultaneously suggests that it is hard to fall out of literature.[17] If one of the things people read for is the kind of absorption that resembles the way Austen frequently figures consciousness, reading also conditions our reception of the outside world, not only of melancholy landscapes, but of overheard voices, and of other people. Austen is ironical here at the expense of women's reading, or perhaps rather of the uses to which it is put. But these passages suggest, as much as *Northanger Abbey* does, that women have learned to feel from literature. The notion that "the pen has always been in their hands," that the true nature of women's feelings falls outside of literature, can only be one moment in what this book has to say on this subject: Austen's ambivalence may have to do as well with its opposite—with a sense that literature has been too much with women.

In *Persuasion*, Austen registers the social threats to women's autonomy, but is skeptical of offering up consciousness as a realm of freedom impervious to others. The novel warns that mental space is always impinged upon. The love plot, far from freeing Anne from the pressures of others, structures the representation of her consciousness in a way that heightens their effects. Austen represents consciousness as a form of resistance only by showing how it is paved over with recollections and repetitions of sensations. Autonomy of mind often appears as an extreme form of absorption which renders one simply incapable of attending to the outside world. I suggested earlier that threats to the mind's autonomy may be represented by the novel's repeated references to bumps on the head. Louisa Musgrove might have to fall on her head to start reading, but for Anne Elliot, it may be that reading is what has already knocked her over the head. Literature, that is, may be another thing that both produces consciousness as a form of resistance to unwanted pressures, and constricts mental space as a realm of freedom or autonomy. At the end of the novel, Mrs. Musgrove worries that Anne's disordered condition after reading Wentworth's letter might be the result of her having "slipped down, and got a blow to her head," and will not rest until she is sure of Anne's "having had no fall" (238). But it is only love, or reading. I noted earlier that there is something "literary" about the temporal structure of *Persuasion*: that Anne's experience resembles a reader's, that the first courtship is to the second courtship as a book is to a reader. For Anne, we could say, the repetition of romance renders her early experience as one she is now quoting. For Anne Elliot, there is no falling out of quotation.

NOTES

1. Jane Austen, *Persuasion*, ed. R. W. Chapman, 3rd ed. (London: Oxford UP, 1933) 3, Vol. 5 of *The Novels of Jane Austen*. Subsequent page references to the novel will be in parentheses.

2. Kenneth Moler, *Jane Austen's Art of Allusion* (Lincoln: U of Nebraska P, 1968) 187–223; see also Claudia Johnson, *Jane Austen: Women, Politics, and the Novel* (Chicago: U of Chicago P, 1988) 149–50.

3. On Austen and Wordsworth, see Stuart Tave, "Jane Austen and One of Her Contemporaries," *Jane Austen: Bicentenary Studies*, ed. John Halperin (Cambridge: Cambridge UP, 1975) 61–74; A. Walton Litz, "Persuasion: Forms of Estrangement," *Bicentenary Essays* 221–32. Nina Auerbach alludes to Shelley and Keats in "O Brave New World: Evolution and Revolution in Persuasion," *ELH* 39 (1972): 112–28. The most comprehensive treatment of the lyric and romantic nature of the novel is Keith G. Thomas, "Jane Austen and the Romantic Lyric: Persuasion and Coleridge's Conversation Poems," *ELH* 54 (1987): 893–94. For comparisons to Woolf, see Norman Page, *The Language of Jane Austen* (Oxford: Basil Blackwell, 1972) 48, 107.

4. *Mansfield Park* 392, vol. 3 of *The Novels of Jane Austen*.

5. Cf. D. A. Miller on Austen's frustration with this body's resistance to meaning in "The Late Jane Austen," *Raritan* 10 (1990): 60–64.

6. *Beyond the Pleasure Principle*, in *The Standard Edition of the Complete Psychological Writings of Sigmund Freud*, trans. and ed. James Strachey (London: Hogarth Press, 1953–64) 18: 26; Walter Benjamin, "On Some Motifs in Baudelaire," *Illuminations*, ed. Hannah Arendt (New York: Schocken, 1969) 162.

7. Maria Edgeworth, 21 Feb 1818, quoted in *Jane Austen: The Critical Heritage*, ed. B. C. Southam (London: Routledge and Kegan Paul, 1968) 17.

8. See Keith G. Thomas' article [note 2], which also treats the encounters between Anne and Wentworth as lyric moments. While Thomas is similarly concerned with defining the role of the lyric in Austen's novel, he conceives of it as primarily an issue of epistemology.

9. See Mary Poovey, *The Proper Lady and the Woman Writer: Ideology as Style in the Work of Mary Wollstonecraft, Mary Shelley, and Jane Austen* (Chicago: U of Chicago P, 1984) 224–40.

10. Daniel Cottom, *The Civilized Imagination: A Study of Ann Radcliffe, Jane Austen, and Sir Walter Scott* (Cambridge: Cambridge UP, 1985) 122; *Selections from "The Tatler" and "The Spectator" of Steele and Addison*, ed. Angus Ross (Harmondsworth: Penguin, 1982) 463.

11. William Gass, "The Medium of Fiction," *Fiction and the Figures of Life* (New York: Knopf, 1970) 27, cited by Victor Nell, *Lost in a Book: The Psychology of Reading For Pleasure* (New Haven: Yale UP, 1988).

12. On writing and noise: the well-known image from James Austen-Leigh's *Memoir* of his aunt, of Austen writing "in the general sitting room, subject to all kinds of casual interruptions" suggests that the woman writer's scene of writing, like her heroine's consciousness, was surrounded by a domestic "white noise." The "ceaseless slams" and shuttings of doors that punctuate Anne's awareness would have their analogue in the nephew's account, in the creaking of the door that alerted Austen to the presence of others: "There was, between the front door and the offices, a swing door which creaked when it was opened; but she objected to having this little inconvenience remedied, because it gave her notice when any one was coming," James Austen-Leigh, *A Memoir of Jane Austen* (London: Century, 1987) 102.

13. Another moment at the end of the novel where authorial rustlings can be heard is in the odd allusion to Scheherazade's head at the very beginning of chapter 11: Anne wishes to tell Lady Russell the revelations about Mr. Elliot's character, but must "defer her explanatory visit" because she is engaged with the Musgroves: "Her faith was plighted, and Mr. Elliot's character, like the Sultaness Scheherazade's head, must live another day" (229). The allusion reminds us, just as the story is winding down, that the events in Anne's life are events in a story, both deferring and bringing about an ending. This seems especially true since we know that Austen in fact had difficulty writing the ending of *Persuasion*. Dissatisfied with her original ending, she wrote two new chapters—and this allusion appears right at the beginning of the second new chapter. Revision involved adding an extra chapter, deferring both the revelation of Elliot's reputation, and the conclusion of the book.

14. See Tony Tanner, *Jane Austen* (Cambridge: Harvard UP, 1986) 211–12.

15. *The Female Aegis; or, The Duties of Woman From Childhood to Old Age* (London, 1798) 78.

16. *Northanger Abbey* 15, in vol. 5 of *The Novels of Jane Austen*.

17. Daniel Cottom's discussion of the walk to Winthrop has yielded similar insights. He conceives of Austen's characters as existing in an "environment of quotation" in order to stress Austen's apperception of the rigorously social and cultural contents of her heroines' psyches. Cf. his assessment of the love plot of *Persuasion*: "The passage of time intervenes here to characterize love as the repetition or 'quotation' of an earlier experience that is not personal and immediate but cultural and historical, and embodied in literature as in the institutions of society," *The Civilized Imagination* 120.

CLAUDE RAWSON

Satire, sensibility and innovation in Jane Austen: Persuasion and the minor works

*P*ersuasion is Jane Austen's last completed novel. It was written between 8 August 1815 and 6 August 1816. The last three weeks of this period were probably devoted to revising the ending. The two final chapters of the original ending are the only portion from any of her published novels to have survived in manuscript. Austen died on 18 July 1817, and *Persuasion* was published posthumously in December, together with *Northanger Abbey*, whose publication had been long delayed. Ironically, her last and mellowest novel, conspicuous for its tender and underisive treatment of its heroine's affections, appeared side by side with one of her earliest full-length satires of sentimental romances and their readers.

The contrast might be taken to highlight a reversal neatly and finally consummated after a graduated progress in her intervening works, but it would be more accurate to speak of an enlargement of sympathies rather than radical change. The accentuated 'romantic' sympathies of *Persuasion* do not signal any abandonment of satire, although fashionable persons of sentiment distrusted the satirical: a character in *Sense and Sensibility*, Austen's first published novel and one which derided the modish cult of fine feelings, objected to persons she thought satirical, 'without exactly knowing what it was to be satirical', but aware that 'it was censure in common use' (*S and S* 215). *Persuasion*'s heroine Anne Elliot is valued for a warmth of feeling and

From *Satire and Sentiment 1660–1830: Stress Points in the English Augustan Tradition*. © 2000 by Claude Rawson.

an attitude to love on which Austen would have cast a colder eye in her earlier work. And the vindication of Anne's first love for Wentworth, against the prudential considerations which forced her to break off their engagement, represents a reversal, or at least a change of emphasis, from the treatment of Marianne in *Sense and Sensibility*. Nevertheless *Persuasion* is in places a sharply satirical book, and even its stylistic innovations may be seen as developments of some old-fashioned satirical ploys.

After finishing *Persuasion*, Austen began *Sanditon*, a work which contained some of her funniest satire of the cult of sensibility in its most extravagant high Romantic phase. The late novel whose heroine 'learned romance as she grew older', having been unhappily 'forced into prudence in her youth' (33), was followed by an unfinished tale in which a sober-minded heroine is portrayed as properly resistant to the influence of novels and 'any spirit of Romance' (*S* 346), while its absurd hero Sir Edward, 'very sentimental, very full of some Feelings or other', is satirised for his taste in fictions which 'exhibit the progress of strong Passion from the first Germ of incipient Susceptibility to the utmost Energies of Reason half-dethroned' (*S* 353, 357). Austen, then in her final illness, abandoned *Sanditon* on 18 March 1817, two months after she began it and four months before she died. It seems to announce some variations in her customary range, and might have developed in new directions, more 'experimental' and less concerned with realistic depiction, than either *Persuasion* or the early anti-'sentimental' novels, *Sense and Sensibility* and *Northanger Abbey*. But its satirical sequences show considerable continuity with these early works and even more perhaps with the youthful burlesques: the best-known of these, *Love and Freindship* (1790), even has a sentimental hero called Edward, 'son of an English Baronet', who sometimes speaks the same novelistic gibberish as his namesake in *Sanditon* (*MW* 80 ff.).

Persuasion also shows change, prefiguring *Sanditon* in some ways, but its innovations similarly look forward and backward. Its accentuated 'romantic' emphasis does not signal any abandonment of satire, and some traditional satiric routines are closely bound up with what is often regarded as one of the innovative features of Austen's style, her use of 'free indirect speech'. This narrative mode has been much studied since the early years of this century, when Charles Bally and then Proust described its versatile workings in Flaubert. It combines the ostensibly factual reporting of speech and thought with complex and shifting intimations of judgmental perspective: of the attitudes or point of view, for example, not only of a first- or second-hand reporter, or of a narrator (whether 'personalised' or 'authorial'), but also of participants in the reported conversation, and even those of the notional reader. Recent criticism has stressed Austen's role in the evolution (not, of course, the invention) of this technical resource, especially in her later novels: 'it is *Persuasion*', says Norman Page in his good book on Austen's language, 'that offers the fullest and most important use of free indirect speech in Jane Austen's work, and represents a remarkable and fascinating step towards technical experimentation at the end of the novelist's life'. An example, cited by Page as showing 'the power of free indirect speech to embody dramatic elements within the flow of the narrative', can also be seen as a reversion to a stylised Augustan satirical mode.[1] Sir Walter has to be persuaded to rent Kellynch-hall:

> How Anne's more rigid requisitions might have been taken, is of little consequence. Lady Russell's had no success at all—could not be put up with—were not to be borne. 'What! Every comfort of life knocked off! Journeys, London, servants, horses, table,—contractions and restrictions every where. To live no longer with the decencies even of a private gentleman! No, he would sooner quit Kellynch-hall at once, than remain in it on such disgraceful terms.' (18)

The trick is to report actual phrases used, but 'indirectly', so that the narration combines the voice and moral perspective of the original speaker with those of one or more reporting or narrating agents. The words within quotation marks are broadly to be taken as Sir Walter's, though the syntax and grammar (verb tenses, the pronoun 'he', etc.) indicate that he is not being quoted directly, but through the reporting voice of Lady Russell (as we shall see, however, the matter is less simple than this suggests). The same might be said of the two immediately preceding phrases, 'could not be put up with—were not to be borne', which are not in quotation marks. They are not very different from what follows and suggest mimicry by a reporting voice: the quotation marks might well have begun earlier so as to include them. But it is not true of the words preceding *them*, 'Lady Russell's had no success at all', which do not mimic Sir Walter's exclamations, but sound like a report by the narrator of what Lady Russell said in her own name. Though the various statements have various sources, however, all report Lady Russell's difficulties with Sir Walter, and they are grouped in a formal set of three, comically highlighting the rush of activity and denial: 'had no success at all—could not be put up with—were not to be borne'.

Formal triadic arrangements were a feature of eighteenth-century prose, much practised by Johnson. His famous letter to Chesterfield of 7 February 1754, quoted in Boswell's *Life*, is a classic example. His Lordship is accused of treating Johnson 'without one act of assistance, one word of encouragement, or one smile of favour', and of delaying his patronage 'till I am indifferent, and cannot enjoy it; till I am solitary, and cannot impart it; till I am known, and do not want it.' Johnson brought the manner to unusual heights of marmorial dignity, but playful or ironic applications were also possible. They are common in Austen's novels and a familiar feature of eighteenth-century satiric style.[2] They almost invariably signal a retreat from strictly 'realistic' representation. People do not usually talk in triads, and there is a suggestion that absurdities are being anthologised. In Fielding's satiric allegory *Jonathan Wild* (1743), a similar effect is created when the depraved Snap family discover that the young Theodosia is pregnant. Their hypocritical indignation takes the form of a catalogue of the cant of moral outrage: 'An Injury never to be repaired. A Blot never to be wiped out. A Sore never to be healed' (III.xiii).[3] In both Austen and Fielding the impression emerges not of an actual conversation faithfully recorded by a self-effacing narrator, but of a stylised anecdotal performance, bringing out the preposterous and the comically habitual, knowingly aware that the usual sentiments were uttered in the usual phrases.

A further complexity is involved. This does not usually cause difficulties for readers, but it is useful to understand its nature. As we have seen, 'Lady Russell's [requisitions] had no success at all' can naturally be read in the context of the triad as the narrator's report of Lady Russell's phrases, alongside Lady Russell's report of Sir Walter's. But it is equally possible to take the words as the narrator's factual account of Lady Russell's failure, without implication of reported speech. A slight indeterminacy exists as to who is saying what. In the phrases in quotation-marks we know the words to be Sir Walter's, as reported by Lady Russell, and the same is true of the last two phrases in the triad: 'could not be put up with—were not to be borne'. The report is a satirical one, but Lady Russell is not normally satirical in this manner in her own direct speech, and there is a sense that her report is itself reported by a subtly interfering authorial voice. The punctuation reinforces this indeterminacy. While those of Sir Walter's phrases which are outside quotation marks are effectively linked to Lady Russell's voice, the presence of the quotation marks around the phrases officially punctuated as his does not preclude Lady Russell's input from being felt. The movement between the three main voices, Sir Walter's, Lady Russell's, and the author-narrator's throughout the entire report is more fluid than the punctuation suggests. And if the punctuation fails to indicate a formal division of voices, it seems unlikely in this passage that any alternative punctuation would provide unambiguous clarification.[4]

These fluidities and indeterminacies are manifestly under control. The essential distinction, between Sir Walter's utterances and the judgmental ironies projected on to them by a reporting consciousness, is secure and sharply realised. What we are neither able, nor invited, to discriminate between at this particular point are the perspectives of Lady Russell and the narrating author. The effect of this, however, is to convey not confusion, but consensual interplay. In some later novelists, in James or Ford, and perhaps elsewhere in Austen, such discriminations are essential to an exact apprehension of important nuances in the text. Even here, the consensus is hardly habitual. *Persuasion* is full of instances in which authorial sympathies and values are at variance with Lady Russell's. The incentive to distinguish between them in this passage is withheld not from any sense that there are no differences, but because the satirical description of Sir Walter is most effectively projected through an assumption of shared judgment as to its absurdity. The passage is less concerned with capturing elusive perceptions or with the shifting interplay between perceiver and perceived than with a more traditional mode of satiric typification. Satiric effects require, or at least flourish in, an atmosphere of fixed standards and normative certainties. They are also characteristically, in some classic eighteenth-century forms, concerned with follies or transgressions that are habitual to a type or a social group rather than to individuals. Just as Sir Walter's ritual exclamations enact a comic stereotype of imprisoning pretensions of rank, so the ironies of disapproval are of a kind, common in the rhetoric of Augustan satire which assume broad agreement among all sensible parties, rather than emanating from the private perspective of an individual character. Although Lady Russell, as a character, is described only a page earlier as having herself 'a value for rank and consequence, which blinded her a little to the faults of those who possessed them' (17), she functions here, without any marked feeling of inconsistency, as part of the consensus.

Seemingly disjointed sequences like 'had no success at all—could not be put up with—were not to be borne' give an impression of abbreviated notation, as though salient phrases had been jotted down for later elaboration. Brian Southam has identified a similar feature in the manuscript of *Sanditon*, begun a few months after *Persuasion* was finished, and he argues that the disjointed note-like effect was a calculated one: where we 'expect much of [the] briskness and concentration to disappear in revision ... the effect of the alterations to the manuscript is in the opposite direction'.[5] He seems to regard this as part of a broader innovative quality in *Sanditon*, but the specific tendency is visible in the published novels at least as early as *Emma*: 'Was she a horse-woman?—Pleasant rides?—Pleasant walks?—Had they a large neighbourhood?' (*E* 171). Such fragmented impressionism appears especially arresting in a style more often remembered for its 'Augustan' qualities of firmly orchestrated patterning and closure. Southam describes some interesting interactions between the two manners in the *Sanditon* manuscript, and other critics like to stress in *Persuasion* a less formal, 'more relaxed and conversational manner' as well as a more 'personal and dramatic form'.[6] In the instances I have cited, the 'disjointed' lists are traditional routines of satiric summarising, coexisting and collaborating with formal Augustan sentence-structures, not at all antithetical to that style. 'No success at all—could not be put up with—were not to be borne' has more in common with Fielding's itemising of the Snap family's moral indignations than with any later experiments in dislocated syntax. The buoyant enumerative disposition, the predilection for triadic groupings, the anthologising of stock phrases and attitudes in abstraction from syntax or meaning, as well as from their natural conversational context, project a definitional command, rather than tentative explorations of consciousness or any pressing sense of incomprehensible disconnection.

There are places, perhaps increasingly frequent in *Persuasion*, in which, as Page says, 'the abrupt phrases and the absence of coordination' are as far from 'the Johnsonian model' as they could be. An interesting example occurs in the important scene where Anne Elliot first sees Wentworth at Uppercross Cottage, almost 8 years after their engagement had been broken off because her father and Lady Russell thought the match unsuitable. Wentworth is now prosperous, and a successful naval officer, and, having returned to the neighbourhood, visits the cottage where Anne's married sister Mary Musgrove lives:

> Mary, very much gratified by this attention, was delighted to receive him; while a thousand feelings rushed on Anne, of which this was the most consoling, that it would soon be over. And it was soon over. In two minutes after Charles's preparation, the others appeared; they were in the drawing-room. Her eye half met Captain Wentworth's; a bow, a curtsey passed; she heard his voice—he talked to Mary, said all that was right; said something to the Miss Musgroves, enough to mark an easy footing: the room seemed full—full of persons and voices—but a few minutes ended it. Charles shewed himself at the window, all was ready, their visitor had bowed and was gone; the Miss Musgroves were gone too, suddenly resolving to walk to the end of the village with the sportsmen: the room was cleared, and Anne might finish her breakfast as she could. (60)

This beautifully executed scene has elements of the manner which Southam noted in *Sanditon*, and one sees what Page means when he says that it seems 'much closer to *Mrs. Dalloway* than to *The Rambler.*'7 This is sensitively observed. The passage has a delicate particularity, a vivid immediacy in its projection of Anne's observations and feelings, which are seldom found in the eighteenth-century novelists who were Austen's predecessors and models. Its prose-rhythms are not of the formal symmetrically structured kind which is characteristic of much of Austen's writing, and which derives variously from Augustan satire, from the satirical novels of Fielding, and from the moral discourses of Samuel Johnson, whom Austen deeply admired. It has a directness in both observation and style which looks forward to some later women novelists.

At the same time, however, the rush of perception, the kaleidoscopic impressionism of the scene, are conveyed in an idiom of quick summarising despatch which resembles the ironic knowingness of Austen's more traditional satirical manner, stripped only of part of its sting: 'he talked to Mary, said all that was right; said something to the Miss Musgroves, enough to mark an easy footing'. The vivid fluidities of perception which seem to anticipate the stream-of-consciousness writing of a hundred years later blend curiously with these sharply efficient summations. As we read them, we are not always able to determine how much they represent Anne's awareness, sensitised and accelerated by flustered embarrassment, and how much is to be attributed to the more comprehensive and summarising perspective of the author or narrator herself. An interplay between the two is sensed throughout the passage. Anne's feelings and perceptions are conveyed not directly in her own words or thoughts, but through an approximate report of these, selective and knowledgeable, from a remoter narrative voice disengaged from the action. If parts of the scene at Uppercross Cottage resemble Austen's more usual satirical idiom, stripped, as I suggest, of part of its sting, much of the writing of *Persuasion* preserves all the sting, and this is especially true of passages sometimes singled out for their innovative qualities, like the passage about Sir Walter's reluctance to move out of Kellynch-hall.

The earlier passage, with its summary anthologising and its notation of cant-phrases, also has more fully developed modern analogues not considered by Page. These are perhaps to be found, at an opposite extreme of extensive elaboration, in Flaubert's *Bouvard et Pécuchet* or, at an opposite extreme of staccato selectiveness, in Mr Deasy's letter to the paper, as glimpsed by Stephen Dedalus: 'May I trespass on your valuable space. That doctrine of *laisser faire* which so often in our history. Our cattle trade ... Pardoned a classical allusion ... By a woman who was no better than she should be. To come to the point at issue ... Dictates of common sense. Allimportant question ...'8 The latter is in fact a satirical boiling-down of a pompous cliché-letter of the kind Mr Collins writes out in full in *Pride and Prejudice*, I.xiii (*P and P* 55–6). In this pair of examples the stylised satiric selectiveness occurs in the modern stream-of-consciousness writer rather than in the Augustan prototype, and Page's view that Austen's syncopated syntax 'sometimes anticipates the stream-of-consciousness fiction of a hundred years later' acquires an unexpected literalness.[9] It seems that in such places the 'moderns' whom Austen most resembles may be those who, like Flaubert and Joyce, were closest to the anthologising habits of the eighteenth-century satirical masters, principally Swift. Swift, as I suggested in chapter 6, looks forward to Flaubert in an enumerative exhaustiveness, an obsessive *jusqu'auboulisme*, which Austen cannot be said to have shared. Her manner derives from a variant style of selective knowingness, popularised in the early eighteenth century in the *Tatler* and *Spectator*, and sharpened by Fielding for novelistic use. In this matter she displays a greater affinity with Fielding than with either Richardson or Johnson, and greater than she might altogether have cared to admit. Perhaps Johnson offers no more reliable a norm for the traditional elements in Austen than Woolf does of her modernity.

Both Fielding and Austen were exuberant cataloguers of dialogue and 'received ideas'. Fielding tended to signpost them, with varying degrees of explicitness, as set-pieces, both within and outside the novels, as in the 'smart Dialogue between some People, and some Folks' and the 'Dissertation concerning high People and low People' in *Joseph Andrews* (II.V, xiii), or the 'Scenes of Altercation, of no very uncommon Kind' between Mrs Honour and Mrs Western's maid in *Tom Jones* (VII.viii), or the 'modern Glossary' in his periodical the *Covent-Garden Journal* (No. 4, 14 January 1752): the latter in some ways a mini-prefiguration of Flaubert's uncompleted *Dictionnaire des idées reçues*, but characteristically compact and selective rather than exhaustive. Austen is less given to such bumptious procedures, at least in her novels, though her habit of assimilating dialogue to a satirical list belongs to the same narrative mode. Her unpublished burlesques, on the other hand, from the earliest juvenilia to her very last fiction, *Sanditon*, are remarkable for the tearaway buoyancy of their satire. They often tend, with or without labelling, towards the satirical catalogue, the *sollisier* of the cant of 'sensibility' and the fatuities of what she called 'novel slang' (*L* 404). The two are unusually congruent. There was in Austen's time, as not in Fielding's, a direct correspondence between the conversational clichés of novels and the real-life affectations of passionate feeling or refined sensibility by devotees of the cult of sentiment, because novels had become the prime literary expression and favourite reading-matter of that fashionable cult. In this Austen's burlesques differ from Fielding's *Shamela*, which they otherwise resemble in their quick-paced zaniness and their surreal stylishness of parodic reduction.

Austen had an exceptionally strong grasp of these verbal affectations, including the affectation by which proponents of fashionable cant professed themselves to be fashionably hostile to cant. This fastidiousness over 'jargon' and 'hackneyed metaphor' was derided in Marianne Dashwood (*S and S* 83, 285; also 38), presumably from social observation, but an underided self-consciousness on the matter is displayed as early as 1767 by the hero of Hugh Kelly's novel *Memoirs of a Magdalen*.[10] *Sanditon*'s Sir Edward Denham, who was 'very sentimental ... and very much addicted to all the newest-fashioned hard words', and who 'had read more sentimental Novels than agreed with him', finds it necessary in turn to declare his contempt for 'the mere Trash of the common Circulating Library' (*S* 353, 357–8). Real-life analogues for *Sanditon*'s 'wild and strange' characters, including Sir Edward, are a matter of record.[11] Austen's anthologising habit was not confined to conversations or to fashionable cant. It naturally extended to typical novelistic situations, and there are several summary-treatments, of which the late 'Plan of a Novel' (*MW* 428–30) is the best known. Among the juvenilia, 'The Beautiful Cassandra' is 'a novel in twelve chapters' which runs to three pages (*MW* 44–7) and 'Amelia Webster' an epistolary novel telescoped into two pages (*MW* 47–9).

But the main survival of the enumerative-summarising style in the mature novels is found, much subdued by comparison with these extravagant exercises, in dialogue, with its tendency to the free indirect form. Behind these enumerative dialogues lie traditions of fictional rhetoric which are still imperfectly understood. Two modes of enumeration are involved, one implying exhaustiveness, the other intimating satirical selection. In fact, both are satirical *and* selective. The first, which includes Rabelaisian as well as Swiftian lists, tends to hint at indefinite extension, but may in practice be as brief as the second, concluding in a Swiftian 'or the like',

> a Lawyer, a Pick-pocket, a Colonel, a Fool, a Lord, a Gamester, a Politician, a Whoremunger, a Physician, an Evidence, a Suborner, an Attorney, a Traytor, or the like ... [*Gulliver's Travels*, IV.xii],

or some other rhetorical *et cetera*. The underlying paradox is that, given unlimited time, a complete catalogue might be compiled, and Swift's *Complete Collection of Genteel and Ingenious Conversation* (1738) is a book-length enactment of this rhetorical tease. The *Collection* is presented as direct dialogue, in 'dramatic' form, and the 'exhaustive' mode seems to encourage unmediated reporting and a pretence of bare factuality, though the case of Flaubert, the other great master of the exhaustive mode, shows that these correlations are not simple. *Bouvard et Pécuchet*, perhaps the purest and most extensive *novelistic* (non-dramatic as well as non-discursive) catalogue of conversational inanity, frequently uses a deadpan mode of free indirect style. It gives off a paradoxical 'summary-effect',[12] based on suggestions of predictable automatism and of a running true to type, even as the sheer mass of the compilation, and the years of labour which he, like Swift, devoted to its assembly, register the ambition of exhaustiveness. In this sense, Flaubert may appear also as a master of the alternative rhetorical mode, that of Fielding and Austen, with its overt tendency to a summarising typicality and an interventionist narration hospitable to the satirical indirect style. Flaubert's doctrine of authorial non-intervention reveals a deep ambivalence on this matter. One might say, alternatively, that it reflects the inclusiveness of his absorption of the whole range of fictional traditions.

It suggests also that the two rhetorical modes are, like all such things, essentially 'untruthful'. They are indeed distinguishable from one another, but as expressions of deep differences of style and outlook which are outside the range of the actual rhetorical claims. If the summarising appearance of free indirect style subverts a sense of the exhaustiveness of the account, the mechanics of its operation may in turn be such as to belie the impression of a summary. The summarising mode may, in fact, be more exhaustive than apparently complete reports in a more unmediated or less ostentatious notation. In the dialogue between Joseph and Parson Barnabas in *Joseph Andrews*, I.xiii, the content suggests a complete record even as the style tends the opposite way: one can learn more of what purports to have been 'actually said' than in Moll Flanders' report, in a more conventional and self-effacing form of *oratio obliqua*, in a parallel scene between herself and the Ordinary of Newgate, despite the greater particularity we have been taught to expect from Defoe.[13] The summary style may even invite a suspicion that it is in excess of what might actually have been said, as Austen's triadic repetitions are open to a suspicion that the anthologising is a *raconteur*'s exaggeration. They display the anecdotal embellishments of a knowing narrator, and the suggestion of summary in such cases tells us not that a selection has taken place, but that the discourse is being managed: not only the creation of consensual feeling of broad agreement between all sensible parties on essential standards of morals and social behaviour, but also the play of irony which reinforces this, implying a complicity among wise judges in uppish mockery of the foolish and the bad.

Fielding provided the model for such management in a way that Austen's favourite Richardson did not. In his 'Biographical Notice', Austen's brother Henry makes clear that Richardson's powers of characterisation, especially in *Sir Charles Grandison*, 'gratified the natural discrimination of her mind', although she avoided 'the errors of his prolix style and tedious narrative'. He adds that 'she did not rank any work of Fielding quite so high' because 'she recoiled from everything gross. Neither nature, wit, nor humour, could make her amends for so very low a scale of morals' (5). These comments, simplified and simplifying though they are, indicate that her admiration for Richardson and her reservations about Fielding were both dominated by moral, rather than technical, considerations, though 'Richardson's power of creating, and preserving the consistency of his characters' naturally has technical implications too. The strongest sign of Richardson's influence on Austen is the fact that all her male heroes are Grandisonian figures. This is especially true of the later heroes, Edmund Bertram, Knightley, and Wentworth, with their somewhat burgherly chivalric uprightness, but it applies also to the reconstructed Darcy and even to Henry Tilney and the unglamorous Colonel Brandon.

Austen was also more broadly fascinated by Richardson, and notably by the main technical feature of his narrative style, his use of an epistolary format. She seems to have experimented with it, but to have been inclined from an early stage to be sceptical of its virtues. The first version of *Sense and Sensibility*, and probably also of *Pride and Prejudice*, were in letter-form, and may have been satirical of it. She abandoned this method in the finalised versions, and did not use it in her other full-scale novels, perhaps concurring with Fielding's opinion, in his preface to Sarah Fielding's *Familiar Letters between the Principal Characters in David Simple* (1747), that it is not the style 'most proper to a Novelist, or ... used by the best writers of this Kind'. Earlier still she had parodied the genre in a series of burlesques of which 'Amelia Webster' is the briefest; and *Love and Freindship* the best known. These are partly directed against Richardson's imitators, but mockery or criticism of Richardson, not invariably affectionate, is found from the earliest juvenilia to her last work, *Sanditon*. Austen did not have Fielding's intense distaste for Richardsonian morality: on the contrary, she shared Richardson's view of Fielding's novels as morally 'very low'. But *Sanditon* is explicitly about the 'exceptionable parts' of Richardson's novels and their corrupting effect (*S* 358), and it has been suggested that Lucy Steele in *Sense and Sensibility* was partly modelled on Pamela.[14] If this suggestion is correct, Austen must have shared something of Fielding's Shamelaic view of Richardson's first heroine. She may not have known *Shamela* itself, or not known it to be by Fielding. But the essentials of that conception of Pamela may be found in *Joseph Andrews* and were, in any case, in wide circulation.

If Austen's epistolary parodies share *Shamela*'s accelerated tempo, as I suggested earlier, the fact does not presuppose a reading of Fielding's pamphlet, and has less to do with Austen's moral view of Richardson than with her artistic instincts about the representation of reality. In stylistic matters, in her technical habits and presentational strategies, her deepest affinities were with Fielding. Like him, she seems to have been resistant to Richardson's pretensions as to the superior authenticity of the novel-in-letters and the immediacy of its 'to the Moment' narration. She probably disliked the idea of such immediacy anyway, and seems to have found uncongenial a narrative arrangement which left the story to the actors, and in which the author remained invisible as in a play. She would have sympathised with Fielding's jeering at the Shamelaic boast that 'You see I write in the present Tense' (Letter vi). Precision timing and clockwork reaction in both behaviour and repartee in *Shamela* are a stylish farcical response to Richardson's pseudo-instantaneities. They are matched in Austen's burlesques by a comedy of instant fainting-fits, accelerated deaths, and love at (or before) first sight, followed within moments by marriage (*MW* 80–2, 99–102, etc.; '*First-sight* Love' was incidentally something of a Richardsonian issue: all his novels contain solemn admonitions against the idea, and one of his essays is ridiculed in *Northanger Abbey* for asserting 'that no young lady can be justified in falling in love before the gentleman's love is declared', *NA* 15).

The clockwork rhythms of farce accelerate time into a species of lunatic and supercharged immediacy which subverts the credibility of all 'to the Moment' pretensions. It also neutralises the related immediacy which surrenders the story-telling to a non-authorial participant. The importance of authorial mediation, guaranteeing a presiding wisdom and a protective filter against the invasiveness of raw experience, was deeply inscribed in an Augustan cultural code of which Fielding was a (sometimes rather loud) spokesman, and to which Austen paid an instinctive allegiance in a modified and subtler form. Richardson's novels were in their nature subversive of this. Parodying him in a format which excluded overt intervention called for stylisations from within which visibly reflected the knowing operations and ironic perspectives of a controlling intelligence. The farcical precisions and surreal coincidences in such narratives are effectively, if not formally, interventionist. Their outrageousness discredits the ostensible narrator, and signals the tacit presence of a satirical raconteur-mimic. Anecdotal routines and automatisms of the 'I said/he said' type, habitual in both *Shamela* and Austen's epistolary burlesques, are readily transferred in the reader's mind from the ostensible speaker to that mimicking presence, especially when the narrative is deadpan in a way that defies an expected or appropriate response. This seems a direct consequence of planting suggestions of farce within a purportedly realistic genre. Although author-figures are not normally visible in stage-compositions, the importation of stage-effects into fictional narratives tends to increase, rather than diminish, a consciousness of authorial presence.

This has particular pertinence because the epistolary genre is 'dramatic' not only in its 'to the Moment' elements, but also in the sense that the narration is left to the actors and the author is notionally invisible as in a play. Richardson was proud of these dramatic features, sometimes accentuating them by introducing dialogue in play-script form. That such effacement of the author was no more congenial to Austen than to Fielding seems amusingly confirmed by a dramatic adaptation of *Sir Charles Grandison*, once attributed to a niece, but now shown to be probably by Austen herself.[15] This work (a good-humoured travesty rather than an attack, and perhaps as much directed at popular abridgements and adaptations of Richardson's novel as at the novel itself) was composed intermittently between the early I egos and 1800. It resembles some of the early burlesques in its comic telescoping of a huge novel into a short space (as *Shamela* boils Pamela down to a brief pamphlet) and in its speeded-up action and dialogue. It is also especially insistent in its stage-directions, the one area where an author can intervene directly in a play's written text. Southam says these leave 'little to chance or to the player's uncertainty' (*G* 12) and speaks of this as a practical matter, concerned with managing inexperienced players in family productions, but the directions sometimes hint at the same accelerated zaniness as the burlesque narratives: 'She gets halfway through the door and he, in shutting it, squeezes her. She screams and faints. He carries her away in his arms to a chair and rings the bell violently. Enter MRS. AWBERRY ...' (*G* 43). Southam stresses the difference between this slight family piece and the major published works, but like the burlesques it displays, in unsubdued and unprocessed form, characteristics which Austen refashioned and transformed in the mature novels.

It has long been recognised that Austen's novels, like Fielding's, contained 'dramatic' or at least theatrical elements of their own. Fielding had been a professional playwright, and had written over twenty plays before he began writing novels. The genres he practised were stylised ones: dramatic burlesques, comedies of witty repartee, *Rehearsal*-plays which contain a playwright-character producing a play-within-the-play (in some ways the prototype of authorial figures in the novels who comment not only on the action, but also on the writing of the story). Austen's stage-experience was not on this scale, but there was a strong tradition of private theatricals in her family, partly reflected in a well-known episode in *Mansfield Park*; and, in addition to the Grandison play, she wrote some dramatic sketches, scraps of which survive among the juvenilia (*MW* 49–57, 172–5). The novels of both authors show many marks of this experience: a keen sense of plot; chapters or episodes framed as set-pieces, analogous in shape and length to a scene in a play; comic reversals and resolutions; semi-autonomous *tableaux*; a sharp ear for dialogue and especially a highly-developed feeling for character-revealing stylisations in dialogue; the 'playfulness and epigrammatism' (*L* 300) in *Pride and Prejudice*, often reminiscent of repartee in wit-comedy; a whole repertoire of stage-routines, including well-timed coincidences, contrived meetings, comic misunderstandings, conversations overheard at cross-purposes. Such theatrical elements were the opposite of those through which Richardson might claim to have achieved dramatic illusion. What they took from the drama were its artifices rather than its immediacies, and they contain further examples of the way in which a pointed importation of stage-effects into narrative tends to maximise, rather than reduce, the impression of authorial management.

In Austen's mature novels, such things are less ostentatiously paraded than they are in Fielding, and we can sometimes sense a specific instinct to moderate them. An important difference between the manuscript draft and the final version of the last chapters of *Persuasion*, finely discussed by Southam, shows a drawing away from stereotyped comic contrivance to a more natural account of the clarification between Wentworth and Anne.[16] This is a particularly impressive late development, but in this as in other respects *Persuasion* extends, rather than departs from, the other novels. Her stylised self-projections, 'dramatic' and other, are on a smaller scale than Fielding's. Her novels have no 'introductory' chapters of the kind Fielding prefixed to each of the eighteen books of *Tom Jones*, only occasional overt appearances, 'brisk and ironic', which, as Page says, anticipate George Eliot and E. M. Forster more than they recall Fielding.[17] At times, as I shall argue, one even senses a momentary withdrawal of authorial certainty very unlike Fielding's parade of bossy assurance.

The subordination of both conversation and incident to authorial performance and satirical perspective is, in Fielding, sustained over large tracts of narrative, and seldom gives way to underisive particularities of observation or the sober analysis of situation and motive. This is not so in Austen. The indirectly reported account of Sir Walter's refusal to leave Kellynch-hall is quickly followed, as it would not be in Fielding, by paragraphs of lucid, low-key analysis: 'There had been three alternatives, London, Bath, or another house in the country. All Anne's wishes had been for the latter ...' (19). Satiric triumphalism gradually gives way to a respect for the factuality of fact and motive, whereas Fielding's modulations are normally in an opposite direction, into a massive flow of explanatory sarcasm or an extended mock-heroic elaboration. Even a deliberate drop into the real, like the portrait of the heroine in *Tom Jones*, IV.ii: 'Sophia then, the only Daughter of Mr. Western, was a middle-sized Woman; but rather inclining to tall', comes over less as a concession to fact than as a pointedly contrastive gesture, trumpeting its difference from the surrounding burlesque rant. The performative set-pieces in Austen are not only more subdued. They come in waves, more intermittent, but with certain perceptible rhythms. Sir Walter's refusal to leave Kellynch-hall had, in the emphatic nature of its report, been comically set up for reversal. He changes his mind in less than a page, even before the analysis of alternatives. The next comparable orchestration of dialogue occurs in the following chapter, where a renewed and more elaborate pattern of reversal is unfolded.

The lawyer Shepherd reports to Sir Walter his discovery of a suitable tenant:

> Mr. Shepherd hastened to assure him, that Admiral Croft was a very hale, hearty, well-looking man, a little weather-beaten, to be sure, but not much; and quite the gentleman in all his notions and behaviour;—not likely to make the smallest difficulty about terms;—only wanted a comfortable home, and to get into it as soon as possible;—knew he must pay for his convenience;—knew what rent a ready-furnished house of that consequence might fetch;—should not have been surprised if Sir Walter had asked more;—had inquired about the manor;—would be glad of the deputation, certainly, but made no great point of it;—said he sometimes took out a gun, but never killed;—quite the gentleman. (26–7)

As in the earlier example, there is a degree of indeterminacy as to who is saying what: where Croft's speeches end and Shepherd's gloss begins, and where authorial mimicry is travestying either or both. Punctuation offers no guide here, not even the faintly confusing signal whereby, in the earlier passage, some of Sir Walter's phrases but not others are given within quotation-marks. Another difference is that in the earlier passage a sympathetic character was reporting an unsympathetic one, thus inducing an impression of solidarity between the reporter and the overall narrator. Here, the process is reversed. The reporter is repellent, and it is the reportee who generates sympathy, though this has to work its way through the distorting medium of the report. The automatism imputed to Admiral Croft's statements by Shepherd's narration reflects discredit on Shepherd, not Croft.

It is Shepherd's nastiness that presents Croft's accommodating and good-natured phrases as mechanical routines, though to the extent that it comes naturally to Croft to say good-natured things the automatism itself, unusually, becomes a sign of grace.

The detail about the Admiral's gun, that he sometimes took one out 'but never killed', may strike some present-day readers as more of a bizarrerie than it really is. It involves the issue of blood-sports, more quotidian then than now, but it has an odd eruptive force in the otherwise banal catalogue of the Admiral's easy-going concessions, and the word 'killed', without suggesting anything that gentlemen do not often do, disturbs the insipid surface of the lawyer's recital. Even in its negative form, since the Admiral *does not* kill, it announces a small sudden violence within that 'little bit (two inches wide) of Ivory' (*L* 469) to which Austen compared her fictional world, much as, on another plane, some stinging acerbities of her own violate the decorous idiom of that world.

The main point of the detail is the Admiral's moral soundness. The 'never killing' vouches for that, as Willoughby's being 'a very decent shot' (*S and S* 37) perhaps hints at the opposite; while the Admiral's having the gun at all presumably assures us, as it assures Mr Shepherd, that he could pass for a country gentleman. 'Quite the gentleman', says the lawyer twice, toadyingly ironic, suggesting an 'it will do' gentility, better than one might expect, but not enough to take *him* in. Shepherd's cheap lazy phrasing, and his whole get-it-over-with summary of the Admiral's attitudes, are a staple of the satirical repertoire of free indirect reporting (compare the it-will-do laxities of Parson Barnabas in *Joseph Andrews*, I.xiii). They establish the lawyer as sanctimoniously complicitous and irredeemably low: he is treated *de haut en bas* by Austen, even as she derides the uppish pretensions of himself and Sir Walter (another standard satiric ploy, habitual in Fielding and others). The Admiral emerges as an honest, heart-of-the-matter figure, generously eccentric in a social milieu whose accepted forms of behaviour might seem suspect by comparison. He represents an ideal of unrefined decency against the self-importance and fetid politeness of Sir Walter and his hangers-on.

The portrait comes as a local climax in an extended debate about the social acceptability of Navy officers, regarded by Sir Walter as a coarse species with unseemly weather-beaten features. The Navy is one of the few intrusions from the wider world which Jane Austen allows into the two inches of ivory, and in *Persuasion* it is especially prominent. It brings hints of distant places and reminders of foreign wars. Its hardships, as weathered by Mrs Croft, are a focus for the novel's insistence on the rightness of taking risks for the sake of love, though Wentworth's opposition to the idea of letting women live on board ship suggests that Austen's endorsement of Mrs Croft has its limits, as least on the specific point. Two of Austen's brothers were naval officers and became admirals, so she had, as we are often reminded, a soft pot for the service. *Persuasion* is one of the two novels (*Mansfield Park* is the other) where the professions, specifically the naval and the clerical professions, play an important part, and where professional duty is held up as an especially important value. In both novels, the idea is entertained that what you do is more important than who you are. Again, one suspects some ambivalence. By the time Anne marries Wentworth, he is not only a successful naval officer but has a substantial fortune. The Crofts, warmhearted, forthright and lovable, are nevertheless 'character parts', marginalised by their amiable eccentricities. The Navy is presented as disconcertingly outside the customary divisions of rank, and even as a challenge to them, especially offensive to Sir Walter 'as being the means of bringing persons of obscure birth into undue distinction, and raising men to honours which their fathers and grandfathers never dreamt of' (24). In any contest with Sir Walter for the reader's sympathies, the Crofts cannot lose.

The decision to vacate the house and to lease it to the Crofts, much fussed and agonised over, suddenly becomes a matter of quick summarising despatch: 'The house and grounds, and furniture, were approved, the Crofts were approved, terms, time, every thing, and every body, was right; and Mr. Shepherd's clerks were set to work, without there having been a single preliminary difference to modify of all that "This indenture sheweth"' (35). It is as if the narrator had wearied of the details, and is in fact the expression of a long standing Augustan *pudeur* over retailing events merely because they occurred: a *pudeur* which Defoe and Richardson did not share, which was in its way contrary to the essential character of the novel-form, but which acted as a vitalising constraint in the work of novelists who, like Fielding and Austen, retained a commitment to older canons of 'polite' style. The rule, as Fielding put it in the Preface to the *Voyage to Lisbon*, that you should not mention a 'merely common incident ... for its own sake, but for some observations and reflections naturally resulting from it', was for many writers a matter of deep cultural predisposition (it had a non-literary counterpart in the rules for conversation propounded in courtesy books). It was not a demand for conciseness as such, and was sometimes the occasion for self-conscious and even prolix disclaimers or mock-disclaimers of mere particularity, in Swift, Fielding, and others. Breaches of the rule implied vulgarity and an unhealthy and unregulated surrender to the flow of events. A prolixity which resulted from this was especially culpable. Richardson's novels seemed to Fielding and others a paradigm-case of stylistic solecism in this matter.

Whatever Austen's view of Fielding, she too disliked 'the errors of [Richardson's] prolix style' (5). The summarising account of the agreement to lease Kellynch-hall is uniquely Austenian, but it has much in common with Fielding's summary ironies and has no counterpart in Richardson. Its blend of circumstantial reticence and amused critical irony declares the account to be under selective and discriminating management. In this and in other ways it is part of a more general tendency of individual elements in the novel towards the set-piece; the closures, symmetries, reversals that suggest the shaped autonomy of a fable, a scene in a play, an instructive irony of motive or circumstance. But such periodically recurrent passages of accelerated and summary narrative also contribute to a larger rhythm of tension and relaxation in the movement of the novel as a whole, akin to some of the more extended patterns of reversal. The paragraph which summarises the conclusion of the deal is followed by a ballet of symmetrical reversals, in which the snobbish baronet ends up with an enhanced opinion of the admiral, while the good-hearted admiral develops a genial contempt in return:

> Sir Walter, without hesitation, declared the Admiral to be the best-looking sailor he had ever met with, and went so far as to say, that, if his own man might have had the arranging of his hair, he should not be ashamed of being seen with him any where; and the Admiral, with sympathetic cordiality, observed to his wife as they drove back through the Park, 'I thought we should soon come to a deal, my dear, in spite of what they told us at Taunton. The baronet will never set the Thames on fire, but there seems no harm in him:'—reciprocal compliments, which would have been esteemed about equal. (35)

On the surface, this seems like the kind of plague-on-both-houses irony which is one of the virtuoso routines of Augustan satirical rhetoric, as in the comment on the violent inclinations of extremists of opposing factions in Swift's *Sentiments of a Church-of-England Man*: 'And this is *Moderation*, in the *modern* Sense of the Word; to which, speaking impartially, the Bigots of both Parties are *equally* entituled.'[18] The seesawing reciprocities, and the stinging finality, are also present in Austen in a less ferocious but equally pointed form. In Swift, they are the climax of an argument and the closing words of the first part of a political tract. In Austen, they occur inside a chapter, at no specially strategic point, a momentary crystallisation in a continuing narrative: despite appearances, they are not merely, nor even mainly, an irony of reciprocal blame, since the admiral is not really blamed.

They look like a Swiftian sarcasm, but they function less as a localised epigrammatic aggression than as part of an intricate system of narrative ironies. The admiral who was under hostile scrutiny passes the test, while the baronet who sat in judgment fails, his pretensions to superiority upstaged by a reversal which puts his presumed inferior on top. This fable of the uppish upped is replayed when the Crofts come to Bath and Elizabeth and Sir Walter decide that they should not be introduced to Lady Dalrymple as 'we ought to be very careful not to embarrass her with acquaintance she might not approve' (157), while the Crofts are totally innocent of any desire for such company: they 'knew quite as many people in Bath as they wished for, and considered their intercourse with the Elliots as a mere matter of form, and not in the least likely to afford them any pleasure' (159). Once again Sir Walter ends up more excluded than excluding: 'He was not at all ashamed of the acquaintance, and did, in fact, think and talk a great deal more about the Admiral, than the Admiral ever thought or talked about him' (159). These recurrent fabular elements not only form a thread of their own within the larger economy of the book. Individually they register an organisational impulse to create local autonomies of significance, rather than surrender an episode to the continuous flow of event or circumstance, even as the narrative is ostensibly committed to reporting that flow.

Ironic reversals and finalities of summation are in some ways a narrative counterpart to the syntactical rhetoric of much Augustan satire, with its stinging definitional containments and its sarcastic paradox-laden antitheses. Narrative is a more spacious and perhaps in Jane Austen a gentler medium, and her fictional world is one that normally excludes the teeming energies of transgression and folly that are the subject-matter of Swift or Pope. The phrase 'regulated hatred'[19] has been applied, in a memorable essay, to her style, and finely conveys its mixture of hard-edged perception and decorous restraint. There are occasional intensities which are not covered by that phrase, and perhaps the most startling of these occurs in *Persuasion*. In I.vi the memory of a deceased son of the Musgroves who had once served in the navy under Wentworth briefly enters the story. Louisa reports that her mother was 'out of spirits', having been reminded of him by a report that Wentworth was coming back. Louisa thinks they should divert her mind from 'such gloomy things'. At this point the narrator weighs in:

> The real circumstances of this pathetic piece of family history were, that the Musgroves had had the ill fortune of a very troublesome, hopeless son; and the good fortune to lose him before he reached his twentieth year; that he had been sent to sea, because he was stupid and unmanageable on shore; that he had

been very little cared for at any time by his family, though quite
as much as he deserved; seldom heard of, and scarcely at all
regretted, when the intelligence of his death abroad had worked
its way to Uppercross, two years before. (51–2)

This is not spoken by a character whose callousness might be the focus
of attention. Unlike some other passages registering malicious attitudes,
there is no suggestion of even a shadowy traffic between the authorial voice
and any less official consciousness within the story. It comes over as a starkly
authorial intervention, especially gratuitous since the young man had not
hitherto been any part of the story. The eruptive force is almost surreal, in
the context of a surrounding narrative whose ironies are more indirect and
low-key, and in a novel whose prevailing atmosphere is usually felt to be
kindlier and mellower than the rest of Austen's work. The paragraph has the
aspect of a formal 'character', a prose counterpart to some of the portraits in
Pope's *Moral Essays*. But one of the remarkable features of this explosion of
definitional bravura is that, unlike Pope's portraits, it contains little
definition. We learn almost nothing specific about what the young man was
like, and the aggressive play of balance and antithesis consists more of *ex
cathedra* adjudications than of a precise detailing of the person's
characteristics. It is so out of keeping with its context that one senses an
unbalancing focus of private malice, a secret settling of scores. It is brought
startlingly into relief, unlike its Popeian analogues, which are more naturally
accommodated within the generic frame of a satirical epistle engaged in a
listing of types, and whose settling of scores is neither secret nor anomalous.

Austen won't let this subject go away, and the deceased Richard
continues to exercise his surviving family for the remainder of the chapter.
The interplay of outlooks between author and characters is resumed. In a
follow-up reflection by the author, harsh summation gives way to a
pretended incomprehension: 'that Mrs. Musgrove should have been
suddenly struck, this very day, with a recollection of the name of Wentworth,
as connected with her son, seemed one of those extraordinary bursts of mind
which do sometimes occur' (52–3). This seems the antithesis of the earlier
rhetoric of summary definition. It projects an alternative mastery, that of the
unspecific applied to quite precise effects. It resembles the knowing mock-
incomprehensions of Fielding (as when he claims that he has 'never met with
any one able to account for' the frenetic discriminations between high people
or low people, or announces that he will not presume to determine the
motive for some obvious folly or nastiness), but with an enhanced and more
concise sense of the inexplicability of things. Fielding's incomprehensions
imply that he knows the answers, Austen's here that they can't be known,

though both employ a similar rhetoric of sharp certainty as to the fact itself of humanity's irrational ways.

Part of the difference is accounted for by the fact that Austen's discourse even here moves with greater fluidity between the author's perspective and those of her characters. A novelistic manner which cultivates interactions with alternative outlooks, and whose exploitation of free indirect style has a greater intimacy and finesse than Fielding's, is more naturally adapted to projecting an incomplete or unresolved comprehension. A sentence like 'Anne sighed and blushed and smiled, in pity and disdain, either at her friend or at herself' (170) would be unlikely to occur in Fielding except, perhaps, in a bouncy parade of omniscience as he conveyed to the reader that both of them know perfectly well what he does not pretend to have grasped. But the remark about 'those extraordinary bursts of mind' is closer to Fielding than this, though in a more subtly manipulative manner. No reader would find them extraordinary. A mother is reminded of the death of her son, and we do not usually marvel at the phenomenon. The shocking insistence on inexplicability forces into relief not the oddity of the mother, but the son's exceptional undeservingness. It is a cunning irony of displacement, as tight as any epigram, without the epigram's accoutrements of verbal wit, registering incongruities of circumstance or character (ironies that eschew verbal wit are more in the style of Johnson, a more freely admired predecessor, than of Fielding). The perverse or contrary character is all in the (alleged) facts, so strange that they do not invite explicit summations, but hardly inexplicable.

Nevertheless, the 'absurdity' of Mrs Musgrove on the point continues to engage Austen as the mother of the son is gradually assimilated into the flow of narrative. Two chapters later, Wentworth is shown being tactful to her. Anne surmises that, as the boy's commanding officer, he had 'probably been at some pains to get rid of him', but he 'shewed the kindest consideration for all that was real and *unabsurd* in the parent's feelings' (67: italics added). *Unabsurd* is a word brilliantly chosen, its slightly laboured inelegance conveying exactly the limits of grudging concession, a word that Richardson might have used, but not Pope or Fielding, more fastidious as they were in their displays of the masteries of style. And Wentworth's determination to maximise the unabsurdity is then surrendered to a merciless fantasia of comic obesity and social gaucherie. Anne and Wentworth

> were actually on the same sofa, for Mrs. Musgrove had most readily made room for him,—they were divided only by Mrs Musgrove. It was no insignificant barrier indeed. Mrs. Musgrove

was of a comfortable substantial size, infinitely more fitted by nature to express good cheer and good humour, than tenderness and sentiment; and while the agitations of Anne's slender form, and pensive face, may be considered as very completely screened, Captain Wentworth should be allowed some credit for the self-command with which he attended to her large fat sighings over the destiny of a son, whom alive nobody had cared for. (67–8)

The *tableau* is very funny, and the extent to which it is a *tableau*, framed within the sofa as a composition, is striking. The present-tense description of how Anne's sitting position 'may be' visualised, an unusual show of surrendering tight narrative management, almost suggests a stage-direction, and even more perhaps a film scenario. The preceding paragraph had offered intimations of Anne's perspective into the exchanges between Wentworth and the bereaved mother, but by now we are more unequivocally back to an official authorial voice, and this seems confirmed by the paragraph which immediately follows:

Personal size and mental sorrow have certainly no necessary proportions. A large bulky figure has as good a right to be in deep affliction, as the most graceful set of limbs in the world. But, fair or not fair, there are unbecoming conjunctions, which reason will patronize in vain,—which taste cannot tolerate,—which ridicule will seize. (68)

The idiom again approximates briefly not to Fielding or Pope, but to Johnson. The style looks back to his way, pondered and literal-minded, of giving to commonplace observations a peculiar combination of pathos and gravitas. The Johnson who has been described, honorifically, as a satirist *manqué*, whose literal truthfulness and compassionate instincts shrank from the ironic distortions and the cruelty of satirical discourse, and who responded instead with palliating explanations, seems to be at work. The reader is here reminded that the grief of fat people is also grief. But the concession is then withdrawn, in an unjohnsonian way, perhaps even with an arch note of parody of the Johnsonian version of the rhetorical triad: 'which reason will patronize in vain,—which taste cannot tolerate,—which ridicule will seize'—an amusing variation on the mini-anthologizing discussed earlier in connection with Sir Walter's reluctance to move from Kellynch-hall ('had no success at all-could not be put up with-were not to be borne').

The later Christmas scene at the Musgroves', with their noisy children and grandchildren, has something of the effect on Anne and Lady Russell that Fanny Price's return to her Portsmouth family had on her (*MP* 343ff.), except that the degrading squalors of indigence at Portsmouth do not exist at Uppercross. 'It was a fine family-piece', the account concludes, and the sarcastic phrase implies, once again, a framed composition, parodying the happy family *tableaux* which were a stereotype of the novel of sentiment: Mrs Musgrove guarding the Harville children from her own grandchildren, Mr Musgrove trying to talk to Lady Russell above 'the clamour of the children on his knees', 'a roaring Christmas fire' (127). Anne, thinking of Louisa's illness, 'would have deemed such a domestic hurricane a bad restorative of the nerves', but Mrs Musgrove's happy comment on the proceedings is 'that after all she had gone through, nothing was so likely to do her good as a little quiet cheerfulness at home' (128). It is usually difficult, in the portrayal of this kindly lady, to distinguish between affection and contempt. If the portrayal is not merely the product of unprocessed animus, it may mark an incipient sense of the radical incomprehensibility of 'character', unusual in the earlier novels.

Contributing to the Christmas *brouhaha* were the Harvilles' children, brought over 'to improve the noise of Uppercross, and lessen that of Lyme' (127), and it may be that the Harvilles are also mildly derided as types of domestic devotion and felicity, surviving difficult times. This is not a sign that Austen was against families, but that she may have been exercised by ambivalent feelings about another fictional stereotype, that of the virtuous family in stricken circumstances, especially frequent in the novel of sensibility and even found, with varying degrees of irony, in the more 'sentimental' parts of Fielding's novels: the Heartfrees in *Jonathan Wild* and the Booths in *Amelia* provide some examples. Harville is, for the most part, a solid fellow and a good naval officer, greatly liked by Wentworth, and 'no reader' (96), unlike his sentimental friend Benwick, who reads Byron and Scott and to whom Anne has to recommend a dose of prose-reading (98–9, 104, 106, 158: in all Austen's novels, people's characters are defined by whether they read, and what). But he has a pointedly 'novelistic' name, recalling Mackenzie's Man of Feeling, Harley, and Burney's Orville, among others, and is in this respect unusual among serious characters in Austen. (The early burlesques contain a Sir George and Lady Harcourt, and a half-page novel, 'The Adventures of Mr. Harley', about a young man 'destined by his father for the Church & by his Mother for the Sea' and who, 'desirous of pleasing both', combined the careers of future Austen heroes by becoming a chaplain 'on board a Man of War', *MW* 33ff., 40). The Harvilles have something of the same faintly insipid passivity as Fielding's Heartfrees, and are exposed to similarly good-natured, but unmistakably uppish, put-downs from their creator: 'Captain Harville, though not equalling Captain

Wentworth in manners, was a perfect gentleman, unaffected, warm, and obliging. Mrs. Harville, a degree less polished than her husband, seemed however to have the same good feelings' (95). 'Perfect gentleman' has unsettling echoes of Mr Shepherd on Admiral Croft: 'quite the gentleman' (26–7). Harville's lameness, a vaguely Byronic trait, is the result of a war-wound (92, 95), but such romantically 'interesting' debilities tend to get short shrift in Austen's novels. In this regard, her outlook may not have changed much from the time when the unreformed Marianne could find something erotically 'interesting ... in the flushed cheek, hollow eye and quick pulse of a fever', but has to settle instead for Colonel Brandon and his rheumatism (*S and S* 31–3). In *Persuasion* Austen goes out of her way to make sure that the Crofts, who are the novel's only example of a truly successful and long-standing love, are given unromantic ailments: the Admiral has gout and Mrs Croft a blister 'as large as a three shilling piece' (155, 157, 161).

The example of the Harvilles, and in an opposite sense that of the Crofts, suggest that Austen experienced a certain awkwardness in assimilating the 'sentimental' sympathies which, as many readers agree, are given fuller expression in *Persuasion* than in most of her previous work. The Crofts seem to show a special determination to give these sympathies a middle-aged expression. It is not merely that they are happily married, but that emphasis is given to them as models for young lovers, even as their middle-aged eccentricities and ailments, and their headlong accident-prone way of life, come over as almost ostentatiously unglamorous. Early in the novel they come to represent for Anne an ideal of happy love equal to what she had once felt between herself and Wentworth: 'with the exception, perhaps, of Admiral and Mrs. Croft, who seemed particularly attached and happy, (Anne could allow no other exception even among the married couples) there could have been no two hearts so open, no tastes so similar, no feelings so in unison, no countenances so beloved' (63). That this middle-aged couple are in their married state comparable to a hero and heroine in courtship, is not merely glimpsed by Anne in her nostalgia for her courtship days, now seemingly over. Nor is the observation confined to a serious-minded heroine like herself, whose view of such things might not be dependent on the glow of romance. Even more strikingly, Louisa Musgrove sees the Crofts in the same way, and tells Wentworth: 'If I loved a man, as she loves the Admiral, I would be always with him, nothing should ever separate us, and I would rather be overturned by him, than driven safely by anybody else' (83).

Austen's insistence against all 'romantic' expectation in investing this pair of aging eccentrics with an aura of emotional grace normally confined to young protagonists is evidently self-conscious. The Admiral himself seems almost aware of the generic reversal when he accuses Wentworth, the novel's official romantic lead, of lacking gallantry. It is a passage of exquisite irony because it pits the values of the Crofts against codes of conduct to which, in any final analysis, Jane Austen would give her endorsement. The issue is Wentworth's unwillingness to admit ladies on board ship, except for brief visits, because as Wentworth replies, life on a ship is too rough: 'There can be no want of gallantry ... in rating the claims of women to every personal comfort *high*.' Mrs Croft reacts warmly to this 'idle refinement': she has lived on board ship with her husband, and she hates to hear Wentworth 'talking so, like a fine gentleman, and as if women were all fine ladies, instead of rational creatures' (68–9). At this point, where present-day readers might be most inclined to acquiesce in Mrs Croft's general position, it seems likely that Austen's own assent is being withheld. There is no suggestion, when Anne eventually marries Wentworth, that she will live on his ships as Mrs Croft did. Mrs Croft's declarations about her happiness on board ship have symbolic value for the case of Anne and Wentworth, because they speak of the value of putting love before prudential considerations. As literal models for them to follow they have nothing to offer, however, and their comic dimension as generous eccentrics safely preserves the novel from taking them seriously in any precise operational sense. They are so remote from prevailing custom in the society of Austen's novels that they acquire the privileges and limitations of Quixotic irresponsibility.

That Austen should have denied the Crofts a centre-stage position in the story does not take away from their uniqueness in her fiction, though it could be argued that love in Austen's novels almost always has a middle-aged, or at least an unyouthful, aspect. The heroes are usually substantially older and wiser than the heroines, and sometimes display a quasi-paternal authority over them. Some of the younger heroines (Marianne, Emma) marry men in their middle or late thirties. These things are not usually made an issue of, or presented as romantically anomalous. In *Sense and Sensibility*, where the issue arises of marrying an older man against the heroine's original wishes, there is a last minute attempt to salvage some of the proprieties of romantic love: 'Marianne could never love by halves; and her whole heart became, in time, as much devoted to her husband, as it had once been to Willoughby' (*S and S* 334). But whereas Brandon represents for Marianne a safe and rational choice, the Crofts, middle-aged on both sides, represent the success of the exact opposite, and their example speaks poignantly to Anne of all that she has missed by holding back. As Marianne had been unwisely led by 'romance' in her youth and eventually became prudent, so Anne, who 'had been forced into prudence in her youth ... learned romance as she grew older' (33). Age is partly, of course, a rhetorical matter: Mrs Croft is 38, and her younger brother Wentworth is by now 31. But Anne (now 28) and Wentworth remain, several years after their first courtship, cast in the role of *jeunes premiers*, in a situation where their author wishes to assert that status with all the conventional novelistic honours, while insisting at the same time, without entire artistic conviction, on the rights of the middle-aged to such things.

Lady Russell is of interest in this context. She plays what would, in a conventional romantic plot, be the role of the interfering elder who tries to manipulate the heroine along mercenary or prudential lines, like an underided Mrs Western. What is interesting is not only that (although shown to be wrong) she is represented in a respectable and even sympathetic light, but that Austen has gone out of her way to indicate that she had a warm loving nature: 'She was a benevolent, charitable, good woman, and capable of strong attachments' (17). In this regard, she resembles another Fielding character, Squire Allworthy, who stands for the civic virtues and admonishes the impetuous Tom Jones for his lack of prudence, but whose gravity has to be shown against the evidence not to be obstructive or stuffy: 'he had possessed much Fire in his Youth, and had married a beautiful Woman for Love' (VI.iv). The disclosure has absolutely no function in the story of *Tom Jones*, other than to maximise sympathy for a character whose identification with prudential values might seem unattractive to readers (and authors) whose main sympathies are with the young lovers. It is interesting that Austen should have made a similar point of stressing Lady Russell's ardent nature, somewhat in opposition to her thematic role, even where the official purposes of the novel require her to be seen to be mainly in the wrong.

That indeed is Jane Austen's main problem. Lady Russell partly upholds Elinor's values at a point in Austen's evolution when her sympathies have moved closer to Marianne. It is not exactly a case of 'reckless middle-age' finding itself 'restrained' by the primly moral young.[20] The middle-aged Austen has not exploded into passion, but mellowed towards it. The most active energies of her earlier imagination were, perhaps paradoxically, critical ones: whatever secret sharing there may have been in the portrayal of Marianne's loving and sensitive side, one is conscious of a strongly willed drive to restrain or ridicule it, as the exuberant unprocessed energy of the early burlesques testifies. We should not forget that exuberant derision of 'sensibility' did not cease with Austen's youth: as we have seen, the unfinished *Sanditon* is slightly later than *Persuasion*. The case is at all stages fraught with ambivalence, but a redistribution of sympathies is evident within the 'serious' novels, which are the works which embody the author's fullest imaginative engagement with her material, and in which the material is human rather than merely bookish. One of the issues for Austen in *Persuasion* was how to project some strong anti-prudential sympathies without, so to speak, being disloyal to Elinor.

Lady Russell is the result. Her influence has to be discredited without forfeiting affection or respect. Hence the assurances of her capacity for feeling, and the curiously weighted assertion that 'she was a woman rather of sound than of quick abilities' (16): a combination traditionally prized in English estimates of social worth, often given, in Swift's approving words, to paying 'more Regard to good Morals than to great Abilities', but subject also to imputations of mediocrity and often dedicated to obstructing persons of more remarkable character or talent, as Swift also noted, with withering sarcasm.[21] Jane Austen seems poised between the two valuations not, like Swift, in separate contexts of equal and opposite affirmation, but in a single inclusive and slightly unfocused view. Lady Russell's early response to Wentworth is a revealing example. She 'had little taste for wit; and of any thing approaching to imprudence a horror'. Thus Frederick Wentworth, charming, witty, confident, 'full of life and ardour', seethed to her dangerously 'brilliant' and 'headstrong' (30–1).

Wentworth is sometimes taken by critics at Lady Russell's valuation, as an unsound type whose 'personal philosophy approaches revolutionary optimism or individualism'. Marilyn Butler's vivid and otherwise compelling chapter on *Persuasion* seems to me part of a consistently reductive misjudgment of Wentworth which extends Lady Russell's censures in the very direction where Austen, as well as Anne, believe them to be most misguided. The dangerous 'revolutionary optimism' is apparently to be discerned in Wentworth's praise to Louisa Musgrove of '"resolution", "decision", "firmness", "spirit", and finally, in truly Godwinian phraseology, "powers of mind"'. These phrases are, in fact, being applied to no more revolutionary a character than Louisa herself, in a fit of gallant speech-making which contrasts Louisa's 'firmness' with some vacillating behaviour by her sister Henrietta earlier in the day. They occur in the same conversation as his mock-pompous oration on the virtues of the nut ('Here is a nut ... To exemplify,—a beautiful glossy nut, which, blessed with original strength, has outlived all the storms of autumn ...', 86), an exercise in rhetorical parody in the genre of Swift's famous 'Meditation upon a Broom-Stick', and delivered, as Austen tells us, 'with playful solemnity', which Butler reads as the serious reflections of a man 'of high moral aspirations ... in the grip of ... a personal bias that perverts his judgement'.[22] The 'personal bias' is not a matter of wilfulness, still less of revolutionary optimism or dogmatism, but bitterness at Anne's failure to exercise 'firmness' when Lady Russell 'persuaded' her to break off their engagement. This is how Anne interprets the 'serious warmth' she detects in the more 'earnest' parts of his speech (86), and this is surely their natural impact on the reader. But even without this inappropriately solemn reading of the discourse on the nut, and the tenuously grounded politicisation of Wentworth's outlook, Butler's view of Wentworth's imputed deficiencies is overstated. As Mary Poovey says, it 'needs to be qualified both by Austen's approving treatment of the naval meritocracy in *Persuasion* and by the personal pride she took in her own brothers' advances in the navy'.[23] It must also be qualified by much in the novel itself, by the evidence of Wentworth's own generosity and good sense, by the affection and respect in which he is held by the other characters, and above all by Anne's feelings for him.

Nevertheless, Lady Russell's perspective is not wholly repudiated, despite all the havoc it has caused in the lives of Anne and Wentworth. Anne insists even at the end that she was right to take Lady Russell's advice, though the advice itself was wrong. Even that concession is cautiously phrased: 'I am not saying that she did not err in her advice. It was, perhaps, one of those cases in which advice is good or bad only as the event decides.' Anne adds that she herself would never 'in any circumstance of tolerable similarity, give such advice', but she sticks to her other point (232). Austen completes the rehabilitation at the end, when she grants that Lady Russell 'had been less gifted' than Anne in 'quickness of perception', but adds (as she had found it necessary to add at beginning) that her emotional priorities were the right ones: 'if her second object was to be sensible and well judging, her first was to see Anne happy'. Austen concludes with a striking quasi-parental variation on her treatment of Marianne's eventual whole-hearted acceptance of Brandon at the end of *Sense and Sensibility*, her warm and loving nature conquering earlier resistance. Lady Russell 'loved Anne better than she loved her own abilities; and ... found little hardship in attaching herself as a mother to the man who was securing the happiness of her other child' (235).

Even Lady Russell's 'prejudices on the side of ancestry' (17), which may to present-day readers seem the least defensible elements in the combination of misjudgments which disrupt Anne Elliot's life, are ones which in an only slightly modified form are broadly endorsed in Austen's fictional world. If *Persuasion* shows ambivalence over this, it differs from the other novels not in the fact of ambivalence, but in the degree of discomfort, the feeling of conflicting loyalties unresolved, which are more acutely evident in this novel than elsewhere. The elaborate pieces of summary-portraiture of Lady Russell at the beginning and end, even more than the presentation of her in the main course of the action, suggest not so much a complexity of which the author has a comprehensive grasp, as an uncertainty as to which of her characteristics is to be approved or disapproved. This uncertainty extends to some of the other characters, and not only to the extent that part of our view of them is filtered through hers, or responds to behaviour precipitated by her. Although Austen seems to have maintained in principle her faith in traditional notions of 'character' as stable, definable, and subject to clear moral judgment, and although she specifically admired Richardson for 'preserving the consistency of his characters' (5), she may in this last novel be on the edge of a more open and destabilised perception of human personality and behaviour.

NOTES

The following abbreviations for works by Jane Austen are used in this chapter. Page references, unless otherwise noted, are to the World's Classics editions of Jane Austen's novels (numerical page references without indication of title are to *Persuasion*):

E	*Emma*;
G	*Jane Austen's 'Sir Charles Grandison'*, ed. Brian Southam,Oxford, 1980;
L	*Jane Austen's Letters*, ed. R. W. Chapman, 2nd. edn., Oxford, 1952;
MP	*Mansfield Park*;
MW	*Minor Works*, ed. R. W. Chapman, Oxford, 1954;
NA	*Northanger Abbey*;
P and P	*Pride and Prejudice*;
S	*Sanditon* (as included in *NA* above);
S and S	*Sense and Sensibility*

I have retained the uncorrected title of *Love and Freindship*, despite recent practice.

1. Norman Page, *The Language of Jane Austen*, Oxford, 1972, pp. 127, 135–36.

2. On triadic groupings, see Page, *Language of Jane Austen*, pp. 109ff. (also 93, 99, 104). For Johnson's letter, see Boswell, *Life of Johnson*, ed. G. B. Hill and L. F. Powell, Oxford, 1934–64, I 261–2.

3. Henry Fielding, *Jonathan Wild*, III.xiii. For a discussion of this passage and of satirical forms of free indirect speech in Fielding and others, see Rawson, *Order from Confusion Sprung*; pp. 288, 261–310.

4. *Persuasion* appeared posthumously, and its punctuation was not verified by Jane Austen. (See Chapman's 'Introductory Note' to *Northanger Abbey and Persuasion*, in his edition of the *Novels of Jane Austen*, Oxford, 1923–54, V, p. xiii, which reports that nevertheless 'the text is good'). As the ensuing discussion suggests, a different punctuation would not have been likely to alter the main drift of the present argument.

5. Brian Southam, *Jane Austen's Literary Manuscripts*, Oxford, 1964, p. 108.

6. Southam, *ibid.*; Page, *Language of Jane Austen*, pp. 49, 52.

7. Page, in *The Jane Austen Companion*, ed. J. David Grey and others, New York and London, 1986, pp. 262-3 (hereafter referred to as *Companion*).

8. James Joyce, *Ulysses*, London, 1955, p. 30.

9. Page, in *Companion*, p. 267.

10. Hugh Kelly, *Memoirs of a Magdalen, or the History of Louisa Mildmay* (1767), Cooke's Edition, n.d. I. 20 (letter 3): 'I will not address you in the hacknied forms of commonplace courtship', he says, before going on to do just that.

11. Southam, *Jane Austen's Literary Manuscripts*, p. 110.

12. Page's useful phrase, *Language of Jane Austen*, p. 129.

13. Defoe, *Moll Flanders*, ed. G. A. Starr, London and Oxford, 1976, pp. 277–8. See *Order from Confusion Sprung*, pp. 292ff.

14. F. W. Bradbrook, *Jane Austen and her Predecessors*, Cambridge, 1966, pp. 84–6.

15. See *Jane Austen's 'Sir Charles Grandison'*, ed. Brian Southam, Oxford, 1980.

16. Southam, *Jane Austen's Literary Manuscripts*, pp. 88f.; Marilyn Butler, *Jane Austen and the War of Ideas*, rev. edn., Oxford, 1987, pp. 28ff.

17. Page, in *Companion*, p. 228.

18. Jonathan Swift, *Works*, II.13.

19. D. W. Harding, 'Regulated Hatred: An Aspect of the Work of Jane Austen', *Scrutiny*, 8 (1940), 346–62. Reprinted in Ian Watt, ed., *Jane Austen: A Collection of Critical Essays*, Englewood Cliffs, NJ, 1963, pp. 166–79.

20. The words are from W. B. Yeats's epigram, 'On Hearing that the Students of our New University have Joined the Agitation against Immoral Literature', in *Poems*, ed. Finneran, p. 94.

21. On this, see *Order from Confusion Sprung*; pp. 351f.

22. Butler, *Jane Austen and the War of Ideas*, pp. 275, 278.

23. Mary Poovey, *The Proper Lady and the Woman Writer*, Chicago and London, 1984, p. 268 n. 12.

Chronology

1775	Jane Austen is born on December 16 in the village of Steventon, Hampshire, to George Austen, parish clergyman, and Cassandra Leigh Austen. She is the seventh of eight children. She and her sister Cassandra are educated at Oxford and Southampton by the widow of a principal of Brasenose College, and then attend the Abbey School at Reading. Jane's formal education ends when she is nine years old.
1787–93	Austen writes various pieces for the amusement of her family (collected in the three volumes of Juvenilia), the most famous of which is *Love and Friendship*. She and her family also perform various plays and farces, some of which are written by Jane, in the family barn.
1793–97	Austen writes her first novel, the epistolary *Lady Susan*, and begins the epistolary *Elinor and Marianne*, which will become *Sense and Sensibility*.
1796–97	Austen completes *First Impressions*, an early version of *Pride and Prejudice*. Her father tries to have it published without success. Austen begins *Sense and Sensibility* and *Northanger Abbey*.
1798	Austen finishes a version of *Northanger Abbey*.
1801–2	George Austen retires to Bath with his family. Jane possibly suffers from an unhappy love affair (the man in question is

believed to have died suddenly), and also probably becomes engaged for a day to Harris Bigg-Wither.

1803	Austen sells a two-volume manuscript entitled *Susan* to a publisher for £10. It is advertised, but never printed. This is a version of *Northanger Abbey*, later revised.
1803–5	Austen writes ten chapters of *The Watsons*.
1805–6	George Austen dies. Jane abandons work on *The Watsons*. She, her mother, and her sister live in various lodgings in Bath.
1806–9	The three Austen women move to Southampton, living near one of Jane's brothers.
1809	Jane, her sister, and her mother move to Chawton Cottage, in Hampshire, which is part of the estate of Jane's brother Edward Austen (later Knight), who has been adopted by Thomas Knight, a relative. Edward has just lost his wife, who died giving birth to her tenth child, and the household is now in the care of Jane's favorite niece, Fanny.
1811	Austen decides to publish *Sense and Sensibility* at her own expense, and anonymously. It appears in November in a three-volume edition.
1811–12	Austen revises *First Impressions* extensively and beginning *Mansfield Park*.
1813	*Pride and Prejudice: A Novel. In Three Volumes. By the Author of "Sense and Sensibility"* is published in January. A second edition of it, as well as a second edition of *Sense and Sensibility*, comes out in November.
1814	*Mansfield Park* is published anonymously and in three volumes. It sells out by November. Austen begins *Emma*.
1815	Austen completes *Emma* and begins *Persuasion*. *Emma* is published in December, anonymously, in three volumes, by a new publisher.
1816	A second edition of *Mansfield Park* is published.
1817	A third edition of *Pride and Prejudice* is published. Austen begins *Sanditon*. She moves to Winchester, where she dies, after a year-long illness, on July 18. She is buried in Winchester Cathedral. After her death, her family destroys much of her correspondence in order to protect her reputation.
1818	*Persuasion* and *Northanger Abbey* are published posthumously together, their authorship still officially anonymous.

Contributors

HAROLD BLOOM is Sterling Professor of the Humanities at Yale University and Henry W. and Albert A. Berg Professor of English at the New York University Graduate School. He is the author of over 20 books, including *Shelley's Mythmaking* (1959), *The Visionary Company* (1961), *Blake's Apocalypse* (1963), *Yeats* (1970), *A Map of Misreading* (1975), *Kabbalah and Criticism* (1975), *Agon: Toward a Theory of Revisionism* (1982), *The American Religion* (1992), *The Western Canon* (1994), and *Omens of Millennium: The Gnosis of Angels, Dreams, and Resurrection* (1996). *The Anxiety of Influence* (1973) sets forth Professor Bloom's provocative theory of the literary relationships between the great writers and their predecessors. His most recent books include *Shakespeare: The Invention of the Human* (1998), a 1998 National Book Award finalist, *How to Read and Why* (2000), and *Genius: A Mosaic of One Hundred Exemplary Creative Minds* (2002). In 1999, Professor Bloom received the prestigious American Academy of Arts and Letters Gold Medal for Criticism, and in 2002 he received the Catalonia International Prize.

STUART M. TAVE has taught at the University of Chicago and is the author of *The Amiable Humorist: A Study in the Comic Theory and Criticism of the Eighteenth and Early Nineteenth Centuries* and *New Essays by De Quincy*.

A. WALTON LITZ is Holmes Professor of English at Princeton University and the author of studies on Wallace Stevens, James Joyce, and Ezra Pound, T.S. Eliot, and William Carlos Williams, as well as *Jane Austen: A Study of Her Artistic Development*.

GENE W. RUOFF is Professor of English at the University of Illinois, Chicago. He specializes in British Romantic literature and is the author of *Wordsworth and Coleridge: The Making of the Major Lyrics* and co-editor, with Karl Kroeber, of *Romantic Poetry: Recent Revisionary Criticism*.

JULIA PREWITT BROWN teaches in the English Department at Boston University. She has written numerous essays on Jane Austen and has published *A Reader's Guide to the Nineteenth Century English Novel* and *Cosmopolitan Criticism: Oscar Wilde's Philosophy of Art*.

SUSAN MORGAN is Professor of English at Miami University. She is the author of *In the Meantime: Character and Perception in Jane Austen's Fiction* and, most recently, *Place Matters: Gendered Geography in Victorian Women's Travel Books about Southeast Asia*.

TONY TANNER has written extensively on British and American novelists, including studies of Joseph Conrad, Thomas Pynchon, Henry James, and Norman Mailer. He is also the author of *Adultery and the Novel: Contract and Transgression* and *The Reign of Wonder: Naivete and Reality in American Literature*.

CLAUDIA L. JOHNSON is Professor of English at Princeton University and is the author of *Equivocal Beings: Politics, Gender and Sentimentality in the 1790's*, as well as *Jane Austen: Women, Politics, and the Novel*.

JOHN WILTSHIRE is Professor of English at La Trobe University. He has written widely on Jane Austen and is the author of *Samuel Johnson and the Medical World: the Doctor and the Patient*.

ADELA PINCH is Associate Professor of English at the University of Michigan. She specializes in eighteenth- and nineteenth-century literature and literary theory.

CLAUDE RAWSON is Maynard Mack Professor of English at Yale University. He is the author of *Henry Fielding and the Augustan Ideal Under Stress, Gulliver and the Gentle Reader*, and most recently, *God, Gulliver, and Genocide: Barbarism and the European Imagination, 1492–1945*.

Bibliography

Auerbach, Nina. "O Brave New World: Evolution and Revolution in *Persuasion*." *English Literary History* 39 (1972).

Babb, Howard. *Jane Austen's Novels: The Fabric of Dialogue*. Columbus: Ohio University Press, 1962.

Bloom, Harold, ed. *Modern Critical Views: Jane Austen*. New York: Chelsea House, 1986.

Brown, Julia Prewitt. *Jane Austen's Novels: Social Change and Literary Form*. Cambridge: Harvard University Press, 1979.

Brown, Lloyd W. *Bits of Ivory: Narrative Technique in Jane Austen's Fiction*. Baton Rouge: Louisiana State University Press, 1973.

Butler, Marilyn. *Jane Austen and the War of Ideas*. Oxford: Oxford University Press, 1975.

Duckworth, Alistair. *The Improvement of the Estate*. Baltimore: Johns Hopkins University Press, 1971.

Gard, Roger. *Jane Austen's Novels: The Art of Clarity*. New Haven: Yale University Press, 1992.

Gunn, Daniel P. Gunn. "In the Vicinity of Winthrop: Ideological Rhetoric in *Persuasion*." *Nineteenth Century Literature* 41 (1987).

Halperin, John, ed. *Jane Austen: Bicentenary Essays*. New York: Cambridge University Press, 1975.

———. *The Life of Jane Austen*. Sussex: Harvester Press, 1984.

Hardy, Barbara. *A Reading of Jane Austen*. London: Peter Owen, 1975.

Johnson, Claudia L. *Jane Austen: Women, Politics, and the Novel*. Chicago: University of Chicago Press, 1988.

Lascelles, Mary. *Jane Austen and Her Art*. Oxford: Oxford University Press, 1939; rpt. 1974.

Litz, A. Walton. *Jane Austen: A Study of Her Artistic Development*. London: Chatto and Windus, 1965.

McMaster, Juliet. *Jane Austen on Love*. Victoria, British Columbia: University of Victoria Press, 1978.

Moler, Kenneth. *Jane Austen's Art of Allusion*. Lincoln: University of Nebraska Press, 1968.

Monaghan, David. *Jane Austen: Structure and Social Vision*. London: Macmillan, 1980.

Morgan, Susan. *In the Meantime: Character and Perception in Jane Austen's Fiction*. Chicago: University of Chicago Press, 1980.

Mudrick, Marvin. *Jane Austen: Irony as Defense and Discovery*. Princeton: Princeton University Press, 1952.

Nardin, Jane. *Those Elegant Decorums: The Concept of Propriety in Jane Austen's Novels*. Albany: State University of New York Press, 1973.

Page, Norman. *The Language of Jane Austen*. Oxford: Basil Blackwell, 1972.

Paris, Bernard. *Character and Conflict in Jane Austen's Novels: A Psychological Approach*. Detroit: Wayne State University Press, 1978.

Pinch, Adela. "Lost in a Book: Jane Austen's *Persuasion*." *Studies in Romanticism* 32 (Spring 1993).

Poovey, Mary. *The Proper Lady and the Woman Writer: Ideology as Style in the Work of Mary Wollstonecraft, Mary Shelley, and Jane Austen*. Chicago: University of Chicago Press, 1984.

Roberts, Warren. *Jane Austen and the French Revolution*. New York: St. Martin's Press, 1979.

Ruoff, Gene W. "Anne Elliot's Dowry: Reflections on the Ending of *Persuasion*." *Wordsworth Circle* 7 (Autumn 1976).

Southam, B. C., ed. *Critical Essays on Jane Austen*. London: Routledge and Kegan Paul, 1968.

Spence, Jon. "The Abiding Possibilities of Nature in *Persuasion*." *Studies in English Literature* 21, no. 4 (Autumn 1981).

Tanner, Tony. *Jane Austen*. Cambridge: Harvard University Press, 1986.

Tave, Stuart M. *Some Words of Jane Austen*. Chicago: University of Chicago Press, 1973.

Thomas, Keith G. "Jane Austen and the Romantic Lyric: *Persuasion* and Coleridge's Conversation Poems." *English Literary History* 54 (1987).

Waldron, Mary. *Jane Austen and the Fiction of Her Time*. Cambridge: Cambridge University Press, 1999.

Wiltshire, John. *Jane Austen and the Body*. Cambridge: Cambridge University Press, 1992.

Wolfe, Thomas P. "The Achievement of *Persuasion*." *Studies in English Literature* 11 (1971).

Acknowledgments

From "Canonical Memory" by Harold Bloom. From *The Western Canon:* 253–263. © 1994 by Harold Bloom. Reprinted by permission.

"Anne Elliot, Whose Word Had No Weight" by Stuart M. Tave. From *Some Words of Jane Austen*: 256–287. © 1973 by The University of Chicago. Reprinted by permission.

"*Persuasion*: Forms of Estrangement" by A. Walton Litz. From *Jane Austen: Bicentenary Essays*, edited by John Halperin: 221–232. © 1975 by Cambridge University Press. Reprinted with the permission of Cambridge University Press.

"Anne Elliot's Dowry: Reflections on the Ending of *Persuasion*" by Gene W. Ruoff. From *The Wordsworth Circle* 7, no. 4 (Autumn 1976): 342–351. © 1976 by Marilyn Gaull. Reprinted by permission.

"The Radical Pessimism of *Persuasion*" by Julia Prewitt Brown in *Jane Austen's Novels: Social Change and Literary Form*: 127–150. © 1979 by the President and Fellows of Harvard College. Reprinted by permission of the publisher.

"The Nature of Character in *Persuasion*" by Susan Morgan. From *In the Meantime: Character and Perception in Jane Austen's Fiction*: 166–198. © 1980 by Susan Morgan. Reprinted by permission.

"In Between: *Persuasion*" by Tony Tanner. From *Jane Austen*: 208–249. © 1986 by Tony Tanner. Reprinted by permission.

"*Persuasion*: the 'Unfeudal Tone of the Present Day'" by Claudia L. Johnson. From *Jane Austen: Women, Politics and the Novel*: 144–166. © 1988 by The University of Chicago. Reprinted by permission.

"*Persuasion*: The Pathology of Everyday Life" by John Wiltshire. From *Jane Austen and the Body: "The Picture of Health"*: 155–196. © 1992 by Cambridge University Press. Reprinted with the permission of Cambridge University Press.

"Lost in a Book: Jane Austen's *Persuasion*" by Adela Pinch. From *Studies in Romanticism* 12, no. 1 (Spring 1993): 97–117. © 1993 by the Trustees of Boston University. Reprinted by permission.

"Satire, Sensibility and Innovation in Jane Austen: *Persuasion* and the Minor Works" by Claude Rawson. From *Satire and Sentiment: Stress Points in the English Augustan Tradition*: 267–298. © 2000 by Claude Rawson. Reprinted by permission.

Index